THE LETTERS OF
JUDE AND JOHN

"When He Appears"
(Jude 14-15, 21, 1 John 2:28, 3:2, 2 John 7)

"The Only Master, The Lord Jesus Christ"
(Jude 4, 25, 1 John 2:22, 4:3)

MARC WHEWAY PH.D

Ark House Press
arkhousepress.com

© 2023 Marc Wheway Ph.D.

All rights reserved. Apart from any fair dealing for the purpose of study, research, criticism, or review, as permitted under the Copyright Act, no part may be reproduced by any process without written permission.

Unless otherwise stated, all Scriptures are taken from the New International Version (Holy Bible. Copyright© 1996, 2004, 2007, 2013 by Tyndale House Foundation. Used by permission of Tyndale House Publishers Inc., Carol Stream, Illinois 60188. All rights reserved.)

Some names and identifying details have been changed to protect the privacy of individuals.

Cataloguing in Publication Data:
Title: The Letters of Jude and John
ISBN: 9780645802573 (pbk)
Subjects: Doctrine; Biblical Reference; Biblical Study;
Other Authors/Contributors: Wheway, Marc Ph. D

Design by initiateagency.com

CONTENTS

JUDE

Introduction	ix
Chapter 1—Apostates	1
Perverted Grace	1
Chapter 2—Apostasy	9
Remember What You Once Fully Knew	9
The Judgement of the Great Day	17
A Warning from Sodom	26
Chapter 3—Abandonment	34
In Like Manner	34
Woe To Them!	43
Chapter 4—Hidden Reefs	54
Blemishes On Your Love Feasts	54
Chapter 5—Judgement Day	64
The Lord Came with Ten Thousand of His Holy Ones	64
Chapter 6—Scoffers	75
In The Last Times	75
Chapter 7—Build Yourself Up	86
Keep Yourself in the Love of God	86
Chapter 8—Snatching Them Out of the Fire	95
Have Mercy, Show Mercy, With Fear	95

Chapter 9—Blameless.. 105
    God Keeps Those Who Keep Themselves.. 105
Conclusion & Introduction 115

FIRST JOHN
    Eternal Life
Chapter 1—The Word of Life 127
    From the Beginning.. 127
Chapter 2—Walking in the Light... 135
    Do Not Be Deceived.. 135
Chapter 3—By This We Know... 143
    If We Keep His Commandments 143
Chapter 4—An Old/New Commandment 155
    The Darkness is Passing Away 155
Chapter 5—Overcome.. 165
    Do Not Love the World.. 165
Chapter 6—Antichrist Warning... 176
    It is the Last Hour 176
Chapter 7—When He Appears.. 191
    Do Not Shrink Back 191
Chapter 8—Love... 207
    By this We Shall Know 207
Chapter 9—Test the Spirits 219
    Every Spirit that does not Confess Jesus is Not from God 219
Chapter 10—God is Love 227
    Perfect Love Drives out Fear 227
Chapter 11—Overcoming the World 238
    Everyone who has Been Born of God Overcomes the World 238
Chapter 12—The Testimoney of the Son 246
    The Spirit is the One who Testifies... 246

Chapter 13—That You May Know 253
    All Wrongdoing is Sin, but there is a Sin that Leads to Death 253

SECOND JOHN

Doctrine Matters 271
    Fellowship, Only, with those Walking in Truth and Love 271
Chapter 1—Walking in the Truth and Love 275
    Some of Your Children [are] Walking in the Truth 275
Chapter 2—Deceivers at the Door 280
    Anyone Who Runs Ahead and Does Not Continue in the
    Teaching of Christ Does Not Have God 280

THIRD JOHN

Friends and Foes 295
    Diotrephes and Demetrius 295
Chapter 1—Walk In The Truth 299
    The Truth Attracts Trouble 299
Chapter 2—Do Not Imitate Evil 308
    Do Not Be Like Diotrephes 308
Conclusion 319

JUDE

INTRODUCTION
Contending for the Faith

The book of Jude, like the book of Revelation, is one you will rarely hear anything about. At best, an occasional misquoted verse, such as verse two, "May mercy, peace, and love be multiplied to you" (Jude 2). Again, like many other misquoted verses, the context is absent. Within the book of Jude, the focus, and therefore theme, is "Contend for the faith" (Jude 3, 20-23) by resisting false teachers. Verse twenty-one instructs the follower of Christ to "Keep yourselves in the love of God waiting for the mercy of the Lord Jesus Christ that leads to eternal life" (Jude 21). The word "Keep" also translates as "Guard," "Preserve," and to "Keep watch."

The command to guard, keep watch, or hold on to, is common within scripture. The charge was given to the disciples by Jesus, warning against the riches of this world, "Take care, and be on your guard against all covetousness, for one's life does not consist in the abundance of his possessions" (Lk. 12:15). And again, after teaching on the signs of the times, Jesus said, "But watch yourselves lest your hearts be weighed down with dissipation and drunkenness and cares of this life, and that day come upon you suddenly like a trap. For it will come upon all who dwell on the face of the whole earth. But stay awake at all times, praying that you may have strength to escape all these things that are going to take place, and to stand before the Son of Man" (Lk. 21:34-36). Also, Paul told Timothy, "Keep a close watch on yourself (your deeds) and on the teaching. Persist in this, for by so doing you will save both yourself and your hearers" (1 Tim. 4:16).

Paul's instruction to Timothy is to watch (be on guard, hold firm). His deeds and doctrine are also given through John, relaying the words of Jesus to the church of Philadelphia, "Because you have kept (observed, guarded) My word about patient endurance, I will keep you from the hour of trial that is coming on the whole world, to try those who dwell on the earth. I am coming soon. Hold fast what you have, so that no one may seize your crown" (Rev. 3:10-11).

The promise of Jesus returning for those who "Keep" themselves in the love of God is penned by Jude in verse twenty-one (Jude 21). The verse refers to the rapture where God will have mercy toward those who love Him, removing them from the earth before the wrath (Rom. 5:9, 1 Thess. 1:10, 5:9), an hour of trial (Rev. 3:10). Seven years later, Jesus will return with the saints (including those who were raptured) to judge the nations (Zech. 14:5b, Jude 14-15, Rev. 19:14). In sum, those who keep (preserve) the faith, are kept (preserved) from the things to come - being the tribulation.

Like Jude, there are many more examples of the believer to "Keep watch, guard and hold fast" within the Bible. Every reference warns about false teaching, resulting in worldly behaviour. Like Jude, Peter dedicates an entire letter to the problem (2 Peter), saying, "Be sober-minded; be watchful. Your adversary the devil prowls around like a roaring lion, seeking someone to devour" (2 Pet. 5:8). Satan seeks to destroy through his agents, masquerading as ministers of light (2 Cor. 11:12-15). Like Jude, Peter instructs the 'Called' to 'Be watchful' in view of the coming "Day of the Lord" (2 Pet. 3), where God will judge the nations through His Son, Jesus.

The book of Jude was initially incorporated into the text of Second Peter. And not surprisingly, due to the similar theme. Like Jude, Peter targets the false prophets and teachers who arose among the congregation. Like Jude,

Peter also targets those who scoff at prophecy regarding the return of Jesus Christ (2 Pet. 3:3, Jude 18). John deals with the same Gnostic cults as Jude did in his letters (1, 2, & 3 John). Chief among the cult leaders is Cerinthus, John's archenemy, the Ebionites, the Nicolaitans, and the Valentinians. Included in the mix was Simon Magus (Acts 8), who is called the "Father of Gnosticism" by the early church. So dangerous are these false teachers, John says, "Not to receive [them] into your house or give any greeting for whoever greets [them] takes part in [their] wicked works" (2 Jn. 10, cf. Rom. 16:17, 2 Thess. 3:6, 14, Tit. 3:10). John's warning is like Paul's (Rom. 1:32) regarding those who approve of sexual sin. Both the one who practices sin and approves it will be treated the same way. Both parties will be put to death. That is, everlasting death in hell (Jude 7).

While Jude and Second Peter are similar, unique to Jude's book where he references apocryphal books, in fact, two of them: The Assumption (Testament) of Moses (Jude 10) and the book of Enoch (Jude 14). For this reason, some believed the book of Jude to be noncanonical. Another reason for disputing the Holy Spirit-inspired writings of Jude was its harsh tone and the lack of theological substance.

While some doubt the authenticity of Jude's book, very little is not found elsewhere in the Bible. Furthermore, Jude's credibility comes from his family and familiarity with the church. Jude, or Judas, is the brother of James (Jude 1) and half-brother of Jesus (Matt. 13:35). While James was a disciple of Jesus, Jude and these three other brothers (Jacob, Joseph, and Simon) were not. Jude became a disciple after the resurrection (Acts. 1:13-14), and after some time, he was appointed a church leader. Judah was not a pastor but rather a travelling teacher and missionary; he was not interested in titles but somewhat satisfied to be called a "Servant" (Jude 1a). Jude was first a servant (enslaved person) to Jesus Christ and, therefore, a servant to those called and kept for Christ (Jude 1b), referring to salvation.

In Jude's introduction, he refers to "Common salvation" (Jude 3), considering what God has done (called) and what He will continue to do (kept/keep). Every faithful follower of Jesus Christ is called and kept for Him in preparation for His return (Jude. 14, 21, 25). As mentioned above, while God kept those called, the called must respond by keeping themselves free from sin and deception and in the love of God (Jude 21). Those called by God keep themselves from sin, and for God, by guarding themselves against false teaching (Jude 3).

Within Jude's introduction, critical to salvation, he alludes to the entire Godhead; God who calls, The Holy Spirit who keeps, for Christ to come (Jude 2). Again, those called, and kept for Christ, are being guarded and are on guard against false teachers and apostasy. Those who keep themselves in the love of God (Jude 21) will have the mercy, peace, and the love of God multiplied back to them (Jude. 2).

Clearly, Jude understands that "Common salvation" (Jude 3) is a two-way street. God did and always does His part, and Christians must do theirs and respond and remain. The believer's part does not mean salvation is gained by works but instead insists that good works follow and confirm salvation. While Jude wanted to write more about "Common salvation" (Jude 3) being the "Mercy, peace and love" (Jude 2) of God, he found it necessary to encourage (Jude 3, 20-21, 24, 25), warn (Jude 4), and remind (Jude 5, 17). Jude reminds the "Called" and "Kept" (Jude 2) of what they "Once fully knew" (Jude 5). Some were now doubting (Jude 22), and others were straying (Jude 23) due to accommodating the "Hidden reefs" (Jude 12).

Jude's encouragement was for those "Called" and "Kept" by God to "Contend for the faith" (Jude 3). His warning was about the false teachers who had crept in unnoticed, who pervert the teachings of grace (Jude 4). While Jude does not say much about the false teaching of the Gnostics who have crept in, he does narrow in on their traits and behavior:

Introduction

1. False teachers, loud-mouthed boasters (Jude 4, 16, 18, 19)
2. The denial of Jesus Christ (Jude 4, 8)
3. Sensuality (sexual sin) (Jude 4, 6, 7)
4. Self-serving, greedy (Jude 11, 12, 16)
5. Sowing doubt (Jude 22)
6. Cause to stray (Jude 23)
7. Produce false converts (Jude 8, 12-13, 18, 19)

The above-listed issue of false teachers producing false converts through hyper-grace and prosperity preaching was just as problematic in the early church as they are today. However, chief on the list is the denial and even doubting of the deity of Jesus Christ, resulting in apostasy for the doubters (Jude 5, 15, 23). Yet still, like the apostates, those caught up in sexual sin (perverting grace) will face God's judgement (Jude 6-7, 18), along with the greedy (Jude 11), when He returns with the saints (Jude 14-15).

As seen through the abovementioned, the book of Jude is eschatological, looking to the return of Jesus Christ (Jude 14-15, 21, 34), narrowing in on the last time leading to that event (Jude 18). The big idea of the book of Jude, when Jesus returns, is that He will have mercy on those who have kept themselves in the faith, and He will judge those who have not.

The book is broken up into three parts:

1. Servant of Jesus: Contend for the faith (Jude 1-4)
2. Main body (Jude 5-19)

    a. Part 1. Warning against rebellion (Jude 5-10)
    b. Part 2. Warning against rebellion (Jude 11-13)
    c. Ancient warning (Jude 14-16)
    d. Modern warning (Jude 17-19)

3. Jesus Christ, our Saviour: Contend for the faith (Jude 20-25)

As seen in the three-part summary above, the book of Jude also contains:

    a. A chiastic structure.
    b. Pinpointing the false who blemishes the love feasts.
    c. Opening and closing with Jesus Christ.

A (1:1-2) Servant of Jesus Christ (1:1)
    B (1:3-4) Intruders, who long ago were designated for condemnation (1:4)
        C (1:5-7) Later destroyed those who did not believe (1:5)
            D (1:8-13) These are blemishes on your love feasts (1:12)
        C' (1:14-16) To execute judgement on all and to convict everyone for all the godless deeds they committed and for all the harsh words godless sinners have uttered against Him. (1:15)
    B' (1:17-23) There will be scoffers living according to their own godless desires (1:18)
A' (1:24-25) Jesus Christ our Lord (1:25)

A: Jesus Christ our Lord. B: Godless. C: Judgment. D: Blemishes on the feasts.

The point and purpose of the letter (D. Jude 8-13), as seen within the chiastic structure, is to warn against the false teachers and converts - those who blemish the love feasts. The false teachers/converts are sandwiched between opening and closing references of Jesus Christ, who is God (Jude 25), and will return to judge those who deny Him (Jude 4) and doubt Him (Jude 22).

Those feasting among the believers are "Blemishes" and "Hidden reefs" (Jude 12), shipwrecking unsuspecting victims. Paul warned Timothy of the same, encouraging him to "Hold fast to his faith and a good conscience, by rejecting this, some have made shipwreck of their faith" (1 Tim. 1:19). In other words, they have become apostate, either denying or doubting Jesus Christ and are now a danger to others, particularly when they continue to feast among them.

The 'Hidden reefs' would be likened to a person, or persons, sharing a meal with the believers after the church service today. While seeking to look after themselves (Jude 12), they deceive others (2 Pet. 2:13) with their empty words and dead works (Jude 12). While professing to be 'Christians,' they are dangerous 'Hidden reefs' shipwrecking their unsuspecting victims.

Those denying Jesus (cf. 2 Cor. 11) and the resurrection (cf. 1 Cor. 15) cause others to doubt. These are the ones who blemish the love feasts, feasting with the believers, without fear, while looking after themselves (Jude 12). Peter says something similar, addressing the false teachers and false converts, revealing their deception, saying they are "Blots and blemishes" feasting with you, with their "Hearts trained on greed" (2 Pet. 2:14).

While Jesus will judge those denying and doubting Him, He will lead the ones keeping themselves for Him to eternal life (Jude 21). Therefore, there is judgement for those rejecting Him and mercy for those accepting Him and remaining in Him.

As mentioned earlier, the letter, Second Peter and the book of Jude were once incorporated, both targeting false teachers. While Jude does not write on the subject that he wanted to, "Common salvation" (Jude 3), Peter does (2 Peter 1:1-15). There, Peter's appeal (2 Pet. 1:5-14) to "Those who have obtained faith" (2 Pet. 1:1) is like Jude's (Jude 20-21). While Peter addresses those "Having escaped from the corruption that is in the world because of sinful desire" (2 Pet. 1:4), Jude warns to "Snatch out of the fire" those having doubt (Jude 23), lest they end up worse than they started, as Peter warned, "For if, after they have escaped the defilements of the world through the knowledge of our Lord and Savior Jesus Christ, they are again entangled in them and overcome, the last state has become worse for them than the first" (2 Pet. 2:20).

To snatch those doubting and save these straying out of the fire, the 'Hidden reefs', who are the false teachers, must first be exposed and removed. Only then will the one who is weak in faith be strengthened. In the same way, someone is saved by sound teaching (1 Tim. 4:16) - they are also derailed and damned by false teaching (1 Tim 4:1). Simply put, Jude's message is, "Jesus Christ (alone) leads to eternal life" (Jude 21). Those who have Him find mercy (Jude 2, 21), and for those who deny and doubt Him, judgement awaits (Jude 15).

CHAPTER 1
Apostates

Perverted Grace

In the same way, Jude opens his letter, he closes it, warning about those who have crept in unnoticed, perverting the grace of God (Jude 4). These "Hidden reefs" (Jude 12) have shipwrecked the faith of others (cf. 1 Tim. 1:9), causing doubt and sin (Jude 22-23).

The heresies of the 'Hidden Reefs', causing some to doubt and sin includes:

1. God has not come in the flesh
2. Jesus is not God
3. Jesus was not born of a virgin birth
4. Jesus is not in the linage of King David
5. Jesus was not resurrected from the grave
6. Jesus was not crucified; someone else that looked like Him was in His place
7. We must not study the Old Testament prophets
8. God is not Almighty
9. Creation is not God's work
10. The world was created by angels

11. All sin is covered by grace; there is no further need for repentance
12. Jesus is not coming back

The heresies mentioned above are made known through early church writings, such as Irenaeus, Against Heresies, and Paul's work, Third Corinthians (3 Cor. 1:10-15). In the letters, First and Second Corinthians, Paul warns about false teachers (2 Cor. 11) who deny the resurrection (1 Cor. 15). While Paul's letter, Third Corinthians is not considered to be inspired by the Holy Spirit, hence its absence from the Bible, yet it is still considered to be authentic and contains valuable information, like other writings of the early church fathers. However, the third letter to Corinth is credible based on the inspired text revealing additional letters (cf. 1 Cor. 5:9, 13, 2 Cor. 2:6-8) and the early church father's acceptance of it.

Third Corinthians is a letter sent by Paul, responding to another sent by Stephanus and the presbyters, who are with him, Daphnus, Eubulus, Theophilus, and Xenon (3 Cor. 1:1). The church of Corinth is writing to Paul, who is in prison (3 Cor. 1:5, 2:2, 35), about the Gnostics who have crept in. Paul responds to the church leaders, telling them to "Keep" (preserve) his teachings (3 Cor. 1:4-5). Paul also says he is not surprised; since he is in prison, false teachers have come in (3 Cor.2:2). Paul warned the church of Ephesus of the same before departing, saying, "Even from your own number, men will rise up and distort the truth to draw away disciples after them. Therefore, be alert and remember that for three years, I never stopped warning each of you night and day with tears" (Acts 20:30-31).

The heretics causing problems are named "Simon and Cleobius, who pervert the faith of many through corrupt words" (3 Cor. 1:3). Despite some saying we should not name names; naming heretics is biblical. Paul did it (1 Tim. 1:19-20, 2 Tim. 1:5, 2:17), instructing the church to avoid them and rebuke them publicly (1 Tim. 5:19-20).

While not much is known about Cleobius, Simon is well known and named, "The father of Gnosticism" by the ancient church. Simon, called a magus (magician), was the sorcerer in the book of Acts who wanted to buy the power of the Holy Spirit (Acts 8:9-25). Irenaeus reveals that Simon did not repent of his deeds, as warned by Peter, but continued in sorcery (Irenaeus, Against Heresies, 1.23). Another well-known sorcerer was Bar-Jesus, filled with deceit and fraud. Like Simon, Bar-Jesus was a false prophet and an enemy of righteousness, leading followers of "The way" away from the straight path (Acts. 13:6-12).

Simon and Bar-Jesus operated in the supernatural, deceiving their followers with signs and wonders. Other false teachers work with words. Both Peter and Jude call them "Loudmouth boasters" (Jude 16, 2 Pet. 2:18) and dreamers (Jude 8, 2 Pet. 2:10), rejecting authority (Jude 8, 2 Pet. 2:10), who blaspheme God (Jude 8, 2 Pet. 2:10).

The "Loudmouth boasters" (Jude 16, 2Pet. 2;18) "Crept in unnoticed," and they "Pervert the grace of God" (Jude 4). The outsiders crept in and then secretly established themselves and their destructive teaching (2 Pet. 2:1), claiming authority (Jude 8). While presenting to be teachers and prophets (2 Pet. 2:1), they are false, "Ungodly people" (Jude 4, 15). They are not servants of Christ but instead, "Scoffers, following their ungodly passions" (Jude 18).

In sum, these ungodly and clueless people (Jude 12-13), seeking to "Gain advantage" (Jude 16), have snuck in. They have helped themselves (Jude 12), and have gained influence (authority), teaching heresies, perverting grace, causing some to doubt and sin (Jude 22-23).

"Perverting grace" refers to going outside God's will (breaking His Law). Grace (Gk. Charis) has the sense of "Outworking favor." That is, the outworking of God's goodwill towards the "Called" and "Kept" (Jude 1). Known by the same name, Charis is an American (Word of Faith) ministry claiming Christians no longer need to repent because God has already forgiven everyone. Citing Charis founder Andrew Wommack, he says, "We do not have to ask Jesus to forgive our sin because He has already done it." Scripture disagrees (1 Jn. 1:8-10, 2:1-2, 1 Jn. 5:16)! Every believer in this life will struggle with sin, slipping and stumbling, while striving to please God. For that one, God's grace abounds (Rom. 5:20). For the one who practices (prefects) sin, their deliberate and willful sin testifies against them, suggesting they are not saved (1 Jn. 3:4, 6, 8, 9). Those claiming that their sins (past, current, and future) are already dealt with (by claiming 1 Jn. 2:12, 3:5), using grace as a license to sin, are dangerously deceived.

Regarding sin, John Calvin said, "True repentance is firm and constant and makes us war with the evil that is in us, not for a day or a week, but without end and without intermission."

On the other end of Calvinism is Wesleyan-Arminianism, where John Wesley said this, "Our main doctrines, which include all the rest, are three: That of repentance, of faith, and of holiness. The first of these we account, as it were, the porch of religion; the next, the door; the third, religion itself."

Confirming Wesley's Arminian position, he says, "No man that ever lived, not John Calvin himself, ever asserted either original sin, or justification by faith, in more strong, more clear and express terms, than Arminius has done."

Both Calvin and Wesley, from opposite ends of the theological spectrum, disagree with Wommack, and more importantly, scripture does also. It should be said, however, that Andrew Wommack of Charis Ministries disapproves of willful sin; on the contrary, he is seen to be living a holy life. However, his doctrine concerning repentance is unbiblical, as are his prosperity teachings regarding dominionism, health, wealth, and happiness.

Deceived men deceive others by teaching hyper-grace (I can do whatever I like, and it will be alright). Such were the ungodly men who had crept into the church Jude was addressing, claiming God's grace allowed them and others to live a sinful life. These "Loudmouth boasters" assuming authority, have rejected the authority of scripture and, therefore, Jesus Christ (2 Jn. 1:19). Paul responds to the same problem in Romans, chapter six, by saying, "Are we to continue in sin that grace may abound? By no means!" (Rom. 6:1-2).

Those who have perverted the grace of God have changed it into 'Sensuality' (licentiousness). Licentiousness refers to activity lacking legal or moral restraints, especially disregarding sexual constraints. The immediate context of Jude's letter indicates the rebellion against sexual sin is what Jude implied, referencing Sodom and Gomorrah (Jude 7a), who ignored God's law. The specific sin of Sodom and Gomorrah was homosexuality (Gen. 19:5). God responded to the sodomites with fire raining down from heaven as an example to all (Jude 7b, Gen. 19:24, Lu. 17:29, 2 Pet. 2:6-8).

Paul warned about homosexuality in his letter to the church of Rome (Rom. 1:24, 27, 32), also in his letter to the church of Corinth (1 Cor. 6:9), and to Timothy in Ephesus (1 Tim. 1:10). Clearly, homosexuality was a problem for the early church, as it is today. Jesus said that when He returns, the earth's condition will be like the days of Sodom (Lu. 17:28). More will be said on Sodom and Gomorrah later.

Sexual sin is the worst sin for two reasons, 1). It is within the body, not outside of the body. And 2). It is a sin against Christ. Paul talks about sexual sin in First Corinthians, chapters five and six. In chapter five, Paul tells the church not to associate with sexually immoral people found within the church (1 Cor. 5:9-11). Paul instructs the church to "Judge those inside the church" (1 Cor. 5:12) and to remove the one in sin (1 Cor. 5:13).

In chapter six, Paul continues, saying, "The body is not meant for sexual immorality but for the Lord" (1 Cor. 6:14). To commit sexual immorality is likened to being a prostitute, which should never be (1 Cor. 6:15). The one who joins themselves to a prostitute becomes one with her/him; the two become one flesh (1 Cor. 6:17). Therefore, Paul repeats his instruction from chapter five (1 Cor. 5:9-11), saying, "Flee from a sexually immoral person" (1 Cor. 6:18). The danger of associating with them is that their sinful nature may entice those weak, lacking self-control (2 Pet. 2:14, 18, Jude 23). In the same way, the body of a married person belongs to their spouse (1 Cor. 7:4) - the body of a believer belongs to Christ, "You are not your own" (1 Cor. 6:20).

The sexual sin within the church of Corinth was not isolated between a man and a woman; it included orgies with the same sex (1 Cor. 6:9, cf. Gal. 5:21, 1 Tim. 1:10) and incestuous sin (1 Cor. 5:1). Sexual immorality opens the door. It leads to every other kind of sin (Rom. 1:26-31), resulting in death for those who practice and approve of it (Rom. 1:32). Sexual sin is also the fastest and surest way to come under a curse. Balaam, who could not curse God's people (Nu. 22-24), knew this; therefore, he caused them to sin sexually (Num. 25:1-18, 31:16). Both Jude and Peter mention Balaam (Jude 11, 2 Pet. 2:15). The church of Pergamon was also in danger due to following and practicing the teachings of Balaam, called, "Balaamism" (Rev. 2:14).

In sum, Balaamism is causing God's people to sin and deceiving them into thinking they have the freedom or a license to sin; in particular, sexual sin (Num. 31:16, cf. 25:1-18) and greedy gain (Num. 22-24, Jude 11, 2 Pet. 2:15-17). More will be said about Balaam later.

Making Jude's list, alongside homosexuality, is every other kind of sin. Jude describes the perverters of grace, the false teachers, and prophets by saying:

1. They are sneaky (Jude 4, 2 Pet. 2:1)
2. They pervert grace, license to sin (Jude 4, 2 Pet. 2:19)
3. They deny the only Master and Lord Jesus (Jude 4, 2 Pet. 2:1)
4. They do not believe (Jude 5)
5. They are not in or under authority, and they despise it (Jude 6, 2, 2 Pet. 2:10)

6. They are sexually immoral (Jude 7, 2 Pet. 2:2, 10, 14, 18)
7. They are dreamers (Jude 8)
8. They are blasphemers (Jude 8-10, 2 Pet. 2:2, 10, 12)
9. They lack understanding (Jude 10, 2 Pet. 2:12)
10. They are like [dumb] animals (Jude 10, 2 Pet. 2:12)
11. They are murderous (Jude 11)
12. They are greedy for gain (Jude 11, 12, 2 Pet. 2:3, 14)
13. They subscribe to Balaamism, loving gain (Jude 11, 2 Pet. 2:15-17)
14. They are rebels (Jude 11)
15. They are fearless (Jude 12, 2 Pet. 2:10)
16. They are hidden reefs, blots, and blemishes at the love feast (Jude 12, 2 Pet. 213)
17. They are without substance (Jude 12, 2 Pet. 2:17)
18. They are lost (Jude 13)
19. They are ungodly (Jude 14)
20. They are grumblers and malcontents (Jude 16)
21. They follow their own sinful desire (Jude 16)
22. They are loudmouths (Jude 16, 2 Pet. 2:18)
23. They seek to gain an advantage (Jude 16)
24. They are scoffers (Jude 18, 2 Pet. 3:3)
25. They deliberately overlook the Creation story (2 Pet. 3:5-7)
26. They follow their own ungodly passions (Jude 18)
27. They cause division (Jude 19)
28. They are worldly people (Jude 19)
29. They are devoid of the Spirit (Jude 19)
30. They forsake the way and have gone astray (2 Pet. 2:15)

Hyper-grace, sometimes known as 'Greasy-grace', teaching is nothing new. Although perverted grace teachings plagued the early church, as they do the modern church, abusing and changing grace as a license to sin was also a shared problem for Israel, causing God to judge them.

Remember, the Old Testament serves as an example for us (1 Cor. 10:11a), "On whom the end of the age has come" (1 Cor. 11b). What God did to His people then, He will do again. Therefore, "Contend for the faith" (Jude 4) by "Keeping yourself in the love of God" (Jude 21) and by preserving sound doctrine and the souls of others (Jude 22-23). Be on guard against false teaching. Expose, rebuke and remove false teachers trying to sneak in and spread lies, perverting the grace of God (Jude 4).

CHAPTER 2A
Apostasy

Remember What You Once Fully Knew

The introduction to verse five (Jude 5) is a 'Reminder' of what was once 'Fully known', regarding the destruction of those who once walked with God and then rebelled. Their rebellion resulted in their destruction. Jude points back at those destroyed and then looks forward to the coming destruction. Following the reminder, Jude calls his reader to remember the predictions of the apostles of the Lord Jesus Christ. They said, "In the last days, there will be scoffers following their own ungodly passions" (Jude 17-18). As with the ones destroyed in the wilderness (Jude 4), likewise will be the scoffers, like the angels (Jude 6), who are "Being kept until the day of judgement, and destruction" (2 Pet. 3:7).

In verse four (Jude 4), Jude states that the ones who have crept in, perverting grace, were designated for condemnation long ago. Peter says something similar regarding the false teachers who "Secretly bring in destructive heresies" (2 Pet. 2:1), warning, "Their condemnation from long ago is not idle, and their destruction is not asleep" (2 Pet. 2:3). Again, Jude connects the past and the present future simply stating, "What God did then, He is going to do again."

While there is no surprise that God will judge the wicked, especially those who secretly bring in destructive teachings, the challenge for most in the church is that Jesus will destroy those who were once saved. Verse five confirms it: "Jesus saved a people out of the land of Egypt, afterward destroyed those who did not believe" (Jude 5). The idea that a once saved person can lose their salvation is picked up again in verse twenty-three, where Jude says, "Save others by snatching them out of the fire" (Jude 23).

Clearly, the 'Fire' speaks of eternal judgement, as mentioned in verse seven (Jude 7). The doctrine of eternal, conscious punishment is well supported by scripture (Matt. 13:40-42, 18:8-9, 25:41, Mk. 9:47-48, Lu. 16:19-31, Rev. 14:9-11, 20:14-15), despite some, even within the church, dismissing it in favor of the instant annihilation theory, or universalism.

The one being 'Snatched' or 'Plucked' from the fire is linked to Zechariah's book, chapter three (Zech. 3:2). There, Zechariah was shown the Lord rebuking Satan over Jerusalem. Joshua, the high priest, stood before God in filthy garments, which were removed, and replaced with pure vestments. The exchange implies that the one taking hold of Jesus (the Branch and Stone, Zech. 3:8, 9), holding fast by walking in God's ways (Zech. 3:7), will inherit salvation. While the promise was to all, starting with the Jews, only a remnant qualified (Zech. 8:6, 11, 12, cf. Rom. 9:27).

While some claim the ones being snatched out of the fire are unsaved, the context disagrees. Again, Jude reminds his reader that those who were once saved were destroyed (Jude 5). Peter joins Jude by warning that it would have been better for someone to have never known (experienced) God than to have known and fallen away (2 Pet. 2:20-21). The writer of Hebrews says something similar, warning about apostasy (Heb. 6:4-6, 10:26-27). The writer of Hebrews compares the church, and Israel (Heb. 3:7-4:13), supporting Jude's statement in verse five (Jude 5). The writer of Hebrews and

Jude are reminding and warning their readers about the same event, God destroying Israel (Num. 14), who Jesus Christ once saved.

The event both the writer of Hebrews and Jude discuss, is mentioned in the book of Numbers, chapter fourteen (Num. 14). The context includes a continuation from chapter thirteen (Num. 13), where spies went into Canaan to spy out the land. Canaan was the Promised Land, given to Israel by God (Gen. 15:18-21). After forty days of spying out the land (Num. 13:25), flowing with milk and honey (Num. 13:27), they reported that it was full of giants who had come from the Nephilim (Num. 13:33). Resulting from the bad report (Num. 14:37), Israel lost faith, and grumbled against Moses (Num. 14:1-2). The congregation of Israel said they would have been better off in Egypt (also symbolic of the world, Rev. 11:8) than to be brought to this land (also symbolic of the millennial kingdom, Num. 14:2-3, cf. Heb. 3:7-4:13). Instead of obeying God, the rebellious then sought a new leader who would take them back to Egypt (Num. 14:3-4).

Returning to Egypt is likened to Peter's warning to those escaping the world and returning to it. As mentioned before, it would have been better for them that they had never escaped in the first place, for their end will be worse than the former state (2 Pet. 2:20-21).

Of the entire congregation, only two believed in God, Joshua, and Caleb (Num. 14:6-8). At the time, it was estimated the congregation of Israel numbered 2.4 million people. The books of Exodus (12:37), Numbers (1:46), and (2:32) reveal the populace of men, not including women and children. Numbers (1:21–43) gives an account of each tribe. The combined numbers, provided through the references given typically and traditionally, are used to interpret just over 600,000 adult men, implying a total population about four times that size, or 2.4 million, made up the congregation of Israel. Out of 2.4 million, only Joshua and Caleb obeyed God.

When Joshua and Caleb challenged the congregation to trust God and remain obedient to Him, they sought to stone them. Still, the Lord intervened, saving Joshua and Caleb (Num. 14:10). God saved Joshua and Caleb and was determined to destroy the unbelieving congregation (Num. 14:12), who, after seeing so many signs, chose to "Despise God" (Num. 14:11).

God intervened on behalf of Joshua and Caleb, and then Moses interceded on behalf of Israel (Num. 14:13-19). Moses reminded God He had forgiven Israel from Egypt until now (Num. 14:19), pleading that He would continue to forgive them (Num. 14:18). Because of Moses' plea, God did pardon Israel (Num. 14:19). Instead of being destroyed, they were disqualified from entering the Promised Land (Num. 14:20-23). Joshua and Caleb, alone from the original congregation, who "Fully followed" God (Num. 14:24), entered the Promised Land (Num. 14:24, 30); the rest died in the wilderness (Num. 14:29, 31, 35).

With the mention of being 'Pardoned', there is some confusion regarding whether it meant Israel still inherited salvation. Remember, referencing Numbers, chapter fourteen, Jude said, "Jesus saved these people out of the land of Egypt, and later destroyed those who did not believe" (Jude 5). While Jesus, on the one hand, delivered the whole nation out of Egypt, He also destroyed any who did not believe. The word "Believe" does not only imply believing in God, but rather being committed to Him, to have faith in Him. Believing alone is not enough; as James says, "You believe that God is one; you do well. Even the demons believe—and shudder!" (Ja. 2:19).

The writer of the book of Hebrews mentions the same event as Jude, warning the one who is in danger of apostasy (Heb. 3:12) not to test God (Heb. 3:8-9). When writing chapter three of Hebrews, the writer is quoting Psalm ninety-five (Ps. 95), which is a call to worship, and in doing so, one must "Take care" (Heb. 3:12). The care taken is against unbelief, causing the unbeliever to fall away. Again, the audience is Christian, holy brothers (Heb. 3:1, 12), who

"Must pay closer attention to what [they] have heard, lest [they] drift away from it" (Heb. 2:1). The writer warns the brother, saying (if you drift away), "How will you escape if you neglect such great salvation" (Heb. 2:3).

The Israelites drifted away when they tested God ten times (Num. 14:22), meaning many times. They never stopped believing in Him; they just stopped following. They tested God due to being deceived by sin (Heb. 3:13). Jude, and the writer of Hebrews, were likewise warning against the deception of sin (Jude 22-23, Heb. 3:13) and those who cause it (Jude 4). Sin disqualified Israel from the Promised Land and can disqualify those confessing Christ from the millennial kingdom. Note the condition of salvation: "IF indeed we hold our original confidence to the end" (Heb. 3:14).

Going by the abovementioned, Israel, being pardoned, likely refers to not being destroyed right then and there, as the three thousand were for disobeying God (Exod. 32:28).

In the same way the 'Good news' came to Israel; it has come to us (Heb. 4:2), but to benefit from the message, faith, and obedience must be applied (Heb. 4:2, 6). The Israelite example is a reminder (Jude 5) purposed to point the reader in the direction of the millennial kingdom (Heb. 4:8), encouraging all to "Strive to enter that rest" (Heb. 4:11). Jesus said something similar when asked, "Will those who are saved be few?" (Lu. 13:23). He answered, "Strive to enter through the narrow door. For many, I tell you, many will seek to enter and will not be able" (Lu. 13:24). Those not entering, being denied access, are damned eternally (Lu. 13:27-28).

Paul contributes to the conversation with his letter to the church of Corinth (1 Cor. 10:1-22), again confirming that the recorded event serves as an example to us: "On whom the end of the ages has come" (1 Cor. 10:11) that we might not do what they did (1 Cor. 10:6, 11). With the incident told in Number chapter fourteen (1 Cor. 10:10), Paul incorporates the golden calf event (Exod. 32), warning against idolatry and sexual sin (1 Cor. 10:8), resulting in death. Like the writer of Hebrews, Paul says, "We must not put Christ to the test" (1 Cor. 10:9). Jude is concerned about the same thing; some had perverted grace, saying, "You can do whatever you like, and it will be alright." In sum, the "Hidden reefs" (Jude 12) were shipwrecking the faith of some by giving them a license to sin, deceiving them into believing sin will not disqualify them from salvation.

When comparing the three contributing authors (Paul, the writer of Hebrews, and Jude), each confirmed the Israelites testing God were disqualified and destroyed (1 Cor. 10:9-10, Heb. 3:17, Jude 5) and consequently did not enter God's rest (Heb. 3:11, 4:3, 5). Again, God's rest for Israel was the Promised Land, which is comparable to the millennial kingdom for us (Heb. 3:7-4:13).

Paul, and the writer of Hebrews, provide evidence of losing salvation. In the book of Hebrews, the writer says, "For we share in Christ if indeed we hold our original confidence from to the end" (Heb. 3:14). Further on, the writer says, "If he shrinks back My soul has no pleasure in him" (Heb. 10:38), warning that those who do shrink back, they are destroyed (Heb. 10:39). Paul confirms, the Destroyer destroys them (1 Cor. 10:10). Like the book of Hebrews, Paul says the one who puts Christ to the test (1 Cor. 10:9), through sin, is destroyed. Only a believer can shrink back from Christ or put Him to the test; therefore, Jude was not addressing outsiders when warning against doubting and sin (Jude 22-23). The same is applied to Israel, "Those who did not believe" (Jude 5). The warning was to believers, who were in danger of apostasy, and, therefore, eternal judgement, disqualifying them from "Entering God's rest."

While the gift of "Entering God's rest" is available to all, through Christ alone, only two from the original congregation of Israel escaping Egypt gained access to the Promised Land. A comparison could also be found in the seven letters to the churches, where only two of seven were without the need for repentance. The churches of Smyrna (Rev. 2:8-11) and Philadelphia (Rev. 3:7-13) were the only two churches that were not in danger of judgement. These two churches were promised, on the condition that they endure and hold fast until the end, that they would be rewarded in the millennium (Rev. 2:11, 3:12). The rest were warned to repent, or else!

Every church 'Believed' in Jesus Christ; however, not all were found trusting in Him alone. Interestingly, Ephesus's church was warned that they would lose their lampstand unless they remembered and repented. However, if they did repent, and remained to overcome the world (remain free from sin), then they would gain access to the tree of life, which is in the paradise of God (Rev. 2:7). The tree of life will be accessible to all who enter the millennial kingdom (Rev. 22:2, 14). Those failing the requirement are denied access.

A similar promise is given to the church of Pergamum - if they repent and remain, they will eat of the hidden manna (Rev. 2:17). The promise of "Hidden manna" is an allegorical rendering of end-time fellowship, pointing toward the marriage supper of the Lamb (Rev. 19:6, 9). Again, only those entering the millennium (Promised Land) will be at the marriage supper.

Another similarity is found with the church of Thyatira. A remnant within is promised, providing they hold fast until the end, (Rev. 2:25a) that they will have authority and rule with Christ over the nations (Rev. 2:25b). A similar promise was given to any repenting within the church of Laodicea, providing they repent and remain they too would rule with Jesus (Rev. 3:21). Ruling with Christ occurs in the millennium, following His return, after the tribulation (Rev. 19-20:1-5).

The promise to the church of Sardis also applies to the millennium and is like a quote from Zechariah, chapter three, as mentioned earlier. The ones who repent and remain will be clothed in white garments. As with the vision in Zechariah, chapter three, the promise is fulfilled when standing before the throne of God in the Promised Land. Those failing the requirement, on each account, face judgement.

One of the most convincing arguments, regarding losing salvation, is seen in the letter to the church of Sardis, having a reputation of being alive but was dead (Rev. 3:1-6). Through the letter, the church was warned if they did not wake up, Jesus would come like a thief and then come against them (Rev. 3:3). "Coming like a thief" refers to the rapture and "coming against them" relates to the tribulation. Furthermore, the church is told that the one who overcomes will never be blotted out of the book of life (Rev. 3:5), meaning the one who does not overcome and remains that way will have their name blotted out. For a person's name to have been blotted out, it had to be there in the first place. Not everyone's name is written in the book of life; only believers' names are (Phil. 4:3, Rev. 13:8, 17:8, 20:12, 15, 21:27). The doctrine of "Once saved, always saved" has no reasonable defense against this argument.

In conclusion, the requirement to fully follow and remain is the same throughout each account. The text compares whether it be Israel or the church, or those who will inherit the Promised Land and those who will not. Jude wanted to remind his readers of this fact - although they once fully knew it. It is not that they had forgotten the past; instead, they had been distracted and derailed by the hidden reefs, intending to shipwreck them in their faith. To be shipwrecked, the one once having faith, sailing along, now has unbelief, therefore doubt, and needs saving (Jude 22) by being reminded of what they once fully knew (Jude 5).

Similarly, Paul and the writer of Hebrews provide examples of what God did in the past, indicating what He did then, He will do it again. Subsequently, Jude, verse five (Jude 5) is literal and allegoric. It implies that those saved out of Egypt (the world) are being saved (preserved) for the Promised Land (the millennial kingdom). While those destroyed through deception do not enter God's rest (the Promised Land).

CHAPTER 2B
Apostasy

The Judgement of the Great Day

Following the example of the rebellious Israelites are the rebellious angels from Genesis, chapter six. Jude references these examples in comparison to the "Hidden reefs" (Jude 12) that have crept into the fellowship unnoticed, causing some to doubt and sin (Jude 22-23).

In the same way, the 2.4 million Israelites were led into rebellion by ten spies giving a bad report (Num. 14:37), disqualifying those who did not believe/obey (Jude 5), and the fallen angels did the same. The stories are linked, thereby confirming the disobedient Israelites were indeed disqualified, as mentioned in the previous section. Regarding the angels, two hundred of them were led into further rebellion against God through a select few (Enock 6). The angels, knowing full well of the consequences (Enock 6), took for themselves wives who bore their children. Eighteen fallen angels, commanded by one more, named Semyaza, led two hundred more in this rebellion (Enock 6:7-8).

The fallen angels are those following Satan when he was cast out of heaven (Lu. 10:18, Rev. 12:3-4, 9) for his sin of pride (Ezek. 25:14-18, Isa. 14:12-14). Due to overstepping the mark on the earth, some of the angels were thrown into hell (Jude 6, 2 Pet. 2:4). As mentioned above, the violation involved interbreeding with women, therefore corrupting God's created design by producing an angel-human hybrid creature called Nephilim (Gen. 6:4). The women fell pregnant. They gave birth to the Nephilim, who were giants, up to forty-five feet tall (Enoch 7:2).

While some have trouble acccepting angels can have sex with women, Enoch makes it clear that they can, and did. He says, "I looked at them and I saw and look, all of them let out their organs like horses, and they began to mount the cows of the bulls" (Enoch 86:4). In case anyone missed it, Enoch repeats the story, saying, "And the Lord summoned those first seven white men, and he commanded them to bring before him beginning with the first star that had preceded those stars whose organs were like the organs of horses, and they brought all of them before him" (1 Enoch 90:21). Something similar is seen in Ezekiel's book, where the prophet records God's words regarding whoring Samaria and Jerusalem (Ezek. 23:4), who "Lusted after her lovers there (Assyria, Ezek. 23:5, Egypt, Ezek. 23:8, 19, and Babylon, Ezek. 23:16-18), whose members were like those of donkeys, and whose issue was like that of horses" (Ezek. 23:20). The phrase, "Whose members were like those of donkeys" refers to Israel lusting after earthly power, resulting in their unfaithfulness and idolatry against God. With Israel's pursuit of power and prosperity, they committed both sexual sin and spiritual adultery. The fallen angels did, likewise, producing giants.

The tallest post-food giant recorded in scripture is Og (Num. 21:33-35, Deut. 3:1-7), who was the king of Bashan. Og was thirteen feet tall (Deut. 3:11). Og came out against the Israelites as they were entering the Promised Land. Previously, the Israelites would not enter the Promised Land because it was inhabited by giants (Num. 13:28, 32-33).

The story of angels breeding with humanity has been well told throughout history and was maintained by the early church writers. The book of

Enoch, which best supports the teaching, was quoted by Origen, Irenaeus, Tertullian, Anatolius, and Theodotus, to name a few. Justin Martyr (100-165 A.D.), in the Second Apology (chapter five), writes: "God, when He had made the whole world, and subjected things earthly to man, and arranged the heavenly elements for the increase of fruits and rotation of the seasons and appointed this divine law—for these things also He evidently made for man—committed the care of men and of all things under heaven to angels whom He appointed over them. But the angels transgressed this appointment, and were captivated by love of women, and begat children who are those that are called demons; and besides, they afterwards subdued the human race to themselves, partly by magical writings, and partly by fears and the punishments they occasioned, and partly by teaching them to offer sacrifices, and incense, and libations, of which things they stood in need after they were enslaved by lustful passions; and among men they sowed murders, wars, adulteries, intemperate deeds, and all wickedness. Whence also the poets and mythologists, not knowing that it was the angels and those demons who had been begotten by them that did these things to men, and women, and cities, and nations, which they related, ascribed them to God himself, and to those who were accounted to be his very offspring, and to the offspring of those who were called his brothers, Neptune and Pluto, and to the children again of these their offspring. For whatever name each of the angels had given to himself and his children, by that name they called them."

Like other early church fathers, Justin was familiar with the book of Enoch, which is still used by the church of Ethiopia, and is included within the Ethiopian Bible. It is said that the doctrine that angels interfered with humanity continued without opposition until the Second Century.

In the Second Century, R. Simeon b. Yohai (in the third generation Tannaim, i.e., A.D. 130–60) introduced a new teaching that the "Sons of God" were men, not angels. Many more have accepted this doctrinal position since dismissing the original view. However, Jude's First Century readers would have been familiar with Enoch's book, thereby would have understood and connected the reference to fallen angels marrying women, producing Nephilim (meaning fallen ones) (Enoch 6:1-2, 7:1-2, 9:9).

Like Jude, Jesus also referenced the event from Genesis, chapter six, warning that those days, "The days of Noah," will be repeated when He returns (Matt. 24:37-39, Lu. 21:26-27). The verses quoted by Jesus are Genesis, chapter six, verses five to twelve (Gen. 6:5-12). The Hebrew word "Blameless" (Gen. 6:9) also translates as 'Complete, intact, and without fault', meaning Noah had not been corrupted, as the entire world has been (Gen. 6:11-12). The whole world had been corrupted due to the interference and interbreeding with fallen angels. As a result, the world was contaminated (Enoch 10:11, 12:4, 15:3) and full of violence (Enoch 9:10, 12:6).

Again, the angels involved in the rebellion were cast into prison (Jude 6, 2 Pet. 2:4), and their offspring were destroyed (Enoch 10:13). However, the spirits of the offspring, being then Nephilim, now roam the earth as "Evil spirits" (Enoch 15:9). During the tribulation the imprisoned angels will be released (Rev. 9:1-2, 11, 14, 16:12), and in a sense, reunited with their children, who are the evil Nephilim spirits roaming the earth. Again, Jesus said what occurred in the days of Noah will be repeated during the tribulation, implying the corruption of God's created design and the whole earth being full of demons, and violence, led by the rebellious angles, under Satan. Demons will also perform lying signs and wonders (Rev. 16:14), deceiving even the elect, if possible (Matt. 24:24). For this reason, the tribulation to come cannot be compared with anything previously seen in the history of the world, and nor will it be repeated (Dan. 12:1, Matt. 24:21).

Jude's point in referencing the angels, is that they, like the false teachers who have crept in unnoticed, "Did not stay within their position of authority" (Jude 6), abandoning their home (rightful place) (Enock 12:4, 15:3, 7). By not staying within their position of authority, the angels did not keep, guard, and protect God's decree; therefore, they were imprisoned. The irony here is that the unguarded are now under guard, in prison (Jude 6, 2 Pet. 2:4), and the unguarded false teachers are predestined for the same (Jude 4, 13, cf. 2 Tim. 4:16).

Jude makes a deliberate comparison between the angels and the hidden reefs (false teachers), comparing their destinations and instructing the reader to "Contend for the faith" (Jude 3). The reader is to resist and be guarded against "Certain people (hidden reefs) [who] have crept in unnoticed" (Jude 4a). The hidden reefs are apostate, like the angels who abandoned heaven. Again, the apostate teachers are so, due to being unguarded and rejecting authority (Jude 8). They have rejected the authority of scripture, and therefore they have rejected God, and now, like the angels, they are condemned (Jude 4b, 6, 13). In the same way, the angels were cast into hell (2 Pet. 2:4), so will the hidden reefs be, along with those deceived by them (2 Pet. 2:3), which is why Jude says, "Snatch them out of the fire" (Jude 22-23).

Jude references those already in hell (Jude 6) and those condemned to it (Jude 4, 13, cf. 2 Pet. 2:3, 17) and further warns of those heading that way (Jude 22-23). In doing so, twice, Jude warns that hell is eternal (Jude 6, 13). Enoch has plenty more to say about hell, and its endless horrors (Enoch 13:1; 14:5; 21, 54:3–5; 56:1–4; 88:1), perhaps some of the most confronting verses are found in chapter ten: "And again the Lord said to Raphael: 'Bind Azazel hand and foot, and cast him into the darkness: and make an opening in the desert, which is in Dudael, and cast him therein. And place upon him rough and jagged rocks, and cover him with darkness, and let him abide there forever, and cover his face that he may not see light. And on the day of the great judgement, he shall be cast into the fire" (Enoch 10:4-6).

Alongside Azazel, from Enoch chapter one, the other angels who interfered with humanity, were also eternally judged: "And when their sons have slain one another, and they have seen the destruction of their beloved ones, bind them fast for seventy generations in the valleys of the earth, till the day of their judgement and of their consummation, till the judgement that is forever and ever is consummated" (Enoch 10:12).

The imprisonment of the apostate angels is not the worst of what they will experience, for they are being reserved for another day, the day of judgement, as Enoch later describes: "Here their spirits shall be set apart in this great pain, till the great day of judgement, scourging, and tormenting of the accursed forever, so that (there may be) retribution for their spirits. There He shall bind them forever" (Enoch 22:11, cf. 84:4).

The fate of the fallen angels is also shared by sinners. So terrible will that end be, Enoch says, "It would be better for them if they had not been born" (Enoch 38:2, cf. Matt. 26:24). If the judged person was better off not being born, the final judgement could not imply they no longer exist; instead, it refers to eternal conscious suffering.

Enoch's warning should be compared with Revelation, chapter twenty (Rev. 20:11-15). John's revelation confirms the final place of suffering is eternal, evident by the antichrist and the false prophet being there, "Tormented day and night forever and ever" for one-thousand years before any other joins them (Rev. 19:20, 20:10). Previously, an angel warned, if anyone takes the mark of the beast (666), they too will suffer the same fate (Rev. 14:9-11). They, too, will suffer, being "Tormented with Fire and Sulphur" (Rev. 14:10). "And the smoke of their torment goes up forever and ever, they have no rest day or night" (Rev. 14:11).

The Greek word for "Forever" is "Aion" literally meaning "Forever". The word is used in reference to eternal life (Jn. 10:28), eternal torment (Rev. 14:11), and the eternal God (Rev. 15:7). The same word cannot be applied to some (eternal life and God) and not to all (eternal torment) in the same way. Using the exact word derivative (Aionios), the Bible confirms that the final state of suffering is eternal (Matt. 25:41, 46, Mk. 9:42-50, Lk. 12:4-5 and 16:22-28,

Rev. 14:10-14, Rev. 19:20 and 20:10). Jude uses the word "Eternal" three times (Jude 6, 7, 21).

For the word "Eternal", Jude used the Greek word 'Aidios' (Jude 7), meaning everlasting and timeless. Jude also used the Greek word "Aionios" (Jude 7, 21), meaning continuing forever indefinitely. Verses seven and twenty-one are applied to two different things (punishment of eternal fire and eternal life); both uses of the same word share the same unending application. Jude does something similar with the word "Forever" (Jude 13, 25). As mentioned above, the Greek word for "Forever" is "Aion" and is used in both verses. In verse thirteen, Jude says the hidden reefs are destined to "Gloom of utter darkness, which has been reserved forever." Similarly, the fallen angels are also "Kept in eternal chains under gloomy darkness" (Jude 6). In contrast, in verse twenty-five, Jude says Jesus Christ will have glory, dominion, and authority before all time, now, and forever (Aion), meaning unending.

The place of everlasting, unending suffering involves "The second death," which is mentioned four times in the book of Revelation and is found nowhere else within the Bible (Rev. 2:11, 20:6, 20:14, 21:8). The second death refers to an eternal state of suffering. Those guilty of perverting grace reject the doctrine of everlasting torment; instead, they replace it with the theory of annihilation, or universalism. Others claim that the suffering of hell ends when "Death and Hades" are thrown into the lake of fire (Rev. 20:14). The latter is better supported; however, the Bible verses provided discredit that idea. The book of Enoch, as mentioned above, quoted by Jude, and referenced by the early church, firmly states that the second death, in the lake of fire, is far worse than imprisonment in hell. Again, if a condemned person ceased to exist, once thrown into the lake of fire, the second death would not be worse. In fact, they would be better off. Again, both Enoch and Jesus state, "It would be better for them if they had not been born" (Enoch 38:2, cf. Matt. 26:24).

The final judgement is called by Enoch, "The great day of the Lord" (Enoch 54:6, Jude 6), which is a day to be greatly feared. Enoch's warning of, "The great day of the Lord" is referenced several times in both the Old Testament and the New Testament, referring to the final judgement (Joel 2:11, 31; Zeph. 1:14; Mal. 4:5; Acts 2:20; Rev. 6:17; 16:8). Again, as bad as the first state of imprisonment will be, the latter will be far worse. While Jude does not detail the latter experience, Enoch does, saying, "In those days they will lead them into the bottom of the fire—and in torment—in the prison (where) they will be locked up forever. And at the time when they will burn and die, those who collaborated with them will be bound together with them from henceforth unto the end of (all) generations" (Enoch 10:13-14).

Again, Jude's reference to angelic rebellion, as recorded in Genesis, chapter six, is compared to the hidden reefs that are corrupting members within the church by leading them into rebellion (Jude 22-23). The hidden reefs or false teachers were perverting grace, using it as a license to sin sexually in context. Interestingly, Enoch concludes his book with a warning about "Sinners" who "Pervert the words of righteousness in many ways" (Enoch 104:10) - saying, "All our sins will not be searched out and written down" (Enoch 104:7). God assures them, they will be (Enoch 104:7-11).

As mentioned earlier, it is essential to note that Jude cites Enoch (Jude 14-15, Enoch 1:9), giving the book Holy Spirit inspired credibility. Jesus gives the same warning as Enoch, threatening anyone who tampers with His word on eternal judgement (Rev. 22:18). Anyone teaching others that they are free to sin without consequence, tampers with God's word, and therefore are already condemned (Jude 4, 13).

In sum, Jude connects the dots by comparing the Israelite's encounter with the giants (Jude 5), moving to the angels creating the giants (Jude 6), who, like Sodom and Gomorrah, went after "Strange flesh" (Jude 7). The "Strange flesh" was that of humanity, and animals (Enoch 7:5), being not of their kind.

The reference to Sodom and Gomorrah refers to both homosexuality and men wanting to have sex with angels (Gen. 19). Jude links the rebellion with the hidden reefs by saying they rebelled against the authority of God (Jude 6, 8), perverting grace, downplaying God's Law, giving a license to sin (Jude 4). In the same way, God dealt with the rebellious through the Flood (Gen. 7). He will again through fire (2 Pet. 3:10). When God judges the fallen angels, who led mankind astray, He will also judge their wives (Enock 19:1-2), and any other who followed in their footsteps by corrupting humanity. The hidden reefs included those who did not remain within the authority of scripture (Jude 6, 8, cf. 2 Jn. 1:9). Especially those who led others astray (Jude 22-23, cf. Matt. 18:6).

CHAPTER 2C
Apostasy

A Warning from Sodom

Following the reminder and examples of the rebellious Israelites who did not believe/obey (Jude 5) and the angels who did not remain within their position of authority, (Jude 6) is the example of Sodom and Gomorrah (Jude 7). The reminder and examples serve as a caution, warning what God did to them, He will do again. The warning is for the "Beloved" (Jude 3) while addressing the false teachers who have crept in (Jude 4) and those who follow them (Jude 22-23). The warning encourages the "Called" and "Kept" (Jude 1) to "Contend for the faith" (Jude 3), which involves guarding the gospel, resisting false teachers, and saving the unsteady souls who they have enticed (2 Pet. 2:14).

The false teachers (hidden reefs) are known for three things within Jude and Peter's letters. Firstly, they deny Christ (Jude 4b, 2 Pet. 2:1). Secondly, they preach a hyper-grace message, giving a license to sin; sexual sin is what both Jude and Peter narrow in on (Jude 4, 2 Pet. 2:2, 10, 14, 18). And thirdly, false teachers scoff at Bible prophecy; instead of preparing for Christ's return, they follow their own ungodly passions (Jude 18, cf. 15-16, 2 Pet. 2:3).

As a result of their ungodliness (Jude 15, 18) and worldliness (Jude 19), the false teachers cause divisions within the church (Jude 19), and the same is seen today. On the one hand, the holiness preachers are instructing the church to separate themselves from this world, as Peter taught, "Live lives of holiness and godliness while waiting for and hastening the coming of the day of God" (2 Pet. 3:11-12). Jude had a similar application, saying, "Keep yourself in the love of God, waiting for the mercy of our Lord Jesus Christ that leads to eternal life" (Jude 21). On the other hand, false teachers are denying Christ, His return, and the authority of scripture. They are ungodly, and therefore unholy (Jude 15).

The ungodly, who are guilty of going outside the authority of scripture, (not keeping God's Laws) go further by giving a license to sin (breaking God's Laws) while loving and promoting the things of this world. At the same time, the first group looks to and longs for Christ and His appearing. The latter desires to live a long life in this world and for the further delaying, and if possible, the cancelling of Christ's return. The longer Christ's return is delayed, the worse things will become (cf. Matt. 24:22).

Jude compares the hidden reefs (Jude 12), intending to shipwreck the faith of some (Jude 22-23), to the examples previously given. In the same way, God destroyed the rebellious Israelites (Jude 5), the angels who interfered with humanity (Jude 6), and Sodom and Gomorrah (Jude 7), He will also destroy the false teachers (Jude 4, 13). Alongside the false teacher will be those deceived by them (Jude 23). The deceived also perish. This is the warning from Sodom.

As mentioned earlier, the specific sin Jude narrows in on is the same now being approved by the hidden reefs: Sexual sin (Jude 4). While all sex outside marriage is sinful in God's eyes, sex outside of male and female is worse. In fact, God calls same-sex relations an "Abomination" (Lev. 18:22, 26, 27, 29, 20:13). Any kind of sexual perversion is an abomination, including cross-dressing (Deut. 22:5), which leads to the topic of gender confusion. Genderfluidity is a form of idolatry, which, alongside sexual perversion, is an abomination before God. The Bible has much to say about the abomination of sexual perversion and idolatry, warning that both result in eternal judgement.

Following the example of angels desiring strange flesh (Jude 6), Jude links Sodom and Gomorrah. Sodom and Gomorrah are mentioned many times within scripture, and in the Apocrypha, as an example of God's righteous judgement (Deut. 29:23; Isa 1:9; 13:19; Jer. .49:18; 50:40; Lam 4:6; Amos 4:11; Zeph. 2:9; Matt 10:15; Luke 17:29; 2 Pet 2:6; Jude 7; cf.; 2 Esdr. 2:8; 3 Macc. 2:5). Sodom was known to be an evil place (Isa 1:10; 3:9; Jer. 23:14; Ezek. 16:46–50), which was also used allegorically for the world (Rev 11:8).

As mentioned above, Jude connects his previous example by providing another (Jude 7), applying that the population of Sodom, guilty of sexual perversion, namely homosexuality, and wanted to have sex with angels, perished. "In a similar manner" (Jude 8a) others will. Like the fallen angels, the Sodomites likewise overstepped the mark, and now they "Serve as an example by undergoing a punishment of eternal fire" (Jude 7b).

The words "In a similar manner" confirm the compared rebellious sins of the first two examples with the third, and the current one; therefore the judgement for all is the same. As stated in the previous sections, while some say the Israelites (Jude 5) were not eternally judged, the connection here is clear. They were, and so will it be for any in the church following in their footsteps (cf. Rom. 11:22), which is the point of the "Example" (Jude 1:7, 2 Pet. 2:6), and the words, "In like manner" (Jude 8).

Again, the specific sin of Sodom is sexual immorality and perversion, especially homosexuality. The latter part of the verse says they "Pursued unnatural desire" (Jude 7b). Peter addressed the same issue (2 Pet. 2:6-10), stating the people of Sodom and Gomorrah "Indulged in the lust of defiling passion and despised authority" (2 Pet. 2:10). The incident both Jude and Peter refer to is recorded in Genesis (Gen. 19:4-11).

The Genesis account mainly focuses on the sin of homosexuality, which Peter describes as a "Defiling passion" and Jude as an "Unnatural desire." Those guilty have "Despised authority" (2 Pet. 2:10, Jude 8) by violating God's laws, which forbid the mixing of things, including sexes (Deut. 22:5, 9-11). Desiring sex with the same flesh (homosexuality) is prohibited by God. Those who practice this sin, and those who approve of it, are guilty of the same and thereby are judged together (Rom. 1:32). Anyone agreeing with or accommodating those practicing homosexuality will be condemned alongside the participator to everlasting fire (1 Cor. 6:9, Rev. 21:8).

As mentioned above, connecting the previous example where angels had sex with women, the sexual sin of Sodom refers to homosexuality and to having sex with angels. In the apocryphal Testament of Naphtali, the eighth son of Jacob and Bilhah, it is written, "But ye shall not be so, my children, recognizing in the firmament, in the earth, and in the sea, and in all created things, the Lord who made all things, that ye become not as Sodom, which changed the order of nature. In like manner, the Watchers also changed the order of their nature, whom the Lord cursed at the flood, on whose account He made the earth without inhabitants and fruitless" (Naph. 3:4-5).

The apocryphal Testament of Benjamin is similar, also linking the sin of Sodom to the transgression of Enoch's day: "And I believe that there will be also evil-doings among you, from the words of Enoch the righteous: that ye shall commit fornication with the fornication of Sodom, and shall perish, all save a few, and shall renew wanton deeds with women; and the kingdom of the Lord shall not be among you, for straightway He shall take it away" (Benj. 9:1).

As seen through the above writings, there is no doubt that the sin Jude had in mind included homosexuality and sex with angels. Both sins corrupted all involved. In the Work of Philo, who is a contemporary of Josephus, Philo Judaeus writes: "As men, being unable to bear discreetly a satiety of these things, get restive like cattle, and become stiff-necked, and discard the laws of nature, pursuing a great and intemperate indulgence of gluttony, and drinking, and unlawful connections; for not only did they go mad after women, and defile the marriage bed of others, but also those who were men lusted after one another, doing unseemly things, and not regarding or respecting their common nature, and though eager for children, they were convicted by having only an abortive offspring; but the conviction produced no advantage, since they were overcome by violent desire; and so, by degrees, the men became accustomed to be treated like women, and in this way engendered among themselves the disease of females, and intolerable evil; for they not only, as to effeminacy and delicacy, became like women in their persons, but they made also their souls most ignoble, corrupting in this way the whole race of man, as far as depended on them. At all events, if the Greeks and barbarians were to have agreed together, and to have adopted the commerce of the citizens of this city, their cities one after another would have become desolate, as if they had been emptied by a pestilence" (On Abraham 135-136).

Note the words of Philo, in comparison to today's gender confusion: "By degrees, the men became accustomed to be treated like women, and in this way engendered among themselves the disease of females." Enoch says something similar, "And now I swear unto you, to the wise and to the foolish, for ye shall have manifold experiences on the earth. For ye men shall put on more adornments than a woman, And coloured garments more than a virgin: In royalty and in grandeur and in power, and in silver and in gold and in purple, And in splendour and in food they shall be poured out as water. Therefore, they shall be wanting in doctrine and wisdom, and they shall perish thereby together with their possessions; And with all their glory and their splendour, and in shame and in slaughter and in great destitution, their spirits shall be cast into the furnace of fire" (Enoch 98:1-3).

Josephus aggress with Philo, saying, "And when God had replied that there was no good man among the Sodomites; for if there were but ten such men among them, he would not punish any of them for their sins, Abraham held his peace. And the angels came to the city of the Sodomites, and Lot entreated them to accept a lodging with him; for he was a very generous and hospitable man who had learned to imitate the goodness of Abraham. Now when the Sodomites saw the young men to be of beautiful countenances, and this to an extraordinary degree, and that they took up their lodgings with Lot, they resolved themselves to enjoy these beautiful boys by force and violence; and when Lot exhorted them to sobriety, and not to offer anything immodest to the strangers, but to have regard to their lodging in his house; and promised, that if their inclinations could not be governed, he would expose his daughters to their lust, instead of these strangers—neither thus were they made ashamed" (Antiquities 200-2001).

Noted above, Philo notes the transition where men become like women, endangering themselves and the entire human race. Philo states that if the Greeks had adopted this practice, they would have been destroyed, as Sodom was. Today the world has done just that; it has accepted and even celebrates homosexuality. Even worse, the world is indoctrinating children with it. This perversion is the prophecy in fulfillment.

Jesus said, when He returns to judge this world, it will be like the days of Lot (Lu. 17:28-37). As with the "Days of Noah" (Lu. 17:26), the "Days of Lot" (Lu. 17:28) are compared. The commonality is sexual immorality, homosexuality, and that angels were having sex with women (Gen. 6), and men wanted to have sex with angels (Gen. 19). Apart from that sexual sin, there was the love of this world, evident with Lot's wife, who "Looked back" (Gen. 19:26, Lu. 17:32). The term "Looked back" has the application of "Wanting to go back" (cf. Lu. 9:62). The same is applied to the scoffers who deny Bible prophecy regarding the return of Jesus. Instead, they want to remain in this world, being satisfied in sin (Jude 18). Peter warns that the one who escapes this world and then returns to it will be worse off than if they never escaped in the first place (2 Pet. 2:20-21). Both Peter and Jude narrow in on the issue of greed (2 Pet. 2:3, 14, Jude 11, 12), which is characteristic of the false teachers (cf. 1 Tim. 6:3-5, Tit. 1:11). Jesus warned when teaching on the coming kingdom (Lu. 17:20-37), do not "Turn back" (Lu. 17:31). Do not bother with worldly goods that are perishing, or else you will perish with them; that is the warning.

Another similarity between the story of the fallen angels and Sodom is that fire is used to destroy both. The angels are kept in eternal chains until the judgement of the great day (Jude 6), resulting in being cast into the lake of fire (Rev. 20:14), and Sodom was destroyed by fire (Gen. 19:24-28), and the Sodomites are eternally punished with fire (Jude 7). Jude's reference to the eternal fire tormenting sinners is the same as what John recorded in the book of Revelation (Rev. 14:10-11, 19:20, 20:10, 11-15, 21:8). As mentioned in the previous section, eternal punishment in the lake of fire is just that, eternal, unending, conscious suffering, without rest (Rev. 14:11). Today, it is common to say "Rest in peace" when someone passes. However, the Bible states there is no peace for those outside of Christ. The fourth book of Maccabees says it this way, "Because of this, justice has laid up for you intense and eternal fire and tortures, and these throughout all time will never let you go" (4 Mac. 12:12).

In conclusion, following the two previous warnings, Jude offers another warning from Sodom. The notice is to the "Beloved" (Jude 3), "Reminding them of what they once fully knew" (Jude 5). God judged those who rebelled, and He will do it again. The hidden reefs (false teachers) are already condemned (Jude 4, 13), and the "Unsteady souls enticed by them" (2 Pet. 2:14) are in danger of condemnation (Jude 22-23). Some, who were once saved, have already been shipwrecked. Therefore, "Contend for the faith!" (Jude 3). Resist false teachers and their teaching, saving those seduced by them by snatching them out of the [hell] fire (Jude 23).

The sin that Jude and Peter narrow in on about Sodom is homosexuality. Those practicing or even approving of homosexuality are condemned to the same death (Rom. 1:32). The destruction of Sodom serves as an example of what God did in the past and what He is about to do again.

CHAPTER 3A
Abandonment

In Like Manner

Following the examples of rebellion and judgement (Jude 5-7), Jude introduces another, with the words "In like manner" (Jude 8) What the hidden reefs (Jude 12) do is the same as the rebellious Israelites, fallen angels, and Sodom. Jude calls the hidden reefs "Dreamers" (Jude 8), who claim to have divine revelation, yet know nothing of the things to come against them (Jude 4, 13). They claim to have prophetic vision, yet they are blind scoffers, understanding nothing (Jude 10) of their coming judgement (Jude 18, 14-15).

The term "Dreamer" refers to having prophetic insight and is often used within the Bible favourably regarding those who have received revelation from God. However, in Jude's case, the term is like what Moses used (Deut. 13:1, 3, 5) and Jeremiah, referring to the false prophets in their time (Jer. 23:25, 28; 29:8). Through Zechariah, God addressed the same (Zech. 10:3).

Those claiming to be "Seers" (dreamers) do so to gain an advantage (cf. Jude 16) and superiority, affording them authority and positions within the church, allowing them to influence others. Remember, the "Dreamers" (Jude 8) had "Crept in unnoticed" (Jude 4) and have since established themselves, causing some to doubt and others to sin (Jude 22-23) by going outside of God's commands.

The difference between the false teachers and God's elect is that the elect of God stays within the boundaries of scripture. The false teacher rejects the authority of scripture and, therefore, God (Jude 8). Remember, the false teachers are guilty of "Perverting the grace of God" (Jude 4), which refers to giving a license to sin. By giving a license to sin, they have become "Lawless" (cf. Matt. 7:21-23). The Greek for "Lawless" (Gk. Anomia) applies to Lawbreakers, who do not keep the law or stay within its boundaries. Jesus warned those guilty of breaking and ignoring the law of God will be cast into everlasting darkness (Matt. 7:23), which is the predestined fate of those Jude is warning against (Jude 4, 13.2 Pet. 2:12). The false teachers, whom Jude was warning of, not only broke the law, but they also added to it (Jude 8) with "New knowledge, and special revelation."

In this post-Apostolic age, divine revelation must be based on scripture; there is no "New revelation," which is what the false teachers claimed. For this reason, Jude called them "Dreamers" (Jude 8) and "Waterless clouds swept along by the wind" (Jude 12). Jude also said they were loud-mouthed boasters (Jude 16), having plenty to say but nothing of any worth. Peter adds to the conversation, saying the false teachers, "Speak loud boasts of folly" (2 Pet. 2:18). Today, there are many loud-mouthed 'preachers' filling pulpits and television screens, who promote 'Special revelation', often with the introduction, "I had a dream or a vision, or God told me..." Remember again, the false prophets during Jeremiah's time said the same thing, "I have dreamed a dream" (Jer. 23:25), yet God called them out, calling them liars (Jer. 23:26). God adds, "Let the prophet who has a dream tell the dream but let him who has My word speak My word faithfully" (Jer. 23:28).

Prophetic revelation must be tested against scripture, which was not the practice of the church Jude was addressing. The evidence for this is that the false teachers had crept in unnoticed and had gained authority within the church, enticing, and corrupting unsteady souls (2 Pet. 2:14, Jude 22-23). The false teachers had themselves "Gone astray, following in the way of Balaam" (2 Pet. 2:15). The fact that they had "Gone astray" confirms they were once on the right path, assuming they may once have also been saved. Now, like the apostate examples provided by Jude (Jude 5-7), they are condemned (Jude 4, 13) and endanger the weak at the love feast (2 Pets. 2:13); shipwrecking them of their faith (cf. 1 Tim. 1:19).

The application for Jude's readers, including us, is that we must fearfully test prophecy (1 Thess. 5:20-21, 1 Jn. 4:1). While we should not despise prophecy, we must abstain from evil (1 Thess. 5:22). In the case of Jude, evil was dwelling among the beloved (Jude 3), yet undetected through the hidden reefs who were perverting grace (Jude 4), proclaiming dreams, while rejecting (scriptural) authority (Jude 8), and doing so, without fear (Jude 12).

While the believer is to "Fearfully work [things] out" (Phil. 2:12), the false teachers were "Without fear" (Jude 12). The one working out their salvation with fear and trembling does so without grumbling, without blemish, and by holding fast to the word of life (Phil. 2:14-16). This is contrary to the false teachers who were grumblers (Jude 16) and blemishes (Jude 12), and rejecting scripture (Jude 8). As a result of rejecting scriptural authority (Jude 4b), the false teachers defile their bodies (Jude 4a) and "Blaspheme the glorious ones" (Jude 8). The examples previously provided compare defilement through sexual sin (Jude 4) with the fallen angels (Jude 6) and Sodom and Gomorrah (Jude 7). As mentioned previously, the false who rejects authority is directly applied to Christ, which is why Jude makes a point of acknowledging His Lordship, Deity (Jude 4, 25), and return (Jude 14, 21).

Not only do the blasphemous teachers (hidden reefs) reject the authority of Jesus (and scripture), but they also slander God's holy angels (Jude 9). While some state that the false teachers were slandering fallen angels, the context disagrees. Jude would not have taken issue with anyone shaming and insulting fallen angels but rather dishonouring God's holy angels. To give honour to evil would be evil itself. While some teach that slandering fallen angels is wrong, Paul did it. (2 Cor. 11:14, Gal. 1:8). Peter confirms that the Gnostics were slandering holy angles: "Those who indulge in the lust of defiling passion and despise authority. Bold and wilful, they do not tremble as they blaspheme the glorious ones, whereas angels, though greater in might and power, do not pronounce a blasphemous judgment against them before the Lord" (2 Pet. 2:10b-11).

The context of the letter reveals that the false teachers, in the same manner (Jude 8) as the rebellious Israelites (Jude 5), the fallen angels (Jude 6), and the Sodomites (Jude 7), were evil. With each example, Jude demonstrates how all rejected God, and His authority, which is now connected with blaspheming angels (Jude 8).

The connection is further developed in verse nine (Jude 9), where Jude cites The Assumption of Moses, another apocryphal work. Although thought to be lost, the bulk of that manuscript is said to be contained in the Testament of Moses. In the Bible, the same story of Moses' death is found in Deuteronomy (Deut. 34:4-6). As cited by Jude, the Testament of Moses provides more revelation of the interaction between Michael the archangel and the devil over Moses' body (Jude 9). Michael is mentioned three times in the book of Daniel (Dan. 10:13, 21, 12:1), revealing him to be the great prince over Israel. Like Jude's account, Michael will again fight with Satan and overcome him during the tribulation (Rev. 12:7) and again at the end of the seven-year ordeal. When Jesus returns, Michael will cast Satan into the bottomless pit (Rev. 20:1-3). Michael is also referenced by Enoch as one of four powerful angels set over humanity (Enoch 20:5, 40:9).

Like Enoch's book, Jude's mention of Michael, and the surrounding circumstance, is not foreign to his reader. Remember, Jude was reminding them of what they once fully knew (Jude 5); therefore, they were fully aware of the contention between Michael and Satan over Moses' body. Michael is a servant of God, a holy angel, chief among many, and the protector of Israel. During the tribulation, Michael will "Fly" Israel into the wilderness, escaping the dragon's (Satan) rage (Rev. 12:6, 14).

Again, while the meaning of Jude's quote is lost for most today, his reader would have been familiar with it. The context again is about the blasphemous false teachers who knew no boundary (Jude 8) and had no fear (Jude 12). Jude writes of Michael, "He did not presume to pronounce a blasphemous judgment" (Jude 9, ESV). The NKJV says this: "When he disputed about the body of Moses, [he] dared not bring against him a reviling accusation." The phrase (dared not) relates to risk and shame (cf. Mk. 12:34). For comparison, there is a reference in the book of Acts (Acts 7:32), revealing, "Moses trembled and dared not look." Stephen cites Moses (Exod. 3:6) concerning the story of the burning bush (Exod. 3). Moses feared God, unlike the false teachers, like the Israelites (Jude 5), the angels (Jude 6), and Sodom (Jude 7). Because Moses had a healthy respect and fear of God, he knew and remained within the set boundaries. He stayed within his proper place concerning whom he is, compared to God (cf. Jude 6).

The connection between Moses and Michael is that both remained within their proper place. Michael, the archangel (Jude 9), was unlike the fallen angels who left heaven and interfered with humanity (Jude 6). Again, the false teachers are compared to the fallen angels, who were referenced as an example. In the same manner (Jude 8), the hidden reefs (Jude 12) are blasphemers (Jude 8, 10), unlike Michael, who was not blasphemous (Jude 9, 2 Pet. 2:11).

The mention of Michael not slandering the devil does not suggest smearing his character, for there are several verses in the Bible doing that (e.g., Jn. 8:44; Acts 13:10; 1 Jn. 3:8; Rev 12:9). Therefore, the application is about judgement. Michael did not overstep the mark by judging Satan, for that is God's role alone (Zech. 3:2). In contrast, the ungodly accuse the godly without cause (cf. Rev. 12:10), without fear (Jude 12, 2 Pet. 2:10) and without understanding (Jude 10). Not only do they reject Christ, but they also slander Him and his servants.

Jude contradicts the false teachers, who, by definition (teacher), should have knowledge, by saying they are without knowledge and, therefore, are without substance (Jude 10, 12-13). While claiming superior knowledge through special revelation (dreams), they are ignorant, biblically illiterate fantasists. So ignorant are they that Jude and Peter liken them to dumb animals who are destined to be destroyed (Jude 10, 2 Pet. 2:12). Both Jude and Peter's comparison of the false teachers to animals destined to slaughter is like Jeremiah's complaint and prayer of the wicked and false prophets (Jer. 12:3b). The end of the false prophets was a reversal of what they wanted to do to Jeremiah (Jer. 11:18-20). Despite the teaching that God does not see, and that judgement will not come (Jer. 12:4), God destroyed the rebellious through the Babylonian invasion. Just as God set Jeremiah apart for the task of preaching the gospel (Jer. 1:5), Jeremiah wanted God to set the troublemakers apart for destruction (Jer. 3b), -which He did. The troublemakers desired that Jeremiah would be slaughtered, like a gentle lamb, without cause (Jer. 11:19). What they desired for Jeremiah, God gave to them. The same will be true for the false teachers (Jude 4, 13) who have crept in unnoticed, perverting the grace of God (Jude 4).

Likened to the dumb animal destined to slaughter, the false teachers only follow their instinct, which in context refers to sexual immorality (Jude 4, 6, 7, 2 Pet. 2:2, 6-10, 14, 18) and greed (Jude 12, 2 Pet. 2:3, 14). In fact, the shared sinful instinct is within every person, resulting from the Adamic nature. The only solution is Christ, who is also likened to a beast, a gentle Lamb, slaughtered without cause (sin) in our place (Isa. 53). Jesus Christ exchanged places with us, and without Him, none have any hope (Rom. 6).

This is the reason Jesus, His teachings (scripture) and servants come under attack. The blasphemers (slanderers) attack the only means of salvation, causing some to doubt and stray (Jude 22-23). The very things the false teachers dismiss (Jesus and scriptural authority) and promote (sexual sin and greed) destroyed them (Jude 10) and their followers (Jude 23).

Regarding greed, Enoch adds this: "Be it known unto you (ye sinners) that the Most High is mindful of your destruction, And the angels of heaven rejoice over your destruction. What will ye do, ye sinners, and whither will ye flee on that day of judgement, when ye hear the voice of the prayer of the righteous? Yea, ye shall fare like unto them, against whom this word shall be a testimony: "Ye have been companions of sinners." And in those days the prayer of the righteous shall reach unto the Lord, and for you the days of your judgement shall come. And all the words of your unrighteousness shall be read out before the Great Holy One, and your faces shall be covered with shame, And He will reject every work which is grounded on unrighteousness. Woe to you, ye sinners, who live on the mid ocean and on the dry land, Whose remembrance is evil against you. Woe to you who acquire silver and gold in unrighteousness and say: "We have become rich with riches and have possessions; And have acquired everything we have desired. And now let us do what we purposed: For we have gathered silver, and many are the husbandmen in our houses." And our granaries are (brim) full as with water, Yea and like water your lies shall flow away; For your riches shall not abide but speedily ascend from you; For ye acquired it all in unrighteousness, and ye shall be given over to a great curse" (Enoch 97:1-10).

Enoch's warning of the unrighteous claiming riches at the expense of the righteous is like the false prophets of Jeremiah's day (Jer. 5:27) and it should also remind the reader of another warning from Jesus Christ, which is found in the book of Luke, chapter twelve, being the parable of the rich fool (Lu. 12:13-21). Like Enoch, Jesus concludes, warning the rich fools, on the day their soul will be required of them, answering for all that they have done (Lu.

12:20). Note also with Enoch's passage, where the wicked says, "We have become rich with riches and have possessions; And have acquired everything we have desired. And now let us do what we purposed." Today, the words and warning of Enoch apply equally to the false teachers, preachers, and prophets who deceive the masses, by saying, "Sow your best seed (money) to my ministry, and God will give you a hundred-fold in return."

In sum, these false teachers are ministers of Satan (2 Cor. 11:13-15), promoting another way (cf. Jn. 14:6), or "Another Jesus," through a "Different spirit," resulting in a "Different gospel" (2 Cor. 11:4), often motivated by greed. Remember again, from the first section of this work, the agenda of the gnostic teachers was to attack the deity of Jesus Christ. Others simply distract you away from Him through worldly offerings, like Satan's attempt with Jesus (Matt. 4:1-11). The false teachers will also attack anyone and anything that proclaim Christ and command a lifestyle of repentance and holiness. Peter counters their teaching by calling God's people "To live lives of holiness and godliness, waiting for and hastening the coming of the day of God" (2 Pet. 3:11-12). Jude says something similar, "Keep yourselves in the love of God, waiting for the mercy of our Lord Jesus Christ that leads to eternal life" (Jude 21).

One of the fastest and surest ways of being led away from God, through the pursuit of holiness, apart from sexual sin, is greed. That is why the Bible has so much to say about the danger of money, going in the oversite direction to what the prosperity gospel teaches. The Bible teaches that God gives us prosperity for purpose, being that He will supply your 'Need' in accordance with His calling (Phil 4:19; Matt. 6:25-34), not self-centered greed or fleshly desire. Prosperity, for many, is an idol of the heart (Ezek. 14:1-11). Modern-day idols are fleshly desires that can quickly lead us astray (Mark 4:19; 2 Pet. 1:4b). Unsurprisingly, Scripture has plenty to say about those who preach and chase after prosperity (for example: 2 Cor. 2:17; 1 Tim. 6:3-10, 3:3b; Jude 11b). Scripture clearly states not to toil to acquire wealth (Prov. 23:4;

28:20), neither desire it, love it, or put your trust in it (Matt. 6:19; 1 Tim. 6:9-10; Heb 13:5).

In conclusion, the gnostic teachers, without fear, attack Christ, His teachings, and His servants, including holy angels, thereby "Reject [their] authority" (Jude 8). The loud-mouthed boasters (Jude 16) reject the authority of anything and anyone godly to promote themselves and their false teaching. Remember, their heart is "Trained in greed" (2 Pet. 2:14), and "In their greed, they will exploit you with false words" (2 Pet. 2:3), telling you what you want to hear (cf. 2 Tim. 4:3), by perverting grace (Jude 4), "You can do whatever you like, and you will be all right." Jude warns that the false teachers are as full of themselves as they are devoid of Christ (Jude 4), His Spirit (Jude 19), and the Truth (Jude 10).

CHAPTER 3B
Abandonment

Woe To Them!

After condemning the false teachers to hell (Jude 4, 8-10, 13), likening them to the three previous examples of the rebellious Israelites, the fallen angels, and Sodom, who also perished, eternally, Jude wastes no time providing another three examples. Like the first three examples, the following three (Jude 11) also took the road to hell, the road most travelled (cf. Matt. 7:13-14). Jude piles up the examples, one after the other, confirming the same outcome for all, warning those remaining, who had let the hidden reefs in (Jude 4), and who were doubting and sinning (Jude 22-23), of the endless punishment of eternal fire (Jude 7b).

Note that the warning is to the church, not to the false teachers designated for condemnation long ago (Jude 4), for whom utter darkness has been reserved forever (Jude 13). Remember again - the false teachers are apostates (2 Pet. 2:15), like with the examples of the three previous groups, the Israelites who knew God, the angels who saw God, and Sodom, who heard the preaching of righteous Lot. All knew, saw, and heard about God, yet fell away and failed to remain within their proper place (Jude 6). All despised God and His authority, like the false teachers who reject the authority of

Scripture (Jude 8), twisting it (2 Pet. 3:16) for their own greedy gain (2 Pet. 2:3, 14, Jude 11-12, 16). Woe to them, as it was for Cain, Balaam, and Korah (Jude 11) fiery judgement awaits.

Jude's "Woe" (Jude 11) is likened to Isaiah's warning, and woe to Jerusalem and Judah (Isa 3:9, 11), due to following in the arrogant footsteps of Sodom. Note that Isaiah, chapter two (Isa. 2:10, 19, 21) has similarities to Revelation, chapter six (Rev. 6:14-17). Isaiah goes on to say, "Woe to those who call evil good and good evil, who put darkness for light and light for darkness, who put bitter for sweet and sweet for bitter! Woe to those who are wise in their own eyes, and shrewd in their own sight!" (Isa. 5:20-21). Woe to those who have led others astray by their perverted values, which is what false teachers of Jude's letter did.

Hosea does something similar (Hos. 7:13) - condemning those who have strayed from God. While they offer lip service, they only do so for selfish gain (Hos. 7:14, 16). Interestingly, God says through the prophet Hosea that He would have redeemed the apostate if they had not continued their lies. Hosea further confirms the issue of apostasy by referencing Adam, who transgressed, and broke the covenant (Hos. 6:7). Like Israel's apostate kings (Hos. 7:7), the nation did the same, committing spiritual whoredom, defiling themselves and the covenant (Hos. 6:10). Like a wandering prostitute Israel went after other gods, who promised health and prosperity, vowing to give them, "Their best life now." Sound familiar?

In the New Testament, Jesus gave a similar warning and "Woe" to the Pharisees, who also used religion for greedy gain at the expense of others (Matt 23:13–36; Luke 6:24–26; 11:42–52). The Old Testament prophets warned Israel and Judah, and Jesus warned the religious teachers, teaching the Law. Now Jude takes the Old Testament examples and applies them to the false teachers within the church, warning the church that they too will meet the same end if they go the same way. Woe to them, and woe to you if you do what they do. John does likewise, saying, "We should not be like Cain, who was of the evil one and murdered his brother. And why did he murder him? Because his own deeds were evil and his brother's righteous" (1 Jn. 3:12).

With every example of rebellion that Jude has given, there was a prophetic announcement of judgement; in the same way, Jude is proclaiming judgement, prophetically against apostates now. Jude warned the church that Jesus is coming back, and when He does, He will execute judgement on all (Jude 14-15). Therefore, "Keep yourselves in the love of God, waiting for the mercy of our Lord Jesus Christ that leads to eternal life" (Jude 21).

The word "Woe" (Jude 11) implies judgement, used serval times in the book of Revelation (Rev 8:13, 9:12, 11:14). When Jesus returns, as Jude mentioned (Jude 14-15, 21), He does so after the tribulation. Throughout the tribulation, God will test humanity by pouring out judgements (Rev. 3:10), providing the whole world with an opportunity to repent and remain. Woe to those who remain in their sin by rejecting the grace of God, enabling them to respond.

Cain is an excellent example of one who refused the grace of God amidst judgement, and subsequently perished. Woe to Cain, and woe to any other following him, "Walking in the way of Cain, abandoning themselves for the sake of gain" (Jude 11a). Note the language in verse eleven again, "They walked in the way of Cain, and abandoned themselves." Peter says something similar, calling the false teachers, "Accursed children. Forsaking the right way, they have gone astray" (2 Pet. 2:14b-15a). Once more, like Peter, Jude narrows in on the apostasy of the false teachers, likened to Cain, who knew God and fell away. The same condition is applied to those following in his footsteps; they are apostates, which is why Peter says it would have been better to have never known than to have known the truth, and then fall away (2 Pet. 2:20-21).

The warning of "Walking in the way" (in the same way) of one beforehand is referenced many times through Scripture (1 Kgs. 15:26, 34, 16:2, 19, 26, 2 Kgs. 8:18, 27, 16:3; 2 Chron. 11:17, 21:6, Ezek. 23:31), always with a warning. "If you do what they do, I (God) will do the same to you!" Those following in the footsteps of Cain, being the false teachers, and those following the false teachers will all suffer the same outcome.

The story of Cain is recorded in the book of Genesis, chapter four. Cain and Abel were Adam and Eve's sons, and Cain was Abel's older brother. Cain murdered his brother Abel due to jealousy, resulting in hatred. Abel offered God an acceptable offering, whereas Cain did not. God's disapproval of his gift angered Cain. Cain's anger and withdrawal (apostasy) from God opened him up to Satan, the tempter, who enticed him to sin (Gen. 4:6-7). Instead of ruling over sin, Cain was ruled by it, acting on temptation and killing Abel. Abel's blood then cried out against Cain, and God heard the cry (Gen. 4:10), which is like the book of Revelation, chapter six (Rev. 6:9-11). Cain was subsequently banished from the presence of God (Gen. 4:16).

Cain's sin against Abel can be viewed metaphorically, exemplifying hatred of one's brothers and sisters (cf. 1 Jn. 3:11). Others, including the early church fathers, have added to the story, indicating Cain was also guilty of sexual sin and greed. Josephus says the following:

"Adam and Eve had two sons; the elder of them was named Cain, which name when it is interpreted, signifies a possession. The younger was Abel, which signifies sorrow. They also had daughters. Now, the two brethren were pleased with different courses of life, for Abel, the younger, was a lover of righteousness, and, believing that God was present at all his actions, he excelled in virtue; and his employment was that of a shepherd. But Cain was not only very wicked in other respects but was wholly intent upon getting - and he first contrived to plough the ground. He slew his brother on the occasion following:

They had resolved to sacrifice to God. Now Cain brought the fruits of the earth, and of his husbandry; but Abel brought milk, and the first fruits of his flocks; but God was more delighted with the latter oblation, when he was honoured with what grew naturally of its own accord, than he was with what was the invention of a covetous man, and gotten by forcing the ground; whence it was that Cain was very angry that Abel was preferred by God before him; and he slew his brother, and hid his dead body, thinking to escape discovery. But God, knowing what had been done, came to Cain, and asked him what was become of his brother, because he had not seen him of many days, whereas he used to observe them conversing together at other times. But Cain was in doubt with himself and knew not what answer to give to God. At first, he said that he was himself at a loss about his brother's disappearing; but when he was provoked by God, who pressed him vehemently, as resolving to know what the matter was, he replied, he was not his brother's guardian or keeper, nor was he an observer of what he did. But in return, God convicted Cain, as having been the murderer of his brother; and said, "I wonder at thee, that thou knowest not what is become of a man whom thou thyself has destroyed." God therefore did not inflict the punishment [of death] upon him, on account of his offering sacrifice, and thereby making supplication to him not to be extreme in his wrath to him; but he made him accused and threatened his posterity in the seventh generation. He also cast him, together with his wife, out of that land. And when he was afraid, that in wandering about he should fall among wild beasts, and by that means perish, God bid him not to entertain such a melancholy suspicion, and to go over all the earth without fear of what mischief he might suffer from wild beasts; and setting a mark upon him that he might be known, he commanded him to depart. And when Cain had travelled over many countries, he, with his wife, built a city, named Nod, which is a place so called, and there he settled his abode, where also he had children. However, he did not accept of his punishment, in order to amendment, but to increase his wickedness; for he only aimed to procure everything that was for his own bodily pleasure, though it obliged him to be injurious to his neighbours. He augmented his household substance with much wealth, by rapine and violence; he excited his acquaintance to procure pleasures and spoils by robbery and became a great leader of men into wicked courses. He also introduced a change in that way of simplicity wherein men lived before; and was the author of measures and weights. And whereas they lived innocently and generously while they knew nothing of such arts, he changed the world into cunning craftiness. He first of all set boundaries about lands; he built a city, and fortified it with walls, and he compelled his family to come together to it; and called that city Enoch," after the name of his eldest son Enoch" (The works of Josephus: complete and unabridged, expounded by R. Wayne Jackson).

Confirmed by Josephus, Cain continued in rebellion against God, fitting the context of Jude's letters. Like the Israelites, the angels, and Sodom, all continued to despise God and His authority. The false teachers are on the same path, and anyone who follows them (Jude 11) is also on the road to destruction (Jude 22-23). As seen through Josephus' writings, among many other early church fathers and historians, Cain is seen as an archetype heretic. Cain is viewed within Jewish tradition as an excellent example of false teachers gone astray, pursuing gain.

Although Cain was born into a life of privilege, taught by his parents, Adam, and Eve, in God's way, and was provided every opportunity by God to respond to His grace, Cain still chose the path of sin, which was "Crouching at the door" (Gen. 4:7). Not only did Cain sin against his brother, his parents and God, he and his descendants grew increasing wicked. Josephus confirms it by saying, "Nay, even while Adam was alive, it came to pass that the posterity of Cain became exceedingly wicked, everyone successively dying, one after the another, more wicked than the former. They were intolerable in war" (Josephus 1.2.2).

Like Cain, "Balaam loved gained from wrongdoing" (2 Pet. 2:15b). He too forsook the right way and went astray (2 Pet. 2:15a); confirmed by Jude, Balaam abandoned himself for the sake of gain (Jude 11). The story of Balaam is found in the book of Numbers, chapters twenty-two to twenty-four. Dwarfing Cain, Balaam is mentioned many more times in scripture due to his wickedness. In the book of Numbers, he is shown to refuse Balak's request to curse Israel for money (Num. 22:18, 24,13). However, in the book of Deuteronomy (Deut. 23:4) and Nehemiah (Neh. 13:2), Balaam is hired to curse God's people. Furthermore, Joshua mentioned Balaam (Josh. 13:23, 24:9, 10), as does Micah (Mic. 6:5). In the New Testament, Balaam is mentioned by Peter (2 Pet. 2:15), Jude (Jude 11), and Jesus, through John, in the book of Revelation (Rev. 2:14).

Peter's mention of Balaam (2 Pet. 2:15-16) plays off his previous statement, where it likens the false teachers to dumb animals to be slaughtered (2 Pet. 2:12). Peter joins Jude in saying the false teachers are loud-mouthed fools (2 Pet. 2:18, Jude 16). It could be argued that Peter is saying the false teachers are even dumber than Balaam's talking donkey. A donkey is known to be a particularly stupid animal, and therefore the association of a 'Donkey' is sometimes used when calling someone stubborn and stupid (e.g., You dumb donkey). However, scripturally, a donkey can also refer to the authority of God's word, as seen through Numbers (Num. 22:21, 23, 28).

The spiritual application of authority also fits within Peter and Jude's letters. The false teachers rejected authority; therefore, they rejected scripture (2 Pet. 2:10, Jude 8). Either way, the suggested statement Peter is making is that the speechless donkey had more sense than Balaam (2 Pet. 2:16) and therefore has more sense than the false teachers, who despise God and reject authority. Unlike Paul, who "Refused to practice cunning or to tamper with God's word" (2 Cor. 4:2), the hidden reefs, peddlers of the gospel (2 Cor. 2:17), and false apostles (2 Cor. 11:13), being agents of Satan (2 Cor. 11:15) have no fear (Jude 12) - therefore no problem twisting scripture, and presenting "Another gospel" (2 Co. 11:4). And like Eve, many are deceived, and led astray (2 Cor. 11:3) by them, as is the case within Peter and Jude's letters (2 Pet. 2:14, Jude 22-23).

In the book of Revelation, Balaam is mentioned in the letter to the church of Pergamum from Jesus (Rev. 2:12-17). The church of Pergamum was charged with holding to the teachings of Balaam and the Nicolaitans (Rev. 2:14-15). Both teachings promoted sexual sin, including orgies at the 'Love-feast', which was the practice of pagans, and was also the case with the false teachers who had crept in and perverted grace (Jude 4). Both Jude and Peter confirm that they were enticing unsteady souls to sin sexually, therefore bringing them into condemnation, in the same way Balaam did with Israel. Such was the case with the church of Pergamum. The same was also true for the church of Thyatira, - it was deceived by the teachings of Jezebel (Rev. 2:20). In each account, the motive is financial gain. In his first letter, Paul warned Timothy against the apostates who corrupt his teachings for financial reward (1 Tim. 6:5-10).

The direct application of Balaam's sin was being an agent to entice the people of God to sin. The sin in Balaam's case was fornication, leading to idolatry, resulting in divine judgement (Num. 25). That is what the early church fathers taught, as seen through Josephus' writings, among others. Josephus wrote the following:

"But Balak, being very angry that the Israelites were not cursed, sent away Balaam without thinking him worthy of any honor. Whereupon, when he was just upon his journey, in order to pass the Euphrates, he sent for Balak, and for the princes of the Midianites, and spake thus to them - "O Balak, and you Midianites that are here present (for I am obliged even without the will of God to gratify you), it is true no entire destruction can seize upon the nation of the Hebrews, neither by war, nor by plague, nor by scarcity of the fruits of the earth, nor can any other unexpected accident be their entire ruin; for the providence of God is concerned to preserve them from such a misfortune; nor will it permit any such calamity to come upon them whereby they may all perish; but some small misfortunes, and those for a short time, whereby they may appear to be brought low, may still befall them; but after that they will flourish again, to the terror of those that brought those mischiefs upon them. So that if you have a mind to gain a victory over them for a short space of time you will obtain it by following my directions:—Do you therefore set out the handsomest of such of your daughters as are most eminent for beauty, and proper to force and conquer the modesty of those that behold them, and these decked and trimmed to the highest degree you are able. Then do you send them to be near the Israelites' camp and give them in charge, that when the young men of the Hebrews desire their company, they allow it them; and when they see that they are enamoured of them, let them take their leaves; and if they entreat them to stay, let them not give their consent till they have persuaded them to leave off their obedience to their own laws and the worship of that God who established them, and to worship the gods of the Midianites and Moabites; for by this means God will be angry at them." Accordingly, when Balaam had suggested this counsel to them, he went his way" (Ant. 4:126-130, expounded by Herbert W Armstrong).

Notice the words, "They have persuaded them to leave off their obedience to their own laws," which repeats what the angels did (Jude 6). Like the false teachers, the Israelites rejected the authority of scripture (Jude 8). Like Balaam, the false teachers entice unsteady souls for greedy gain (2 Pet. 2:14-15).

Following the examples of Cain and Balaam, who had gone astray, is Korah's rebellion (Jude 11). Korah's rebellion is recorded in the book of Numbers, chapter sixteen, albeit he is first mentioned in Exodus (6:21, 24). Like the rest, Korah was once secure within the elect of God, yet "Rose up before Moses" (Num. 16:2), leading another 250 well-known leaders into rebellion against Moses and Aaron (Num. 16:2-3). Korah's charge against Moses and Aaron was that they had set themselves up as holy and Israel's leaders, whereas Korah said, "All in the congregation are holy, every one of them" (Num. 16:3b, 15). When accused of exalting himself, Moses fell on his face, telling Korah that the Lord will decide in the morning, who is His, and holy among the congregation (Num. 16:4-7). The problem is identified in verse ten, where Korah wanted the priesthood for himself (Num. 16:10b). Although Korah had been given other responsibilities (Num. 16:9), he was not satisfied, like Satan, when he wanted to be God (Isa. 14:12-15), followed by his fallen angles who wanted to produce demi-gods, the Nephilim (Jude 6).

Like Satan, Korah has revolted against God by challenging Moses' authority (Num. 16:11). In verse sixteen (Num. 16:16), Moses instructs Korah to be present before God in the morning, when God would judge between Moses and Korah, and company. The following day, Korah and company presented themselves, and the "Glory of the Lord appeared" (Num. 16:19). Moses was told to separate himself from the congregation (Num. 16:20, 24, 26, 27), like with Lot when God was about to judge Sodom (2 Pet. 2:6-9, Jude 7). Once the righteous were separated from the rebellious, God opened the ground underneath Korah and company, casting them alive into hell (Num. 16:30-33).

The link Jude makes between Korah and the false teachers is that they, too, despised authority (Jude 8), teaching something contrary to scripture (Jude 4). In the same way, Korah, and those following him, were destroyed, cast alive into hell, and the false teachers will also be (Jude 4, 13). As Cain was banished, Balaam died in battle, and Korah went alive into hell; all who walk in their ways also end up in hell. The same was true for the rebellious Israelites (Jude 5), the fallen angels (Jude 6), and the people of Sodom and Gomorrah (Jude 7), serving as an example by undergoing a punishment of eternal fire (Jude 7b). Hence Jude's instruction to the church, "Contend for the faith" (Jude 3) and "Snatch [those in danger of apostasy] out of the fire"

(Jude 23). Warning, woe to those who do not listen and do not obey, calling evil good and good evil. Hell awaits!

Like Jude, Moses tried to spare those following Korah (Num. 16:22-27), being in danger of apostasy; however, God consumed everyone involved in the rebellion (Num. 16:35). The next day, another uprising occurred resulting from those objecting to God's judgement of Korah and company (Num. 16:41). Once more, Moses was told by God to separate himself from the grumblers (Num. 16:45). Again, Moses intercedes, attempting to save some (Num. 16:46-48). Some were saved because Moses stood between the dead and the living, albeit 14,700 died before the plague of the Lord stopped (Num. 16:49).

CHAPTER 4
Hidden Reefs

Blemishes On Your Love Feasts

Verse twelve of Jude's letter (Jude 12) is the point of arrival and big idea within the chiastic structure. Remember again; a chiastic structure is where a story told is mirrored on either side of the critical point. The key point of Jude's letter is the false teachers; the hidden reefs have crept in and are shipwrecking the faith of some unsteady souls. The false teachers are blasphemers, feasting with the church, established in positions of power, self-seeking, and greedy for gain (Jude 12).

In the last section, the blasphemers, past and present, who are condemned to hell, were addressed. This section will consider the continuation of Jude's rebuke of the false teachers, the hidden reefs (rocks), who have crept in unnoticed (Jude 4). The false teacher is designated for condemnation from long ago (Jude 4), for utter darkness that has been reserved from them forever (Jude 13, 2 Pet. 2:17), which is why they are "Twice dead" (Jude 12).

These blots and blemishes reveling in deception have worked their way into the fold and are now feasting with the called and kept beloved (Jude 2, 3) - yet they entice unsteady souls (2 Pet. 2:13-14). The apostates, who have forsaken the way (2 Pet. 2:15), are endangering others by luring them onto the road of apostasy with their false words (2 Per. 2:3). Indeed, they have already caused some to doubt and others to sin (Jude 22:23). The false teachers led some away from the straight, narrow, and difficult path (Matt. 7:14), by offering other benefits, such as prosperity (Jude 12, 16, 18, 2 Pet. 2:2, 14), and a license (freedom) to sin (Jude 4, 2 Pet. 2:19).

While offering other advantages, outside of what scripture affords, they have nothing to offer, like with their talk; they have plenty to say, but nothing of any worth (Jude 16, 2 Pet. 2:18). They are spiritually bankrupt. They are waterless clouds, waterless springs, fruitless trees, wild waves, and wandering stars (Jude 12b-13, 2 Pet. 2:17). They reject the authority of scripture (Jude 8) they are without knowledge, without fear (Jude 12), and they are without understanding (Jude 10), yet still, they position themselves among the flock as teachers, apostles, and prophets (2 Pet. 2:1).

The false teachers crept in (Jude 4) and rose from within (2 Pet. 2:1a), secretly bringing in destructive heresies (2 Pet. 2:1b), specifically at the "Love feast" (Jude 12, 2 Pet. 2:13). The love feast is the only meeting or gathering mentioned for the early church. The word "Love" on this occasion is the Greek word "Agape". There are seven commonly known Greek words for love, all with slightly different applications. However, "Agape" love is the greatest of love, meaning "Unconditional love". The love feast is to have the application of unconditional love, flowing from God to the beloved and on flowing to each other. The feast is reserved for the called and kept (Jude 1) by Jesus Christ (Jude 24). Essentially, the love feast is the same as the Lord's supper (1 Cor. 11:17-34). Only those fully committed to Jesus should participate in sacred meals (Jn. 6:53-54). Due to some failing to "Examine themselves" before partaking in it, they become sick and even die (1 Cor. 11:27-31).

The love feast or Lord's supper was to be done in remembrance of Jesus Christ (1 Cor. 11:24), mirroring the "Lords supper" (Matt. 26:26-29, Mk. 14:22-25, Lu. 22:18-20, Jn. 6:53, 1 Cor. 10:16-17 11:17-34), reflecting on what Jesus did through the cross, and will do on His return (1 Cor. 11:26). The entire meeting is a celebration of Jesus Christ, with a sense of renewed commitment to Him by way of "Examining" oneself (1 Cor. 11:28), repenting of any sin, judging oneself (1 Cor. 11:32) in pursuit of holiness and righteousness, in preparation for His return (Jude 21). The focus is on His return, with the believer positioned and prepared by participating (Jn. 6:53-54, Rom. 5:16-21, 1 Cor. 10:16, 18) in His once and for all sacrifice (Heb. 10:10). The problem that Jude and Peter narrow in on is that there are 'Scoffers' at the table, sowing doubt, by saying, there is no sin (Jude 4), and Jesus is not returning (Jude 18, 2 Pet. 3:3), therefore you can do whatever you like. Follow your own sinful desires (2 Pet. 3:3, Jude 18).

The same scoffers were those abusing the meals, "They feast with you without fear, looking after themselves" (Jude 12). Peter says that while "Reveling in deception, they feast with you" (2 Pet. 2:13) and that they are "Insatiable for sin, enticing unsteady souls, having their hearts trained on greed" (2 Pet. 2:3, 14). The hidden reefs helping themselves to the meal and wine do so at the expense of others (1 Cor. 11:21-22). Instead of waiting for all to be fed (1 Cor. 11:33-34), they load up their plates and glasses, times over (1 Cor. 11:20-22), leaving others with empty stomachs and a (false) 'gospel' void of hope when it comes to who Jesus is, what He did, and how the believer must respond (Jude 20-21) in preparation of His return (Jude 18, 2 Pet. 3:3).

The false teachers, Peter and Jude were dealing with, are no different from today's prosperity pimps who exploit their hearers with wrong words motivated by greed (2 Pet. 2:3, 14). They help themselves to the best of everything, leaving others with nothing (Jude 12). There is a vast difference between God's elect and worldly preachers using the 'gospel' for greedy gain, positioning themselves over and above. An example of this is seen with Jesus' disciple, Thaddeus. According to the record of Eusebius, Thomas, one of the twelve disciples, sent Thaddeus, one of the seventy, to the Prince of Edessa, after Jesus' crucifixion and resurrection. The prince had previously sent his couriers to Jesus, as recorded in John's gospel (Jn. 12:20-23), requesting that Jesus would come and heal him. According to Eusebius, Jesus sent a letter saying He had to complete His Father's will. Eusebius' record is consistent with John's gospel (Jn. 12:23-25). Eusebius further states that Thaddeus went - he operated in healing, signs and wonders that accompanied the preaching of the gospel. Abgarus, the Prince, believed and was healed. Many others in the city heard the gospel and were also healed. Abgarus commanded his citizens to listen to the preaching of Thaddeus and afterward ordered them to give the preaching evangelist gold and silver. Thaddeus refused the gift, saying, "If we have forsaken that which was our own, how shall we take that which is another's." Thaddeus' response is consistent with John's gospel (Jn. 12:25-26). Clearly, there is a vast difference between the account recorded by Eusebius, and the many seen today demanding a gift in return for healing or payment to hear to 'gospel.'

The love feast aimed to achieve a common union between all, otherwise known as 'Communion' with Christ and each other, with an application of unhindered fellowship. However, not all were unified. Some were causing divisions, namely the false teachers (1 Cor. 11:18). Paul said, "There must be factions among you in order that those who are genuine among you may be recognized" (1 Cor. 11:19). The faction was between the genuine and the false; the true were confronting false teaching, to some degree, and therefore they were contending for the faith (Jude 3).

On one hand, Paul, and the writer of the book of Hebrews instructs the church to strive for peace (Rom. 14:9, Heb. 12:14) and to be in union with one another (Eph. 4:1-6), and on the other hand, Paul commends the church for resisting false teachers, and so does Jesus (Rev. 2:2, 9-10, 13, 24, 3:4, 10).

The divisions and different groups within the churches addressed in the book of Revelation occurred due to false teaching. However, in Paul's letter, there were factions mainly due to the greedy gluttons helping themselves to more than their fair share of the meal, and wine, leaving little or nothing for the rest (Jude 12, 1 Cor. 11:20-2133-34). Those helping themselves to the best of the offerings put themselves first and above the needs of others. The act was likened to upper-class citizens showing superiority over the poor within the church instead of behaving like one family. The superior mindset is also seen in those appointing themselves as apostles and prophets, many of who are ill-equipped to faithfully handle scripture.

As seen in Jude's letter, no factions were formed, which may be what motivated him to say, "Contend for the faith" (Jude 3). When holding firm to sound biblical doctrine, conflicts, and offshoots (church splits) will follow.

Jude marks the false teachers, calling them "Hidden reefs" (Jude 12), warning the church of the danger of getting too close - like a lighthouse warns ships at night. Without the lighthouse, caught off guard, unsuspecting ships will be smashed against the rocks. The same will happen to the faith of the naive believer and already has (Jude 22-23, 2 Pet. 2:14).

Jude's wordplay, using reefs, or rocks, to describe the false teachers, continues when he calls them blemishes (Jude 12). Peter also calls them blots and blemishes (2 Pet. 2:13). Remember, the love feast is in remembrance of the Lord's supper, which was symbolic of the New Covenant, replacing the Old Covenant. Under the Old Covenant, a sacrifice was to be without blot or blemish for it to be acceptable to God (Lev. 22:20). Jesus was that perfect sacrifice without blot or blemish (1 Pet. 1:19, Heb 9:11-28). The wordplay that Jude uses with the word 'Blemish' confirms that the false teachers have no business even being at the love feast.

Jude's reference to the false teachers being fearless, like the word "Blemish", is specific to the love feast, which is done in remembrance of Christ, the perfect sacrifice. Not only was the love feast in remembrance of what Jesus did and will do when He returns, but it is also a time when Jesus is present (Matt. 18:19-20). Therefore, Paul said, before partaking of the meal, to examine yourself (1 Cor. 11:28). When coming before a Holy God, one must be without sin, blot, or blemish, yet the false teachers were neither clean nor fearful. The fear required is reverential fear, whereas the false teachers were irreverent (Jude 14-15, 2 Pet. 2:10b). They had no fear of God (Jude 4, 8) and, therefore, no thought or care of the consequences (Jude 4, 13).

Like Balaam (Jude 11), the false teachers were only in it for what they could get out of it, oblivious of the dangers ahead. They were confessed seers (prophets) yet, blinded by greed. Again, the danger of allowing the false teachers to attend the love feast is that they mislead some with false words and lying dreams and visions. As mentioned previously, while they have plenty to say, they have nothing of any worth, which is why Jude calls them, "Waterless clouds, swept along by the wind" (Jude 13). The wind sweeping them along is not the wind of the Holy Spirit (Jn 3:8), for they are "Devoid of the Spirit" (Jude 19). Therefore, it is the wind of their vain imagination coming to nothing. They have no water, no fruits (Jude 13), and no clue. Likewise, they have no direction, like "Wandering stars" (Jude 13) that go off course.

The reference to the wandering stars is also linked to Enoch's book, where the prophet calls the fallen angels stars that have left their proper dwelling place (Enoch 21:6, 86:1, 3, 88:1, 3. cf. Jude 6). Isaiah also refers to Satan as a fallen star (Isa. 14:12-15), as does the book of Revelation (Rev. 9:1). Again, Jude compares the false teachers and the fallen angels. They are "Kept in eternal chains under gloomy darkness until the judgment of the great day" (Jude 6, 13). The fallen angels departed from God, as the false teachers have, by departing from the authority of scripture (Jude 8).

Enoch confirms the judgement for the wandering stars, which the false teachers and worthless servants will share in (Matt 8:12; 22:13; 25:30; Matt 25:41), "And I saw one of those four who had come forth first, and he seized that first star which had fallen from the heaven, and bound it hand and foot and cast it into an abyss: now that abyss was narrow and deep, and horrible and dark. And one of them drew a sword and gave it to those elephants and camels and asses: then they began to smite each other, and the whole earth quaked because of them. And as I was beholding in the vision, lo, one of those four who had come forth stoned (them) from heaven and gathered and took all the great stars whose privy members were like those of horses, and bound them all hand and foot, and cast them in an abyss of the earth" (Enoch 88:1-3).

As mentioned earlier, the false teachers promise much but deliver nothing, failing to bear fruit even in the late season of "Autumn" (Jude 13). In the same way, Jesus cursed the fig tree for not bearing fruit (Lu. 13:6); He has already condemned the false teachers to hell (Jude 4, 13). Remember, a prophet is known by their fruit (Matt. 7:15-20); those yielding no fruit or bad fruit are cast into hell (Matt. 7:20), which is why Jude uses the words "Twice dead" and "Uprooted" (Jude 12). The hidden reefs will be uprooted like the trees bearing bad fruit and cast into the fire (Matt. 7:19). They are twice dead because they are dead in their works (dead religion), bearing no fruit, and they will be cast into the lake of fire, which is the second death (Rev 2:11; 20:6, 14; 21:8). While the false teachers are still yet to be uprooted, are cast into everlasting darkness (Jude 13), as mentioned previously, they are already dead, awaiting their final judgement, which has already been pronounced (Jude 4, 13).

Jude continues with his pronounced judgement in verse thirteen (Jude 13), likening the false teachers to "Wild waves casting up the foam of their shame." Here, Jude quotes Isaiah (Isa. 57:20), associating "Mire and mud" (Isa. 57:20) with "Shame" (Jude 13). The opposite of 'Shame' is 'Pride' or 'Indifferent'. The false teachers exhibited both! They are prideful boasters (Jude 16), having no fear (Jude 12), and being indifferent (unmoved) by the judgement to come. The judgement of the prideful false teachers will serve as humiliation in "Gloom of utter darkness, forever" (Jude 13).

Note the use of Jude's words where he says the "Wandering stars" will be bound in "Gloomy darkness" (Jude 6, 13). Stars, also called "Luminaries" by Enoch, that give light, yet these light bearers will be bound in darkness. Angels are light bearing; after Satan fell like lightning (Lu. 10:18), he transformed himself into an angel of light to deceive (2 Cor. 11:14), as his ministers do. Ministers of the gospel are called to be the salt and light of this world, but if they lose their saltiness or light (apostasy), how shall they be restored? (Matt. 5:13).

Jude wraps up verse thirteen (Jude 13) with another parallel where he says the fallen angels and the false teachers are being kept and reserved for the day of judgement (Jude 4, 13), resulting in the second death, contrary to those God has kept (Jude 1), and is keeping (Jude 24) for eternal life. The difference between the two groups (factions) is that the condemned did not keep themselves by remaining in their proper place (Jude 6), fearing God (Jude 12), and respecting scriptural authority (Jude 8), whereas the saved did and so keep themselves in the love of God (Jude 21). Those saved receive God's multiplied mercy, peace, and love (Jude 2, 21), while the other, He punishes with eternal fire (Jude 7).

A similar use of Jude's language and warning is found in the book of Revelation to the church of Sardis. Sardis was a church with a reputation of being alive but was dead due to being in bed with the world (Rev. 3:2). The apostate church had moved away from what they once knew and, by doing so, had soiled their garments (Rev. 3:3, 4). Their garments were now spoiled, blemished by sin. Unless Sardis repents, Jesus will come, like a thief, at an hour they would not know (rapture), leaving them behind (tribulation), where He would then come against them (Rev. 3:3). Those who repent and remain unsoiled, they (alone) would not have their names blotted out of the book of life (Rev. 3:5). However, the 'Blemished' who do not repent and remain, will have their names blotted out, and then will go into the lake of fire, which is the second death.

Enoch also has something to say regarding those having their names blotted out of the book of life - another book which Enoch wrote for his son Methuselah and for those who will come after him and keep the law in the last days:

"Ye who have done good shall wait for those days till an end is made of those who work evil, and an end of the might of the transgressors. And wait ye indeed till sin has passed away, for <u>their names shall be blotted out of the book of life</u> <u>and out of the holy books</u>, and their seed shall be destroyed forever, and their spirits shall be slain, and they shall cry and make lamentation in a place that is a chaotic wilderness, and in the fire shall they burn; for there is no earth there. And I saw there something like an invisible cloud; for by reason of its depth I could not look over, and I saw a flame of fire blazing brightly, and things like shining mountains circling and sweeping to and fro. And I asked one of the holy angels who was with me and said unto him: 'What is this shining thing? for it is not a heaven but only the flame of a blazing fire, and the voice of weeping and crying and lamentation and strong pain.' And he said unto me: '<u>This place which thou seest-here are cast the spirits of sinners and blasphemers, and of those who work wickedness, and of those who pervert everything that the Lord hath spoken through the mouth of the prophets-(even) the things that shall be</u>. For some of them are written and inscribed above in the heaven, in order that the angels may read them and know that which shall befall the sinners, and the spirits of the humble, and of those who have afflicted their bodies, and been recompensed by God; and of <u>those who have been put to shame by wicked men: Who love God and loved neither gold nor silver nor any of the good things which are in the world, but gave over their bodies to torture. Who, since they came into being, longed not after earthly food, but regarded everything as a passing breath, and lived accordingly, and the Lord tried them much, and their spirits were found pure so that they should bless His name. And all the blessings destined for them I have recounted in the books. And he hath assigned them their recompense, because they have been found to be such as loved heaven more than their life in the world, and though they were trodden under foot of wicked men, and experienced abuse and reviling from them and were put to shame, yet they blessed Me</u>. And now I will summon the spirits of the good who belong to the generation of light, and I will transform those who were born in darkness, who in the flesh were not recompensed with such honor as their faithfulness deserved. And I will bring forth in shining light those who have loved My holy name, and I will seat each on the throne of his honor. And they shall be resplendent for times without number; for righteousness is the judgement of God; for to the faithful He will give faithfulness in the habitation of upright paths. And they shall see those who were, born in darkness led into darkness, while the righteous shall be resplendent. And the sinners shall cry aloud and see them resplendent, and they indeed will go where days and seasons are prescribed for them" (Enoch 108).

Note Enoch's words, underlined, regarding the blasphemers who pervert everything the Lord has spoken, which is repeated by Jude (Jude 4, 8). Consider also the following underlined verses revealing the servants and followers of God, who loved not the things of this world, in comparison to the hidden reefs (Jude 12) who were/are greedy for gain (Jude 12, 18, 2 Pet. 2:3, 14). Think about the similarities seen today with those claiming to be ministers of the gospel, who fill their pockets at the expense of the naïve, some of which are already condemned.

Although the false teachers are already condemned (Jude 4, 13), being "Twice dead" (Jude 12), those enticed by them (2 Pet. 2:14), now doubting and sinning, are still within reach of saving (Jude 22-23): "Snatch them out of the [eternal] fire, showing mercy with fear, hating the garment stained by the flesh" (Jude 23). The garment stained by flesh has been blemished by the false teachers, like with the church of Sardis. But Jude instructs the church to save them, showing mercy with fear (cf. 2 Tim. 2:25). Again, showing mercy and fear is the opposite of the false teachers, who show no mercy towards the lost, being the very cause of their apostasy. In doing so, they have no fear of God and the consequences to come (Jude 4, 13).

CHAPTER 5
Judgement Day

The Lord Came with Ten Thousand of His Holy Ones

In the last section, it was confirmed that the critical point of Jude's message is that there are blemishes at the love feast (Jude 12), which should never be. The love feast is reserved for the called and kept by God (Jude 1) through Christ (Jude 24) by the Holy Spirit (Jude 20), for those who keep themselves pure (2 Pet. 3:14) by loving God (Jude 21) and others in fear (Jude 22-23).

The salient difference between the godly who are keeping themselves, and those who are not, is that the godly fear God (Jude 23), while the ungodly do not (Jude 12). The fear of God, or lack of it, makes the difference. The false teachers have no fear due to believing there is no consequence for sin, which is why they pervert grace (Jude 4), promising freedom in sin (2 Pet. 2:19). Whereas the godly, keeping themselves in the love of God, pursue a life of holiness, waiting for and hastening the coming of the day of God (2 Pet. 3:12). The false teacher also speaks against Christ (Jude 15), without fear of the consequences.

On that day, the day the godly are waiting for (Tit. 2:13) when Jesus Christ returns, they will be glorified. As for the ungodly, the example of Sodom and Gomorrah will also be their eternal experience (Jude 7, 2 Pet. 2:6-7). Before the final judgement, those loving God, keeping themselves pure and holy, will be rescued from trials (2 Pet. 2:9), removed from the earth (Jude 21, Rev. 3:10), and then returned at the end of the seven-year tribulation (Jude 14-15).

While the false teachers and prophets (2 Pet. 2:1) introduce 'new teaching' and 'special revelation' through their false words (2 Pet. 2:3) and deceptive dreams (Jude 8), Jude relies on the authority of scripture and ancient writings, such as the book of Enoch. Jude in no way announces new teaching of any kind, but instead remains within the boundary of what is written, as Paul instructed, "Do not go beyond what is written" (1 Cor. 4:6). John warns those who do, saying, "Anyone who runs ahead and does not continue in the teaching of Christ does not have God" (2 Jn. 1:9). The condemned (Jude 4, 13) false teachers did not have God, due to being devoid of the Holy Spirit (Jude 19).

Again, the evidence that the godly do have God is that they have the Spirit (Jude 20); therefore, they remain under Christ's authority (Jude 8) and remain within the bounds of His written word, starting by not perverting grace (Jude 4). Peter adds that the false teachers are "Ignorant and unstable, they twist to their own destruction, as they do the other scriptures" (2 Pet. 3:16), warning the church not to do the same, therefore losing their stability or safe position (2 Pet. 3:17). The warning follows another, where Peter says it would be better never to have been delivered from the world than to be delivered and then go back to it (2 Pet. 2:20-21), which many are now in danger of (2 Pet. 2:14, Jude 22-23).

As seen with his handling of the text, Jude is a faithful Bible teacher, fearfully saving those who have been enticed by the empty promises of the waterless clouds and fruitless trees (false teachers). Jude is attempting to save those who let down their guard, who are now doubting and straying (Jude 3, 22-23). In doing so, Jude cites Enoch, reminding his reader of the expected end for those who fear God and those who do not. Jude's excerpt from Enoch (1:9), under the inspiration of the Holy Spirit (2 Tim. 3:16-17, 1 Pet. 1:20-21), gives the book of Enoch credibility, albeit today, the book is part of the Apocrypha.

Apart from the references to the "Watchers" (fallen angels), there is not a lot within the writings of Enoch that are not found elsewhere in the authorised scriptures. Jude's citation of Enoch's prophecy, found in Enoch chapter one, verse nine (Enoch 1:9, Jude 14-15), is seen many times throughout the Bible; therefore, Jude judges Enoch's prophecy as correct.

Prophecy is tested in two ways, firstly, it must be consistence with scripture, and secondly, it must be tested by time. Jeremiah, chapters twenty-seven to twenty-nine, is an excellent example of true and false prophecy being tested by time.

Like Jude, Jeremiah also dealt with false prophets leading God's people astray, resulting in destruction. The false prophets went against Jeremiah, and therefore God, telling Judah that God would shortly deliver them from Babylon (Jer. 27:16). God said, through Jeremiah, He will not, therefore, do not listen to the false prophets who are prophesying lies (Jer. 27:16). One of the false prophets, Azzur, who was in the "House of the Lord, in the presence of the priests and all the people" (Jer. 28:2), said, "Thus says the Lord of host (armies), I have broken the yoke of the king of Babylon. Within two years I will bring back to this place all the vessels of the Lord's house" (Jer. 28:2b-3a). Note the timeframe, "Shortly" (Jer. 27:16) and "Within two years" (Jer. 28:3). Another false prophet called Hananiah said something similar, "Thus says the Lord: Even so will I break the yoke of Nebuchadnezzar king of Babylon from the neck of all the nations within two years" (Jer. 28:11).

A third way prophecy is tested is by two or three witnesses (1 Cor. 14:27-29). And that "The spirit of the prophets are subject to the prophets" (1 Cor. 14:32). The saying refers to self-control, purposed to warn them to avoid making the excuse, "God took over and made me do it." One prophet is subject to the next, controlling their gift and maintaining order in the church. The false prophets had no self-control due to not being submitted to God (His Spirit), scripture, or each other. Regarding the false prophets of Jeremiah's day, some might have said two or more have said the same thing (Azzur and Hananiah); therefore, it must be God.

The false prophets of Jeremiah's day were identified by their false 'gospel' of peace and security. However, God said, "I did not send these prophets, yet they have run with their message; I did not speak to them, yet they have prophesied. But if they had stood in My council, they would have proclaimed My words to My people and turned them back from their evil ways and deeds" (Jer. 23:21-22). Something similar was repeated in chapter twenty-eight, where God said, "The prophets who preceded you and me for ancient times prophesied war, famine, and pestilence" (Jer. 28:8). "As for the prophet who prophesies peace WHEN the word of that prophet comes to pass, THEN it will be known that the Lord has truly sent the prophet" (Jer. 28:9).

The false prophets prophesied peace, but peace never came, and would not before seventy years of captivity have been fulfilled (Jer. 25:1-12, 29:10). The false prophets said, within two years, God will restore (Jer. 28:3, 11). Death and destruction were unavoidable despite the false proclamation of peace; the majority who listened to the false prophets would perish, and the remaining remnant would be taken captive. For his blasphemy, God pronounced that Hananiah would be removed from the face of the earth within the same year, which was fulfilled in the seventh month (Jer. 28:16-17).

Again, the false prophets said God would restore, while God said through Jeremiah that He would send Judah into exile (Jer. 29:14, 20). Following

Judah's repentance, where they "Call upon [His] name" and "Seek" [God], then "They will find" [Him], "When they seek with all of their heart" (Jer. 29:12-13). The prophecy is still yet to be fulfilled and will be after the tribulation, then fulfilling verse eleven (Jer. 29:11) and chapters thirty and thirty-one (Jer. 30-31), which brings us back to Jude.

Prophesy is tested through time, among other things. In both Peter and Jude's letters, the false prophets scoffed at prophecy because the predictions of Christ's return seemed to be delayed (2 Pet. 3:3-10, Jude 18). Both Peter and Jude note that the scoffer was following their own sinful desires (2 Pet. 3:3) and ungodly passions (Jude 18). Jude calls them, "Worldly people devoid of the Spirit" (Jude 19).

Once more, note the distinction between the true and the false. The false prophets promise peace, prosperity, and security, whereas the true prophet announces judgement, for some to be saved. The false prophet, even amidst judgement, says it will soon be over, and then there will be peace and security (your best is yet to come). However, the genuine prophet says there will be a period, often an extended period, of trouble, purposed to produce the fruit of repentance before peace eventually comes (Jer. 29:11-14).

Remember, before, saying, "Oh, all that judgement was in the Old Testament, and we live in the New, under the covenant, and age of grace." Jude, six times, used examples from the Old Testament to illustrate what God did then; He will do again. Note also, Jude was warning the church! The church Jude was addressing would have been very familiar with the prophets Moses, Isaiah, Jeremiah, and Ezekiel, whom all prophesied about the coming tribulation, and millennial rest, and therefore, the church members would have made the connection between the false teachers then, and now. It is, however, interesting that Jude cites Enoch, not treating it any differently than the authorised scripture.

Again, like the words of Jeremiah, Jude's reference to Enoch's prophecy (Jude 14-15) was laughed at by the false teachers (Jude 18). Peter says the same, adding, "God is not slow to fulfil His promise as some count slowness but is patient towards you, not wishing that any should perish, but that all should reach repentance" (2 Pet. 3:9). Note, God is patient towards YOU, a member of the church, reading this letter. The one God is drawing to repentance that they might be saved includes those in the church who have been enticed (2 Pet. 2:14), those who are doubting and sinning (Jude 22-23), which is why Jude says, "Save them" (Jude 22-23). The attempt to save does not include the false teachers, for they are already condemned (Jude 4, 13, 2 Pet. 2:3, 13b, 3:16), kept for the day of judgement (2 Pet. 2:9, Jude 4, 13).

To establish credibility, Jude points the reader towards Genesis (Gen. 5:18-24), saying, "Enoch, the seventh from Adam" (Jude 14). "Enoch walked with God, and he was not, for God took him" (Gen. 5:24). Enoch was raptured, being the first ever to be snatched away, followed by Elijah (2 Kgs. 2:1-14), whom the church follows (Rom. 5:9, 1 Cor. 15:51-52, 1 Thess. 1:10, 4:16-17, 5:9, 2 Thess. 2:7, Tit. 2:13, Rev. 3:10, 4:1), and then will be followed by the two witnesses (Rev. 11:12). The church and saved Israel, with the two witnesses, will return with Jesus at the end of the tribulation (Jude 14). The two witnesses, being either Enoch and Elijah or Elijah and Moses, will appear at the beginning of the tribulation, preaching repentance and holiness (Rev. 11). The purpose of the tribulation is to save. Remember, God would have none perish, but all reach repentance (2 Pet. 3:9).

Enoch, the seventh from Adam, is also mentioned in Enoch's book (Enoch 60:8, 93:3). Enoch was of the seventh generation, seven meaning perfection. The point of saying so is that both Jude and Peter point to Christ's return, which commences the millennial dispensation in the seventh year. Then, a time of peace and prosperity will be a reality. Enoch states that it will be seven thousand years before the sin is thoroughly dealt with (Enoch 93). Peter says something similar, saying that after seven thousand years, there will be a New Heaven and New Earth (2 Pet. 3:8-13). In the same way, Enoch walked with God; followers of Christ will also walk with Him in the coming kingdom for one thousand years.

As mentioned earlier, the idea of the Messiah coming to judge is not foreign to the Old Testament (Isa 63:1–6, Isa 66:15, Zech. 14:5); however, the New Testament reveals that the awaited Messiah is Jesus (Matt. 24:29-31, 1 Thess. 3:13, 2 Thess. 1:7, Jude 14-15, 21, Rev. 1:7, 6:12-17, 19:13, 15, 22:12, 20). Jude's reference, found in the book of Enoch, regarding "Ten thousand holy ones," is also mentioned by Moses (Deut. 33:3). The references apply both blessing and judgement.

The Synoptic gospels state seven times, Jesus is returning to judge (Matt. 16:27, Mk. 8:38, Lu. 9:26, Matt. 24:30–31, Mk. 13:26–27, Matt. 25:31, Lu. 12:8–9), Zechariah (Zech. 14:5) and John (Rev. 6:12-17) and reveal what that day looks like, and how people will respond. On that day, there will be two different responses. One group will mourn over their sin, receiving mercy (Zech. 12:10-13:1). In contrast, the other group will mourn in fearful expectation of judgement (Matt. 24:30). Zechariah, like Enoch says, the Lord (Jesus) will come with all the holy ones (Zech. 14:5, Enoch 1:9, Jude 14) to execute judgement. Daniel says something similar, "A river of fire was flowing, coming out from before Him. Thousands upon thousands attended Him; ten thousand times ten thousand stood before Him. The court was seated, and the books were opened" (Dan. 7:10).

The purpose of the judgement is to repay the ungodly for their rejection of Jesus Christ and blasphemy. Unlike the blessed, who are on watch for Jesus's return (Matt. 24:46, Lu. 12:37), the cursed who are scoffing at the prophecies (Jude 18, 2 Pet. 3:3), who have spoken against Jesus (Jude 15), the loud-mouthed boasters, now face dire consequences. The consequences are so great because they have rejected the only means of salvation, they have perverted the grace of God (Jude 4), and twisted scripture to suit themselves (2 Pet. 3:16).

Jude lists the specific sins of the ungodly, who are committed to ungodliness, as opposed to holiness (2 Pet. 3:11), starting with them speaking, "Harsh things against [Jesus]" (Jude 15). The accusation, leading to their judgement, is first mentioned in verse four (Jude 4). Jude moves quickly from the opening greeting of the letter to an accusation, "Certain people have crept in unnoticed - ungodly people who pervert the grace of our God into sensuality and deny our only Master and Lord Jesus Christ." The ungodly (Jude 4, 15) speak harsh things by denying the deity of Christ and, thereby, blaspheme Him (Jude 8, 10) in their loudmouth boasting (Jude 15). The loudmouth boasters claim superior knowledge by twisting scripture and giving false words and dreams (2 Pet. 2:3, 3:16, Jude 8).

As mentioned previously, every word Jude writes has been carefully selected. The phrase "Harsh words" may have been drawn from Enoch's book: "But ye—ye have not been steadfast, nor done the commandments of the Lord, but ye have turned away and spoken proud and hard words with your impure mouths against His greatness. Oh, ye hard-hearted, ye shall find no peace. Therefore, shall ye execrate your days, And the years of your life shall perish, And the years of your destruction shall be multiplied in eternal execration, and ye shall find no mercy" (Enoch 5:4-5, cf. 27:2, 101:3). Enoch has pronounced judgement on the fallen angels; however, their judgement is shared by the ungodly following in their footsteps (Matt. 25:41).

The number one charge against the false teachers in Jude and Peter's letters is that they speak against God (Jude 4, 8, 10, 15, 18-19, 2 Pet. 2:1, 10, 13, 18, 3:3, 16). While their behaviour will also condemn them, their words are more of a concern due to their influencing others (2 Pet. 2:14, Jude 22-23). For this reason, although being "Very eager to write about common salvation" (Jude 3a), Jude "Found it necessary to write appealing to [the church] to contend for the faith" (Jude 3b). In other words, watch (guard) your life and doctrine (1 Tim. 4:16) and preserve sound biblical doctrine by resisting false teachers.

The conclusion of Jude's accusations against the false teachers is that they are "Grumblers, malcontents (moaners), following their own sinful desires" (Jude 16). The word "Grumblers" is connected to verse five (Jude 5), where Israel grumbled against Moses, and God, resulting in their disqualification from the Promised Land. Remember, under the section addressing that sin, it was said that while some say the Israelite's disqualification is from serving God, not eternal life, Jude makes it clear it is the latter, eternal life, hence the connection in verse sixteen (Jude 16).

Verse eleven (Jude 11) could also be linked with Korah's rebellion against Moses. Paul warned against the same, saying, "We must not put Christ to the test, as some of them did and were destroyed by serpents, nor grumble, as some of them did and were destroyed by the Destroyer. Now, these things happened to them as an example, but they were written down for our instruction, on whom the end of the ages has come. Therefore, let anyone who thinks that he stands take heed lest he fall" (1 Cor. 10:9-12). Here, it should be repeated for those still believing God it was somehow different in the Old Testament than the New. The Old Testament events serve as an example for all living under the new covenant. Like Paul (1 Cor. 10:6, 11), Jude also makes that explicitly clear (Jude 7).

Included in Paul's list of sins, serving as an example, is idolatry and sexual immorality (1 Cor. 10:7-8), resulting in their destruction (1 Cor. 10:10), repeated by Jude (Jude 5, 7, 11). Also serving as an example is that most of those once saved out of Egypt (the world), God was not pleased with because of their sin; therefore, they were destroyed (1 Cor. 10:5). Although they all had the same opportunity (1 Cor. 10:1-4), few remained faithful, enduring to the end, thereby, passing the test.

Besides being grumblers, the false teachers were malcontents (moaners). The Greek implies that they were complaining about their fate. However, it is doubtful they were complaining about their eternal fate, for they were ignorant of that; therefore, it could be argued they were complaining against the appointed leadership like the Israelites, and what Korah did (Jude 5, 11). The false teachers could also have been disgruntled over God's sacrificial requirement like Cain was (Jude 11), reinforced by Peter's instruction to live holy lives (2 Pet. 3:11), which supports their need to twist Scripture (2 Pet. 3:16) and pervert the grace of God (Jude 4).

The next accusation: "Following their own sinful desires" (Jude 16, 18), also supports the abovementioned argument. The ungodly had no desire to live godly, holy lives; therefore, they twisted the Scriptures and perverted grace. The context of the desires of the ungodly is desiring evil over good.

Note that Jude's charge has a chiastic structure starting and ending with the false teachers' words. They speak "Harsh things," and they are "Loud-mouthed boasters" (Jude 16). Peter says it this way, "For, speaking loud boasts of folly, they entice by sensual passions of the flesh those who are barely escaping from those who live in error. They promise them freedom, but they themselves are slaves of corruption. For whatever overcomes a person, to that he is enslaved" (2 Pet. 2:18). When likened to Daniel (Dan. 11:36), there is a connection to the antichrist (Rev. 13:5), with the false teachers having the spirit of the antichrist due to their rejection of Jesus (1 Jn. 4:1-6). In the same, Antiochus (a type of antichrist) made boastful claims, flattering God's people to gain favour (Dan. 11:21, 32). The same is seen again with the false joining themselves to the faithful through flattery (Dan. 11:34). Paul warns about them in his time, saying, "For such persons do not serve our Lord Christ, but their own appetites, and by smooth talk and flattery they deceive the hearts of the naïve" (Rom. 16:18), stating, flattering someone to gain something is not something he ever did (2 Thess. 2:5).

No doubt, the false teachers flatter those with something to give in return, like the wealthy and church leadership. After all, the blemishes were greedy for gain, seeking positions and prosperity. The reference to gaining favour could be connected to Balaam (Jude 11), which applies to 'ministering for money'. The teaching of Balaam (Rev. 2:14) refers to luring someone into sin by rejecting the authority of God's word to gain favour and financial advantage. Whichever way it is, "Showing favouritism to gain advantage" implies that some are disadvantaged. Remember again from the last section, at the love feast, everyone was to be treated equally, as a family in Christ (1 Cor. 11:20-22, 33); however, the blots and blemishes are helping themselves, without fear, at the expense of others (Jude 12).

As mentioned in the previous section, the blots and blemishes (2 Pet. 2:13) should not have even been at the table - only those "Without spot or blemish" (2 Pet. 3:14) were invited. The only ones without sin are those trusting in Jesus, who He will present blameless (sinless) before God on the day of judgement (Jude 24). On the contrary, the loud-mouthed boasters who had rejected Jesus by speaking harsh things against Him, condemned themselves to everlasting fire (Jude 4, 13), which will be executed when "The Lord [comes] with ten thousand of His holy ones (Jude 14).

CHAPTER 6
Scoffers

In The Last Times

In the previous section, it was revealed that the false teachers and prophets, the dreamers, who had crept in unnoticed, rising among the faithful, enticing unsteady souls, causing them to doubt and sin, would face Jesus when He returned to execute judgement. As stated beforehand, the hidden reefs are already judged, prejudged, and predestined to hell (Jude 4), albeit the judgement of fire (Jude 7) and gloomy darkness (Jude 13) is yet to be executed.

While the threat of judgement was aimed at those causing trouble in Jude's lifetime two thousand years ago, the reality is that Jesus will return in ours - so, the fulfilment of the prophecy will occur within three decades. When the judgement is executed, every false teacher, perverting grace (Jude 4) and twisting scripture (2 Pet. 3:16), will face the full consequence.

As mentioned above, the execution of God's righteous judgement will occur within three decades from now. We know the season (timeframe) from the lesson of the fig tree (Matt. 24:32-35), where Jesus said the generation that witnesses Israel's rebirth would see His return. Israel was reborn in 1948; therefore, the youngest of that generation 'witnessing' that event is seventy-four years old today. The maximum length of life nowadays is one hundred years, albeit few live that long. According to the Life Expectancy Index and the Worldometer, the average length of life is in the early eighties, depending on which country a person lives in. The average expected length of years has nearly doubled since 1950 when only forty-seven years could be anticipated. Countries with the highest life expectancies are Switzerland, Hong Kong, Iceland, Australia, and Singapore (82 years on average). At the other end of the spectrum, those living in certain African nations can expect fifty years, and South Africa is slightly higher at sixty years.

Reiterating the point detailed above is this - the generation living at the time of Israel's rebirth has less than three decades left. On average, less than two decades are expected. In the best case, a select few may live longer than the average expected lifespan; therefore, up to one hundred years could be achieved at the outside. Whichever way it is, Jesus will return within three decades from now, by 2048 or before.

The statement suggests that there is additional evidence supporting a specific timeline or chronology, which is linked to the Essene calendar. According to this calendar, the end of the year six thousand (which refers to a period of time in Jewish history) coincides with the return of Jesus and the establishment of a thousand-year reign or millennial kingdom. The statement further *suggests* that this event is expected to occur in 2075, based on the Essene calendar.

The millennial kingdom commences on the seventh day, symbolic of a day (1000 years) of rest. Enoch (Enoch 91-93) gives the same timeline. However, from Second Esdras (chapt. 4), we learn that from the time of Ezra, there are 3925 years, and the time before Ezra was around 3445-3485 years. Starting at the time of Ezra, from creation (3485), less the years of Ezra (midpoint) until Christ (460), less the years from Christ to the current day (2023), (=5968, with 32 years remaining before the start of the millennium, the seventh day). By adding thirty-two years to the year 2023, the year of Christ's return could be in 2055 A.D. Then subtract seven years for the tribulation, placing the rapture in the year 2048 - precisely one hundred years after the rebirth of Israel (1948). The calculation works with less time from Ezra to the resurrection (2055) (Esd. 4:45, 50) than from the time that has already passed (3485).

If Jesus returned in 2048, the youngest person of the generation witnessing Israel's rebirth would be one hundred years old. Again, only a few people live that long; most, in the best case, can only expect eighty (something) years, including Israel, where the average expected number of years for males and females is eighty-two. Therefore, Jude's prophesy, given by Enoch (Enoch 1:9), will be fulfilled within our lifetime. At the fulfilment, every false teacher and prophet will be repaid for their apostasy and apostatising of others. The hidden reefs will be eternally judged alongside the fallen angels, where together, they will be tormented day and night forever and ever.

Interestingly, the fallen angels, who corrupted humanity, hid among human beings, taking on the form of humanity, 'Veiling' themselves from the heavenly angels, who were terrifying the two hundred watchers, according to the book of Giants. Unlike the false teachers, the watchers knew their day of judgement was coming; in fact, they knew it would be executed in one hundred and twenty years (Gen. 6:3, cf. the book of Giants). From there on, they would have "No peace, Placed in fire and taken to face eternal damnation" (book of Giants).

According to the book of Giants, the fallen angels believed that they would never lose their power; however, the keeping of power was of no value because where they would spend eternity, they would be powerless. Furthermore, while in hell, with their offspring, the giants, and every false teacher, the "Righteous will fly over the fire of damnation and gloat over the souls inside it" (book of Giants). While the prophecy is challenging, Isaiah says something similar: "And they shall go and look on the dead bodies of men who have rebelled against Me. For their worm shall not die, their fire shall not be quenched, and they shall be an abhorrence to all flesh" (Isa. 66:24). Jesus cited Isaiah when warning those who cause "Little ones believing in Jesus to sin" about their eternal designation in hell (Mk. 9:42-28). The one's causing "Little ones" to sin includes the false teachers who "Entice unsteady souls" (2 Pet. 2:14), causing some to doubt and sin (Jude 22-23).

The fulfilled timing of Isaiah's prophecy is set for the end of the seventh day (7000 years), commencing on the eighth. The eighth day is what Peter prophesied (2 Pet. 3:8-13), where everything would be made new. Among other prophets, Peter was quoting verses from Isaiah (Isa. 24:17-32, 30:31-33, 65:17-25, 66:15-24).

In Isaiah's quoted verses, there are three different events being fulfilled at three different times. First, there is the return of Jesus Christ, after seven years of tribulation where, "On that day the Lord will punish the host of heaven in heaven (Satan), and the kings of the earth, on the earth" (Isa. 24:21). The following verse describes the cosmic events happening at the return of Jesus Christ (Isa. 24:23). Isaiah, chapter thirty (Isa. 30:31-33) is speaking about the same event; though, chapter sixty-five (Isa. 65:17-25) comes with mixed opinions. Within the passage, there is reason to believe the prophet is talking about the millennial kingdom and the eighth day interchangeably. Verse seventeen (Isa. 65:17) speaks of a new heaven and earth, which occurs after seven thousand years of history. Nevertheless, the remainder of the passage talks about the millennium. The final chapter (Isa. 66:15-24) talks about the return of Jesus (Isa. 66:15-18), followed by the millennium (Isa. 66:19-), and then the eighth day (Isa. 66:22-24). Enoch's reference to the fallen angels, who hid among human beings, and their offspring, being mocked by the "Righteous [who] will fly over the fire of damnation and gloat over the souls inside it" will be fulfilled after the millennium, according to Isaiah (Isa. 66:22-24).

The time leading up to the abovementioned is "The last time," which both Jude and Peter warn about (Jude 18, 2 Pet. 3:3, cf. Acts 2:17-21). Both rightly believed that they were living in the last days (Act 2:17, Heb. 1:1-2, Jam. 5:3). Their understanding of the last days was from their knowledge of the Old Testament (Isa. 2:2, Hos. 3:5, Mic. 4:1). Paul also wrote about the last days, stating they would be more difficult than the former (1 Tim. 4:1, 2 Tim. 3:1, 4:3, 2 Thess. 2-3-9). Paul likewise believed he was living in the end times, encouraging believers to walk accordingly (Rom. 13:12-14, Eph. 5:15-16, 6:13).

One of the reasons the disciples believed they were living in the last days was the increase of false teaching, which is why Jude reminds the "Beloved" (Jude 3, 17) what the apostles of the Lord Jesus Christ taught (Jude 17, cf. 2 Pet. 3:1-3). Jude began his letter with a reminder of how God dealt with the apostates (Jude 5) and ended it by pointing back to the prediction of the apostles, stating that false teaching will continue and even increase until Jesus returns. The prediction of Christ's return also comes under fire (Jude 18, 2 Pet. 3:3). Here, Jude makes a distinction between the apostles of Jesus Christ and the "Super apostles" Paul warned about (2 Cor. 11:5). The self-appointed false apostles were stealing converts (2 Pet. 2:14) with new teaching, resulting in a different gospel (2 Cor. 11:4, Gal. 1:6-9), and a very different outcome.

The term super-apostles is a reference given to the skilled speakers (cf. 2 Cor. 11:6), who charged for their services (2 Cor. 11:7). While Paul was not a slick speaker and was physically (Gal. 4:15) and emotionally (2 Cor. 1:8-9) suffering. Unlike the super-apostles, he did, however, operate in the power of the true gospel (1 Cor. 4:20). In his letters to the church of Corinth, Paul gave a brief account of the experience and reality of an apostle's ministry, which is one of suffering (1 Cor. 4:6-20, 2 Cor. 1:8-9). The doctrine of suffering was not found anywhere within the teaching of the false prophets;

their gospel revolves around health, wealth, and happiness, accompanied by greasy grace (you can do whatever you like, and it will be all right).

Noteworthy is where Paul mocks the self-confessed and appointed apostles, calling them so-called "Super-apostles" (2 Cor. 11). Paul, like every other true apostle, was appointed by Jesus Christ (Rom. 1:1, 1 Cor. 1:1, 9:1-2, Gal. 1:1, 1 Tim. 2:7), whereas the false apostles are self-appointed and assigned by Satan (2 Cor. 11:13-15).

Today, people still claim to be apostles, even stating we are in a new apostolic age, placing themselves in the same category as Paul. However, they are deeply deceived and a danger to others. The apostolic age began with Jesus' resurrection and ended with the death of John. While there is still the fivefold ministry in operation, which includes apostles (Eph. 4:11), they are not in the same class as the first-century apostles. The evidence is that they do not write scripture. Anyone claiming to be an apostle today is, most likely, delusional. A genuine apostle would not go by a title, they would not have 'Apostle' written on their business card, and they would not be promoting themselves as an apostle on social media. Instead, *IF they were appointed to an apostolic ministry, they would be doing the work of a missionary, probably with next to no worldly recognition and as little financial support.

Another distinction between the apostles, and those claiming to be one, is that there is not a single Bible verse providing evidence of a female apostle. The apostles were all male; sorry, ladies, you do not qualify for the office of an apostle! Remember, the apostles wrote scripture under the influence of the Holy Spirit; a woman never wrote a single verse of scripture. They did not write even Bible books primarily about women (Esther and Ruth).

Today, those called to apostolic ministries are known for their self-sacrifice and teaching, having strong biblical knowledge, and their deeds follow. They are certainly nothing like the dreamers, spewing out a new revelation and special, superior knowledge. Neither would they be preaching prosperity, such as, "God wants you to be rich." No Old Testament prophet or New Testament apostle ever came with that message. The prophets told Israel to repent and return, while the apostles told the church to imitate Christ, remain faithful, and endure hardship.

The false teachers were not interested in sharing the sufferings of Christ (1 Pet. 4:13) or any other (1 Cor. 12:26); after all, they were "Worldly people" (Jude 19), following their ungodly passions (Jude 18, 2 Pet. 3:3). Instead of teaching 'Sound doctrine', they 'Tickled the ear', resulting in 'Turning people away from the truth'. While the super-apostles majored in prosperity preaching and greasy grace, they had nothing to say about the need to "Endure suffering" (2 Tim. 4:3-5). Naturally, their false teaching caused divisions in the church (Jude 19).

Remember again, Jude distinguishes between the apostle of the Lord Jesus Christ and the other self-appointed and Satan-assigned 'apostles'. The false apostles, prophets, and teachers deny Christ's deity (Jude 4, 2 Pet. 2:1) and reject His authority (Jude 8) by twisting scripture (2 Pet. 3:16) and perverting grace (Jude 4). As mentioned earlier, outside of denying Jesus, they are known for their greed (2 Pet. 2:3, 14, Jude 12, 16) and the downplaying of sexual sin (Jude 4, 6, 7, 2 Pet. 2:2, 4, 6-8, 10, 14, 18, 3:3). They are also known for their boastful talk (2 Pet. 2:18, Jude 16). The "Dreamers" (Jude 8) have plenty to say, yet nothing of any value (Jude 10, 12-13, 2 Pet. 2:12-14, 17-19). Moreover, their contribution is not only worthless to anyone's well-being, like a waterless cloud (Jude 12), but it is also very dangerous (2 Pet. 2:2, 14, Jude 22-23), shipwrecking unsuspecting souls.

It is essential to note that Jude's reminder of the predictions of the apostles of the Lord Jesus Christ (Jude 17) is linked to Enoch's prophecy (Jude 14-15), giving him further credibility. Enoch foretold of the Messiah's arrival to judge as the apostles did (1 Cor. 15:51-52, 1 Thess. 4:13-5:1-11, 2 Thess. 2, Tit. 2:13, 2 Pet. 3, Jude 14-15, 21, 24); however, the apostles recognised the

Messiah to be Jesus, as mentioned previously. Enoch and the apostles prophesied about the judgement of the false teachers. The apostles' predictions both accompany Enoch's prophecy and are rooted in the Old Testament (2 Pet. 1:19-21), unlike the "Dreamers" (Jude 8), who are devoid of knowledge (Jude 10), truth, and the Holy Spirit (Jude 19).

Note, in verse seventeen (Jude 17) where Jude switches from the ungodly (Jude 4-16) back to the beloved (Jude 3, 17, 20). The letter starts and finishes by addressing the beloved, brothers, family, and friends in Christ. The first mentioned came with a challenge, "Contend for the faith" (Jude 3), "Reminding [them] of that [they] once fully knew" (Jude 5). The next mentioned comes with a reminder of the apostles' predictions and teachings (Jude 17), followed with, "Beloved, build yourself up in the most holy faith" (Jude 20), countering the false teachers.

Again, Enoch and the apostles warned about false teachers coming into the church. The warnings are eschatological, as an end-time sign. Paul warned in his letter to the church of Thessalonica that one of the most significant end-time signs would be an increase of false teaching, resulting in the great falling away (2 Thess. 2:3). The great falling away does not so much refer to people backsliding into apostasy, such as what Peter addresses (2 Pet. 2:20-21), but rather entire denominations, and movements departing from sound doctrine. Nonetheless, whether it be an individual, or an entire church and denomination, anyone twisting scripture is guilty of denying, and therefore betraying the Jesus of the Bible. Enoch warns that "It would have been good for [those who deny Jesus] if they had not been born" (Enoch 38:2). The warning is like the one Jesus gave, referring to Judas (Matt. 26:24).

As mentioned earlier, false teaching will increase in the last days, being the sign indicating we are in the last hour (1 Jn. 2:18). God allows false teaching for the purpose to prepare those not loving the truth for the coming antichrist, the strong delusion whom He sends (2 Thess. 2:11). God sends the strong delusion to test and separate one from the other (2 Thess. 2:11-12). In the same way, there are those within and competing against the church with antichrist spirits (1 Jn. 4:1-6); there is a coming antichrist. He is the strong delusion, and yet, there are many 'strong delusions' operating today. An example of that is seen with those placing themselves in the same category as the apostles, bringing in new revelation and special knowledge. Dreamers!

Again, the teachings of the apostles revolved around suffering, temptation (1 Thess. 3:4-5) and deception (2 Thess. 2:5), therefore enduring (1 Cor. 4:12, 9:12, 10:13, 13:7, 2 Cor. 1:6, 2 Tim. 2:10, 2:12, 3:11, 3:4, 4:5, 2 Thess. 1:4, Heb. 10:32, 11:27, 12:2, 3, 7, 20, 13:13, 1 Pet. 2:19, 20). Jesus also had much to say about endurance. Among many verses, He ended all seven letters to the churches addressed in the book of Revelation with the command to endure (Rev. 2-3). The word 'Endure' is a far cry from the word 'Enjoy', as in 'Your best life now'.

Again, within the context of Jude's letter, the apostles' prediction is narrowed in verse eighteen (Jude 19) with the words: "They said to you." The prediction is that false teachers would come in and scoff at the prophecies declaring that Jesus will return (2 Pet. 3:3). Remember, Jude led to this point by saying that Jesus will return, and when He does, He will judge the ungodly (Jude 14-16).

As mentioned earlier, 'The last time' applies to Jude's audience and others until Christ returns. Therefore, "Scoffers following their ungodly passions" will continue and increase until the Second Coming of Christ (1 Tim. 4:1, 2 Tim. 3:1, 1 Jn. 2:18). Essentially, what Jude (Jude 18), Paul (1 Tim. 4:1, 2 Tim. 3:1, Peter (2 Pet. 3:3), and John (1 Jn. 2:18) are warning about, is the same. Furthermore, all expected that the threat of judgement would be executed against the false teachers in their time, and instead, the threat remains hanging above their necks, somewhat like a guillotine. Until the day of 'execution,' things will get worse, not better.

As explicitly seen through Paul's prophecies (1 Tim. 4:1, 2 Tim. 3:1), things will get a lot worse before Jesus returns. Jesus also made it clear, leading up to His return, false teachers and prophets will be in abundance, even operating with signs and wonders (Matt. 24:11, 24-26), deceiving and conditioning people for the antichrist, who also operates in signs and wonders (2 Thess. 2:9, Rev. 13:13).

Regarding the word 'Scoffer', remember again, Jude carefully selects every word from the Old Testament and the Apocrypha, not wasting a single one. Consequently, it is likely he is referencing Jeremiah (Jer. 17:15), who said, "Behold, they say to me, where is the word of the LORD? Let it come!" In both accounts (Jeremiah and Jude), they were not addressing atheists but confessing believers who did not believe God was going to judge them. This is why Peter said, "Knowing this first of all, that scoffers will come in the last days with scoffing, following their own sinful desires. They will say, "Where is the promise of his coming? For ever since the fathers fell asleep, all things are continuing as they were from the beginning of creation" (2 Pet. 3:3-4).

The book of Proverbs also addresses the scoffers who ignore the warnings of God (Prov. 1:22-25), stating that when terror strikes, God will laugh at them (Prov. 1:26-17). When they call on His name, He will not answer (Prov. 1:28). In the sermon, "Sinners in the hands of an angry God", Johnathon Edwards applies Proverbs, chapter one, to those cast into hell. The application given is that when those in hell call out to God in terror, He will laugh at them. God will laugh because they refused to listen (Prov. 1:34), they hated knowledge (Prov. 1:22, 29), they would have none of His counsel and despised His reproof (Prov. 1:30). The application of hell is contextually sound based on verse twelve saying, "Like Sheol let us swallow them alive, and whole, like those who go down to the pit" (Prov. 1:12). While the verse refers to the wicked, enticing others, intending to kill (Prov. 1:10-11), God flips the tables, applying it back to them, the scoffers (Prov. 1:22).

Remember, the false teachers are apostates, not atheists, having once been on the right road (2 Pet. 2:15, 20-21); therefore, one could argue they once had the Spirit. While some claim a believer cannot lose their salvation (once saved, always saved), the scripture is clear, you can. Those who grieve the Spirit (Eph. 4:30 [4:17-32]) endanger themselves by searing their conscience (1 Tim. 4:1-2) to the point where it no longer bears witness (Rom. 2:15). The conscience then becomes insensitive to the Spirit, resulting in apostasy (Rom. 1). A sure way of searing the conscience is to follow false teaching (1 Tim. 4:1-2), which renders a person incapable of knowing right from wrong, disqualifying them from eternal life. "Can an apostate dispense the fiery lies of hell without his conscience being seared?" No! One cannot teach and follow false doctrine and expect to end up in the same place as the other, holding fast (cf. Rev. 3:10-11). Jude makes it clear that the false teachers are disqualified from teaching and from Christ; therefore, they are without hope of salvation. The genuine follower of Christ is recognised by their profession of Him, their submission and obedience to Him, their love for Him, and others, their fellowship with His Spirit, and their commitment to scriptural authority. Jude's false teaches do not meet a single condition for salvation; therefore, they are double-dammed, being "Twice dead" (Jude 12).

CHAPTER 7
Build Yourself Up

Keep Yourself in the Love of God

Following the warning and condemnation of the false teachers, Jude shifts from "These" to "You". "These" represents the false teachers, and "You" represents the beloved (Jude 3, 17, 20), the brothers and family of God. The beloved has dropped their guard, allowing the hidden reefs (Jude 12) to sneak in (Jude 4) and shipwreck the faith of some (Jude 22-23). They have enticed unsteady souls (2 Pet. 2:14), promising them the freedom to sin (2 Pet. 2:19) through false words (2 Pet. 2:3). Those who were once clean, without spot or blemish, and at peace (2 Pet. 3:14), have been blemished by the false teachers sitting at the love feast (2 Pet. 2:13, Jude 12). While the false have no fear of God (Jude 12), unbeknownst to the loud-mouthed boasters (Jude 16, 2 Pet. 2:18), they are already judged (Jude 4, 13), which will be executed when Jesus returns (Jude 14-15). Despite the scoffers saying Jesus will not return, therefore He will not judge them (Jude 18, 2 Pet. 3:3), Jude assures the church, He will.

Like Jude, John addressed the false teaching of those saying Jesus will not return, saying, "Many deceivers have gone out [from the church] into the world, those who do not confess the coming of Jesus Christ in the flesh.

Such a one is a deceiver and the antichrist. Watch yourselves, so that you may not lose what you have worked for but may win a full reward" (2 Jn. 1:7-8). John continues to say that those who do not hold to scripture do not have God and that if anyone brings a different gospel, reject them, or join them in judgement (paraphrased) (2 Jn. 1:9-11). Those who twist scripture (2 Pet. 3:16) and pervert grace (Jude 4), alongside those following them (2 Pet. 2:14, Jude 22-23, 2 Jn. 1:11), are damned, which is why Jude says, "Contend for the faith" (Jude 3).

The church that had dropped their guard and may not be walking with Jesus as taught (cf. Col. 2:6-7), are now being instructed by Jude to "Build themselves up." Twice Jude reminds them of what they once knew (Jude 5, 18), yet had forgotten due to being distracted with false worldly teaching; now he says, "Get back to what the apostles of Jesus Christ have taught you" (paraphed).

The false teachers, prophets, and apostles had introduced a different gospel (2 Cor. 11:4), which was quickly received by those passionate about the things of the world; it tickled their ear (2 Tim. 4:3). A 'gospel' promising freedom (to sin), and prosperity, without suffering is very appealing to worldly people; but, the gospel of Jesus Christ is one of suffering and endurance.

Again, Jude instructs his readers to get back into the word, accompanied by praying in the Spirit, resulting in remaining in the love of God (Jude 20-21). For those who do, they (alone) can expect to receive mercy from God when Jesus returns, leading to eternal life (Jude 21b).

Remember the chiastic structure of Jude's letter, finishing with how he starts. Within Jude's instruction to the church, there are three keywords (keep, love, and mercy), also seen in verses one and two (Jude 1-2). Jude opened his letter by addressing the called and kept praying a blessing of mercy, peace, and love over them. Jude now ends his letter by instructing the called and kept, who are remaining in the love of God, that they might experience His mercy

(Jude 21). Jude also acknowledges Jesus, who keeps those (Jude 24) who keep themselves (Jude 21).

Note the distinction between those keeping themselves (Jude 21) and those helping themselves (Jude 12). Jude makes it very clear; mercy is only given to those living sacrificial lives by staying in the love of God, striving to get in (cf. Lu. 13:24). There is no room or excuse for misunderstanding the text - anyone staining their garment with sin (Jude 23), will not get in. They will not receive mercy when Jesus returns (Jude 21). As mentioned earlier, the church of Sardis (Rev. 3:1-6) should be compared to Jude's warning.

Note the seriousness of Jude's warning to the church, following his judgement on the false teachers. Jude is in no mood to waste time or mince his words. Contrary to his gentle introduction, he challenges the church to build itself back up and remain. Jude instructs the church, "This is your responsibility! Jesus has done (Jude 2) and is doing His part (Jude 24), you better do yours!" (paraphrased). Jude, like Paul and Barnabas, also "Urged [the church in Antioch] to continue in the grace of God" (Acts 13:43), for some Jews had "Thrust (the gospel) aside and judged themselves unworthy of eternal life" (Acts 13:46).

Alongside, continuing in the grace of God by returning to the most holy faith (Jude 20a) through sound biblical doctrine is praying in the Holy Spirit (Jude 20b). Those who do these things are counted as "Holy ones" and will return with Jesus to execute judgement on the angels and nations (Jude 14). Contrary to the holy ones receiving mercy when Jesus returns, no ungodly (unholy) person (Jude 14) will; therefore, no one living for themselves will inherit salvation. For this reason, Peter says, "What sort of people ought you to be in lives of holiness and godliness, waiting for and hastening the coming of the day of God?" (2 Pet. 3:11-12). Continuing, "Beloved, since you are waiting for these, be diligent to be found by Him without spot or blemish, and at peace" (2 Pet. 3:14). Like Jude, Peter leaves no room for unholy (sinful) living, assuring any living that way, that they will not find mercy and favor with God.

As mentioned in the previous section, anyone living an unholy, ungodly (worldly) lifestyle grieves the Holy Spirit and sears their conscience, resulting in apostasy. However, the called, and kept, who are keeping themselves (not helping themselves) through the keeping power of the Spirit, are as much kept from sin as they keep themselves from it and are presented blameless through Christ before God.

Jude's reference to the Trinity was noted in the opening section of this work. Here, Jude points out that the Godhead, Three in One, is actively involved in salvation. God the Father sent the Son, the Son made redemption possible for humanity, and the Spirit seals and empowers those confessing and committing to Christ. Jesus then presents His followers, "The holy ones," blameless before God, His Father. Interestingly, the work of salvation also has a chiastic structure.

Again, as already mentioned several times, Jude wastes no time or words in his letter. Every word is carefully selected. The words: "Build yourself up" are no exception, implying a building in disrepair. Jude's statement refers to faith flickering away due to false teaching. Paul taught that the church is the temple, being built up through the teachings of Christ, the Cornerstone, through the prophets and apostles (1 Cor 3:10, 12, 14; Eph. 2:20, Col. 2:7). The apostles built on the teachings of Jesus, (Matt. 16:18. Acts 15:16). Peter said it this way, "As you come to Him, a living stone rejected by men but in the sight of God chosen and precious, you yourselves like living stones are being built up as a spiritual house, to be a holy priesthood, to offer spiritual sacrifices acceptable to God through Jesus Christ" (1 Pet. 2:4-5).

Jude's address to the church likened her to the temple, instructing his reader to rebuild, like the message from the prophet Haggai, "Return and Rebuild." Haggai addressed God's people who had become distracted by outsiders, straying after the things of the world. They had forsaken the temple rebuild to line their own pockets. However, God corrects the remnant (those who responded) through the prophet and gets them back on track. God then revealed that the Messiah was coming, and when He arrives, the ungodly would be judged, and the godly would be rewarded. The godly will be rewarded in the millennium when "The latter glory of the house shall be greater than the former" (Hag. 2:9). Again, in the same way, Judah got off track, and so had the church. As a remnant within Judah returned (to God) to rebuild, so must the church; that is the one Jude addressed and the church in general.

The "Building of the (church) temple" starts by returning to sound biblical doctrine, resisting, and rejecting everything else, thereby "Contending for the faith" (Jude 3). "The faith" (Jude 3) is "Their faith" (Jude 20), "Delivered to the saints" (Jude 3). Jude ordered the church to fight for what they had already been given and what was already theirs because some had already lost it, such as the false teachers. Others were in danger because of the false teachers (2 Pet. 2:14, Jude 22-23, cf. 2 Jn. 1:8). The primary teaching, causing some to depart and others to doubt, is that Jesus is not the Son of God and that He will not return to judge the angels and the nations (2 Pet. 2:1 3:3, Jude 4, 18). John warns anyone holding to that teaching does not have God (2 Jn. 1:7-10).

Again, the church was to pray in the Holy Spirit alongside rebuilding. Jude's instruction is like Paul's (Rom. 8:26, Eph. 6:18), to which Paul adds, "To that end, keep alert with all perseverance" (Eph. 6:18). Jude and Paul's reference to praying in the Spirit directly applies to speaking in tongues. Paul said to the church of Corinth that he wanted everyone to speak in tongues (1 Cor. 14:5), telling them, "Do not forbid speaking in tongues" (1 Cor. 14:39), which includes women "Who pray and prophesy" (1 Cor. 11:5) in the church. The reality is that not everyone speaks in tongues (1 Cor. 12:30), or prophesies, for if they did then and now, no one would not be trying to stop those who did and do.

Like sound biblical doctrine, praying in tongues is for "Building up" (1 Cor. 14:12, 26). Jude instructs the church to rebuild their faith and to build themselves up in prayer, which plays an integral part in persevering (Eph. 6:18). Perseverance, not prosperity, is the mark of a true believer. Instead of being filled with the world and devoid of the Spirit (Jude 19), Paul says, "Be filled with the Spirit" (Eph. 5:18), which means emptying oneself of the world. Remember again, having the Spirit is the evidence of having Jesus Christ (Rom. 8:9), and evidence of having the Spirit is having the gift of tongues; however, it is not the only evidence. There are those who do not speak in tongues and display more fruit of the Spirit (Gal. 5:22-23) than those who do. It is important to note that the idea that someone is not born again unless they speak in tongues is false.

Although the direct application of Jude and Paul's instruction to pray in the Spirit refers to speaking in tongues, it does not only imply speaking in tongues. Paul said that when praying in public, unless there is someone to interpret, then speak in a known language (1 Cor. 14:19). In the same way the Holy Spirit speaks through prophecy, He also speaks through prayer in a known language, as He does through preaching. Whichever way, being built up, filled, and controlled by the Spirit keeps the confessing follower of Christ in the love of God (Jude 21).

Remaining in the love of God is the aim, by being built up in the faith and the Spirit, which is the means to achieving that aim. Contrary to the teaching of Calvinism, stating that because God is Sovereign (over a person's free will), there is nothing anyone can do to get saved (if not called) or lose their salvation (if they have been called), Jude makes it clear, the called and kept have a part to play. Peter states that God is "Not wishing that any should perish, but that all should reach repentance" (2 Pet. 3:9), resulting in salvation.

Obviously, free will is involved for a person to come to Christ and to remain in Him (cf. Jn. 15:9-10).

Note that the "Called and Kept" are already loved by God (Jude 2-3), yet they must remain in that love to inherit salvation (Jude 21), which goes against the false teaching claiming that because God loves you (just the way you are), He will overlook your sin. He will not! Those loved by God can depart from Him, thereby losing salvation. The writer of Hebrews says something similar, "Keep your life free from the love of money, and be content with what you have, for He (Jesus) has said, I will never leave you nor forsake you" (Heb. 13:5). Often, the latter part of that verse is quoted, to say, "No matter what I do, God will never leave me." God will never leave you; however, you can leave Him through your words and actions; in the same way, someone walks away from a marriage, and their spouse can do nothing to stop them. Again, the false teachers who have crept in have already walked away from God (2 Pet. 2:15) to the point of no return (Jude 4, 13), and now others are in danger of doing the same (2 Pet. 2:14). Snatch them out of the (hell) fire before it is too late (Jude 23).

Lastly, alongside rebuilding faith and remaining in prayer, the reader is instructed to, "Wait for the mercy of the Lord Jesus Christ that leads to eternal life" (Jude 21). Jude's conclusion is eschatological and very much connected to verses fourteen and fifteen (Jude 14-15). Jude quotes Enoch word for word (Enoch 1:9, 2:1, Jude 14-15) regarding the return of Jesus; however, His return is in two parts. The first regards the church's rapture, and the second is where Jesus returns to the earth, the Second Coming, seven years later with the holy ones. The holy ones are the Old Testament saints and the church, including those who died in the Lord and those who have been raptured.

Irenaeus (180 A.D), a disciple of Polycarp, who was John's disciple, references Enoch, who was raptured (cf. Heb. 11:5). Irenaeus believed that the church would be likewise caught up in the air (Against Heresies. Bk. 5). Irenaeus holds a pretribulation interpretation of Paul's teaching (1 Thess. 4:15-17, 5:9 [Rom. 5:9], 2 Thess. 2:6-7). Peter could also be interpreted to say the church will be removed before the tribulation (2 Pet. 2:4-9). Similarly, Jesus taught that some would escape the hour of trial (Lu. 21:34-36, Rev. 3:10-11, 4:1, cf. 11:12).

Joining Enoch is Gad, the seer. Gad served King David (approx. 1000 B.C). Unbeknownst to most, Gad wrote the book of Gad, albeit it was not included in the canon of scripture. Like Enoch, Gad prophesied the pretribulation rapture of the church, the tribulation, and judgement in chapter fourteen (Gad, 14). Gad connects the rapture with the feast of trumpets (Rosh Hashanah). At the time, three groups of people will live on the earth—those living for Jesus, those unaware of Him, and those rejecting Him. The first group will be removed before the tribulation begins. The second will receive another chance through tribulation, and the third is already damned. The third group, according to Gad, includes those subscribing to replacement theology (chapters one and two). Replacement theology is where the church, or Islam, has replaced the Jews. The doctrine breeds hatred for God's chosen people, the Jews. At the end of the tribulation, anyone who has not accepted Jesus Christ as Lord during the tribulation will be eternally judged when He returns. The judgement occurs on another Jewish Feast Day called Yom Kippur, also known as, The Day of Atonement. The time between the two Feast Days is seven years (Yamin Noraim), ending with the battle of Armageddon. Following the battle, Jesus commences the millennial kingdom on earth. Gad predicts the events, perfectly fitting pretribulation doctrine as taught today.

Since there are still two prophetic events to be fulfilled, Jude's first reference to Christ's return (Jude 14-15) follows his second (Jude 21). The second reference arguably points to the rapture. Paul said something very similar in his letter to Titus, "For the grace of God has appeared, bringing salvation for all people, training us to renounce ungodliness and worldly passions, and to live self-controlled, upright, and godly lives in the present age, waiting for our blessed hope, the appearing of the glory of our great God and Savior Jesus Christ" (Tit. 2:11-13).

In support of the New Testament references to 'Waiting', the Old Testament has plenty to say, primarily through the prophet Isaiah (Isa. 30:18, 49:23, 51:5, 64:3-4). Other prophets confirm Isaiah's prophecies (Hab. 2:3, Mic 7:7, Zeph. 3:8, Dan. 12:12). There are also verses in the early New Testament showing Jews following the Old Testament prophecies, waiting for the coming kingdom (Mk. 15:43, Lu. 2:25, 38; 23:51). Paul's verse in his letter to Titus (Tit. 2:13) however, is the most well-known with the shift from the Messiah to Jesus. When Jesus returns, whether for those caught up in the air or those at the end of the tribulation, who are looking for Him and waiting, they will receive His mercy.

The word "Mercy" is seen elsewhere in the New Testament (1 Tim. 1:2, 2 Tim. 1:2, 2 Jn. 3), relating to salvation (Tit. 3:5, 1 Pet 1:3), inherited by those who draw near to God (Heb. 4:16). Those drawing near to God, and who are merciful to others (Matt. 5:7), can expect to receive mercy, resulting in eternal life (Jude 21), on That Day (2 Tim 1:18) as opposed to eternal death. The false teacher can have no expectation of mercy when Jesus returns, only terror (Jude 4, 12, 13, 15, cf. Isa. 2:6-22). The terror to come is a repeat of the past (Lam. 2:22), serving as an example of what God did to the rebellious then, He is about to do again. Only the next judgement will dwarf the previous ones.

In conclusion, only those living for and waiting for Jesus, receiving, and welcoming Him on that day, can expect to be received by Him. Those living for themselves, helping themselves (Jude 12), being worldly people (Jude 19), who are not awake and watching for Jesus, nor watching themselves (Lu. 21:34-36), have no hope of receiving mercy - therefore, salvation. Those without hope include the sleepy, worldly church who are being warned, "Wake up" or be left behind, fought against, and blotted out of the book of life (Rev. 3:1-6).

CHAPTER 8
Snatching Them Out of the Fire

Have Mercy, Show Mercy, With Fear

Throughout the chapters of this work, it has been argued several times that with every Jude example Jude provides, six in total, all were once saved before becoming apostates. As an example of rebellion resulting in apostasy, Jude first mentioned the Israelites who refused to conquer and occupy Canaan (Jude 5). Then Jude refers to the angels who did not remain within the proper place (Jude 6). The fallen angels followed Satan when he was kicked out of heaven (Rev. 12:4) for pride (Isa. 14:13-14), interfered with humanity (Gen. 6), producing the Nephilim, or giants. The first and second examples are linked. Israel was to destroy the giants (Nephilim, Num. 13:33a) occupying Canaan. In the giant's eyes, Israel saw themselves as "Grasshoppers" (Num. 13:33b). Later in the story, the Israelites brought a curse on themselves for sexual sin and idol worship (Num. 25:1-3). The Israelites were living in Shittim instead of the Promised Land (Canaan).

The second and third examples are also linked with the angels going after strange flesh, like the Sodomites (Jude 7). The angels desired women (Gen 6), who were not of their kind, while the Sodomites desired men (homosexuality), and unbeknownst to them, they were seeking to have sex with angels (Gen. 19:4-7). The story of Lot (Gen. 19) shows an example of those once saved who then perished. Lot's sons-in-law and his wife were given a way to escape, yet they did not take it or endure. The sons-in-law "Lingered" and were left behind (Gen. 16:16), while Lot's wife "Looked back" and was turned to salt (Gen. 19:26). Both examples are symbolic of loving this world like the Israelites who wanted to go back to Egypt (Gen. 14:2-4). Egypt is symbolic of the world (Rev. 11:8). The world is what they wanted, and the world is what they got.

The following examples were Cain, Korah, and Balaam (Jude 14). Again, all three rebelled against God by pursuing the things of this world. All three were once saved yet fell into apostasy. The six examples of apostasy are used to make the point that the false teachers who have crept in (Jude 4), "In like manner" (Jude 8), they, too, are apostates. The false teachers were once on the right track and have since "Forsaken the way" (2 Pet. 2:15). They have forsaken the way and are now leading others astray (2 Pet. 2:14, Jude 22-23). Those being led astray and in danger of fire were likewise once secure. John warns that believers can lose what they once had; therefore, they must "Watch themselves" by resisting and rejecting the false doctrine from deceivers (2 Jn. 7-11).

The abovementioned presents a problem for Calvinism, subscribing to the false doctrine of "Once saved, always saved," first promoted by the heretic, Valentinus (100-180 A.D.). If that teaching was correct, then who is Jude instructing the church to "Snatch out of the [hell] fire?" (Jude 23). Remember the context; each account is a reminder of those who were once safe yet left their secure place. Jude's statement is aimed at those doubting and sinning; therefore, it does not refer to the world or the unsaved. Instead, Jude addresses the church members, who need to remember what they once fully knew (Jude 5) and what the apostles taught (Jude 17-18). Since Jude is addressing the church, not the world, the question presenting a problem for Calvinists is, "Who among them was, or is to be snatched out of the fire?" Since the one being snatched is directed at the same straying, and the fire refers to hell (Jude 7), the doctrine of unconditional, eternal election, meaning God's elect are predestined to be saved (past, present, and future), no matter what, is problematical.

Adding to the problem is when John Calvin said, "Where there is a danger of burning, we do not hesitate to take violent hold on a man we want to bring out unhurt; it would not be enough to beckon with a finger, or politely hold out one's hand, for we must care for their salvation with the thought that, unless they are roughly handled, they will not come to God" (Calvin's New Testament Commentaries, Matthew, Mark and Luke, Vol. III, James and Jude, p.335). The confusion lies with the words: "Take violent hold" and "Roughly handle." If a person is predestined to be saved, no matter what, where is the need to take violent hold and to handle roughly? Alongside unconditional election, within the five points of Calvinism is irresistible grace.

The Calvinist fourth point of the acronym TULIP is "Irresistible grace", implying that God's will, will happen, no matter what. The idea that God's will eventually come to pass runs contrary to the doctrine of free will. Free will states that man can and does choose whether to accept and obey God or not. With the doctrine of Irresistible grace in mind, Calvinists state that Jude's reference to "Snatching some out of the fire" refers to those predestined for salvation yet are still on the path leading to the faith. Save them! However, as mentioned above, according to "Unconditional election" (predestination), the ones in danger of [hell] fire would never have been in danger of it! Puzzling! As for those not called and chosen, they have no hope of being snatched out of the fire, for they were predestined for eternal damnation, according to Calvinism. Messy!

The acronym TULIP consists of five points:

- Total Depravity (also known as Total Inability and Original Sin)
- Unconditional Election.
- Limited Atonement (also known as Particular Atonement)
- Irresistible Grace.
- Perseverance of the Saints (also known as Once Saved Always Saved)

John Wesley's response to the TUIP: The Wesleyan Perspective:

- Deprivation - Human beings are sinful and without God, incapable (deprived) on their own of being righteous; but, they are not irredeemably sinful and can be transformed by God's grace; God's prevenient grace restores to humanity the freedom of will.
- Conditional Election - God has chosen that all humanity be righteous by His grace yet has called us to respond to that grace by exercising our God-restored human freedom as a condition of fulfilling election.
- Unlimited Atonement - The effects of the Atonement are freely available to all those whom He has chosen, which includes all humanity, "Whosoever will."
- Resistible Grace - God's grace is free and offered without merit; however, human beings have been granted freedom by God and can refuse His grace.
- Assurance and Security - There is security in God's grace that allows assurance of salvation, but that security is in relation to continued faithfulness; we can still defiantly reject God.

The Wesleyan perspective on the Calvinistic TULIP is better balanced and stronger theologically. It also presents no problems when dealing with Jude's reference to "Snatching [some] out of the fire" (Jude 23). Calvinism, however, is inconsistent and is without mercy to those outside the elect. Conveniently, all Calvinists consider themselves to be of the elect, claiming God's "Limited Atonement" (too bad for the rest). In contrast, the Wesleyan perspective subscribes to "Unlimited Atonement", that is, "Atonement" (being made right with God through His Son, Jesus Christ) is available to all and granted to any responding to the work of the cross (Christ's sacrifice, one and for all, cf. Heb. 10:1-18).

The salient difference between Calvinism and the Wesleyan perspective is judgement over mercy. Calvinism teaches that only the elect receive mercy, whereas those who are not elected are predestined to judgement, and there is nothing they can do about it. God created them for destruction. The Bible verses used by Calvinists to support their predestination doctrine are found in the book of Romans: "You will say to me then, "Why does he still find fault? For who can resist His will?" But who are you, O man, to answer back to God? Will what is moulded say to its Moulder, "Why have you made me like this?"

"Has the Potter no right over the clay, to make out of the same lump one vessel for honourable use and another for dishonourable use? What if God, desiring to show His wrath and to make known His power, has endured with much patience vessels of wrath prepared for destruction, in order to make known the riches of His glory for vessels of mercy, which He has prepared beforehand for glory?" (Rom. 9:19-23). In sum, Calvinists interpret Paul's words to say God predestined some for destruction (an eternity in hell) to reveal (to the elect) His wrath, power, patience, and glory.

Mercy (Jude 2, 21), not judgement, is Jude's desire, and it is the theme of the entire Bible (Matt. 9:13, Hos. 6:6). Rather than judging those who are doubting and straying (falling into apostasy), Jude instructs the church to have mercy, and to show them mercy. That is, extend the same mercy, peace, and love toward those sinning (Jude 22-23) as has been extended towards them (Jude 2). Scripture reminds us that we are all sinful and need God's mercy. We were all like the tax collector who said, "God, be merciful to me, a sinner" (Lu. 18:13), and to receive mercy (Jude 21), we must be merciful (Matt. 5:7), which is like, to receive forgiveness, we must first forgive others (Matt. 6:12).

Today, the distinctive doctrines of Calvinism and Arminianism cause confusion within the church. The Wesleyan Methodist Church's position is, Wesleyan-Arminianism. The danger with the Calvinistic doctrine of "Once saved, always saved" is seen within Jude's letter with those perverting grace. Perverting grace applies to those saying, "You can do whatever you like; it will be all right." The immediate context of Jude's letter concerns sexual sin.

Nowadays, some willingly and deliberately sin while believing they are saved (secure) when they are not; others are doubting their salvation because they struggle with sin. Both positions can result in apostasy. Jude's doubters (Jude 22) are no longer sure of what is right or wrong, therefore, no longer commit to either doctrinal position, while others again are siding with the false teachers (Jude 23), going against what they once fully knew (Jude 5), while ignoring the warnings of the apostles (Jude 17-18). In both instances, Jude says, "Have mercy, show mercy" (Jude 22-23) and "Snatch them out of the fire" (Jude 23).

From an eschatological perspective, Jude's reference to "Snatching from the [hell] fire" can be linked with Amos (Amos 4:11-12). From a present perspective, the reference is connected to Zechariah (Zech. 3:2). The present perspective confirms that those who accepted Jesus and are committed to Him through repentance and obedience (alone) have been made clean. They have exchanged their filthy rags of self-righteousness (Isa. 64:6, cf. Isa. 59:12-15, Rom. 3:9-18) for clean garments provided by Christ (Rev. 19:8, 22:14). The exchange has a 'here and now' application, pointing to the 'there and then.' Jude applies both by saying, "Keep yourselves in the love of God, waiting for the mercy of our Lord Jesus Christ that leads to eternal life" (Jude 21). The idea of keeping oneself, leading to salvation, is theologically known as progressive sanctification. A person is secure if they remain; nevertheless, the reality of salvation is not fully experienced until Christ returns.

The prophet Amos makes it clear that God intends to save, even by "Plucking some from the fire" (Amos 4:11); however, most do not respond. No matter what God does, be it good or not, the maturity of humanity rejects Him (Amos 4); therefore, God had no other option but to judge them, as the prophet said, "Prepare to meet your God" (Amos 4:12). While the prophet Amos is addressing Israel, and the passage is prophetic of their judgement in the coming tribulation, it will also apply to apostates within the church, "Who did not return to [Jesus]" (Amos 4:11b). Five of the seven churches in the book of Revelation were told, "Repent" or else (Rev. 2-3). The same warning will apply to the apostate church, left behind to endure the great tribulation, "Repent and return or be prepared to meet your God." Any failing to repent, return, and endure the tribulation, will face the "Wrath of the Lamb" (Rev. 6:16-17) when He returns. The purpose of the tribulation is to "Snatch some out of the [hell] fire" (Jude 23), evidence of God's mercy toward those who would otherwise be eternally damned.

Also, from an eschatological sense, the Greek "Snatch them" (Jude 23) is "Harpazo," which is also the word used for "Rapture" (1 Thess. 4:17) from the Latin word "Ratura" (seize or kidnap) and "Raptus" (carrying off). Paul used the same work when talking about his heavenly experience (2 Cor. 12:2). An application of this is seen in the book of Revelation, where Jesus promises the faithful church of Philadelphia that on the condition that they remain, He will "Keep [them] from the hour of trial [test] that is coming on the whole world to try [test] those who dwell on the earth" (Rev. 3:11).

In the same way, those saved (those reading Jude's letter) are not yet in heaven; those damned are not yet in hell. Moreover, in the same way, those saved can lose what they have (2 Jn. 8), those in endangering of hellfire (Jude 23) can still be saved, which is why Jude says to the saved, "Keep yourself in the love of God," and to "Save others" (Jude 23). Those straying are still within reach, while the saved are not yet out of danger. The image of Jude's statement is one of the flames lapping at the feet of the unprepared, unsteady souls that are easily enticed (1 Pet. 2:14). Once the flame takes hold, they will be forever lost, like the false teachers who are "Twice dead" (Jude 12).

The early church fathers agreed with John. For example, Origen (230 A.D.) said, "One can lose salvation gradually, but not by accident." The early church fathers were also in agreement, teaching that the consequence of not inheriting salvation, or losing it, is eternal, unending conscious suffering. All taught that the soul is immortal. Irenaeus (178 A.D.) said, "Souls are only created once, are immortal, and can be recognized like Abraham and Lazarus." Lactantius (285 A.D.) said the same. Commodianus (240 A.D.) said, "None [Christians] will be tormented in Gehenna for all time." And that, "Hell is eternal." Justin Martyr (160 A.D) said about that those ending up in hell "They will be punished for an endless duration." Justin quotes Isaiah (Isa. 66:24), saying, "We know from Isaiah that the members of those who have transgressed will be consumed by the worm and unquenchable fire, remaining immortal. As a result, they become a spectacle to all flesh." Jesus also quoted Isaiah, confirming that hell is unending torment for the body and soul (Mk. 9:18).

The image of "Fire", and therefore warning, is extended to any who stray from the faith, those whom the hidden reefs have shipwrecked. The command to "Save them" (those straying) is a consistent theme found throughout the New Testament (Matt. 18:15-17, Jam. 5:19-20), starting with oneself (1 Tim. 4:16, Gal. 6:1-2). Jude's application is more about restoring than judging others; however, judgement still applies, recognising that the person needs restoration. Only after there has been some effort made to restore someone sinning does the church accept, they are beyond reach (2 Thess. 3:14–15, 1 Tim. 5:20, Tit. 3:10). While the person is still within reach, the church is not instructed to mark them, but only after they have rejected correction, and cause others to stray (Rom. 16:17-18).

Jude desires to save, not slay. He starts the letter by saying he was "Very eager to write about common salvation" (Jude 3) but instead needed to warn about the false teachers. As a result, some were now in danger of [hell] fire and in need of "Saving" (Jude 23), having, and showing mercy, mixed with fear (Jude 22-23). Remember, the false teachers had/have no fear (Jude 12), doing and saying whatever they like. Still, the church must tread carefully, working out their own salvation with fear and trembling (Phil. 2:12, cf. 1 Pet. 1:17), while attending to the needs of others. Others now also lacking fear, are those influenced by the false teachers, having soiled their garments (Jude 23). The garment refers to salvation, which was once clean, and the defilement of this world has soiled it (cf. Rev. 3:4), again supporting the fact that those in need of saving were once on the right track. Therefore, fear refers to judgement of oneself and others (Heb. 4:1, 10:27, 12:28-29).

The one, now having defiled garments, is a result of the "Flesh" (Jude 23), which is a follow-on from those devoid of the Spirit (Jude 19), because they have defiled their flesh (Jude 8). Therefore, Jude says, "Build yourselves up in your most holy faith; pray in the Holy Spirit" (Jude 20). The immediate context of dirty garments applies to sexual sin, "Defiling the flesh" (Jude 8) The Greek word for clothing is "Chiton," referring to inner clothing touching the flesh. The Bible has much to say about the flesh, warning not to walk in it (Gal. 5:16–19, 24, 6:8, Eph. 2:3, Col. 2:23, 1 Pet. 2:11, 1 Jn. 2:16). While Jude is referring to sexual sin, any form of worldliness also applies (cf. Rev. 3:1-6), which is why Jesus, in the tribulation, says, "Behold, I am coming like a thief! Blessed is the one who stays awake, keeping his garments on, that he may not go about naked and be seen exposed!" (Rev. 16:15).

The one saving another should be built up in faith and prayer and should do so with fear (Gal. 6:1); otherwise, they also stain their garment (Jude 23). The image could be of a person walking on a tightrope, requiring great skill, with fire lapping beneath. Anyone rescuing another is also in danger, such as a fireman entering a burning building - firefighters must do so with great care. The danger with rescuing those in peril is that the rescuer must get close enough to reach one in danger but stay far enough away to preserve themselves. In Jude's case - sin's deception that could trap the unskilled rescuer. As the sinner's clothing is defiled, so can the rescuer. Hence, the reason for required fear is "Hating the garment stained by the flesh" (Jude 23b) when on the rescue mission to save the sinner, who was once safe.

CHAPTER 9
Blameless

God Keeps Those Who Keep Themselves

Jude starts and ends his letter by acknowledging Jesus Christ, the one who has called and kept (Jude 1) and who presents His followers "Blameless" before God (Jude 24). Like other New Testament letters, Jude begins and ends with a positive tone, albeit the bulk of Jude's content is very damning. The conclusion of Jude's letter is to shift focus from the false teachers and the problems they have caused back to God.

The doxological formula Jude uses to end his letter is found elsewhere; Paul uses it (Rom. 16:25-27, Eph. 3:20, 1 Tim. 1:17, Gal. 1:5, Phil. 4:20), and the writer of the book of Hebrews (Heb. 13:20-21), Peter also (2 Pet. 3:18), and angels and the heavenly saints, through John (Rev. 1:5-6, 4:8 [Isa. 6:3], 11, 5:9-13, 7:12, 11:17-18, 15:3b-4, 16:5-7, 19:1-3, 6b-8). A doxology is seen eight times, throughout eight chapters, in the book of Revelation. The Old Testament also contains doxology (1 Chron. 29:10-13, Ps. 41:13, 57:5, 72:18-19, 106:48, 150:1-6, Isa. 6:3, Dan. 2:20). The point and purpose of the hymn is to give God glory (cf. Rev. 14:7), despite the challenges. For those seeking God, He is seen through the visible expression of Jesus Christ, and experienced through the Holy Spirit, who is ever-present. The very real presence of God has been overlooked by the false teachers, who have no fear (Jude 12), and expect no judgement (Jude 18).

Jude assures his readers that the false teachers will be judged and have been already (Jude 4, 12, 13), although the judgement is still to be executed (Jude 14-15) and will be when Jesus returns (Jude 21). However, for the "Blameless" (Jude 24) who are wholly submitted and committed to God, through Jesus Christ, sealed and empowered by the Spirit, there is no fear of judgement (cf. 1 Jn. 4:8). The "Blameless" are so due to the keeping power of Christ (Jude 1, 24). In partnership with Jesus, the believer who has been "Keeping themselves in the love of God" (Jude 21), has also been "Kept" (Jude 1) by "Him who is able to keep [them] from stumbling" (Jude 24). Remember again, the word "Keep" is also translated as "Guard." Jude's opening line encouraged the "Beloved" to "Contend for the faith" (Jude 3), which implies, guard, and preserving doctrine, as taught by the apostles (Jude 17). It also implies guarding themselves (Jude 21) and others (Jude 22-23). By doing so, they will remain to be "Kept" by Christ.

It's important to note, throughout Jude's letter, he gives six examples of those who have not remained on guard and a seventh example of the current false teachers who were once on the right path (2 Pet. 2:15). Every example provided points to apostasy, revealing the reality and danger of it, particularly for those now doubting and sinning (Jude 22-23).

The doctrine of the keeping power of God is seen elsewhere in scripture (Jn. 17:11, 15, 2 Thess. 3:3, 1 Pet. 1:5), always in the context of danger. The danger applies to this world and the one ruling it, Satan. Satan, the ruler of this world (Jn. 14:30), will do everything within his power to entrap the followers of Christ with the things of this world, in the same way, he attempted to with Jesus (Matt. 4:8-9). Jesus kept Himself from sin by quoting scripture (Matt. 4:10) - evidence of Him drawing near to His Father-God - and God responded by sending ministering angels (Matt. 4:11b), and the devil fled

(Matt. 4:11a). The same method is given to the church by James, when we submit to God, we resist the devil, and then he flees (Jam. 4:7). The devil does not flee because a believer tells him to, especially when that person is in sin.

The Christian practice of rebuking the devil is not supported by scripture. In fact, Jude makes a point of saying, do not do it, otherwise be likened to the false teachers (Jude 8-9), who know nothing (Jude 10), and are dammed (Jude 11), being twice dead (Jude 12). Jude states that anyone pronouncing a judgement on the devil is likened to a dumb animal (Jude 10), going the way of Cain (Jude 11). Going the way of Cain refers to rebelling against God and His authority. Anyone rebuking the devil falls under the same category as Jude's false teachers, who operate outside scriptural authority.

The problem with rebuking the devil is that it deceives the rebuker by trusting in themselves over God, thinking more of themselves than they ought. Their focus can also shift from God to evil. The church of Ephesus fell into this sin, departing from their first love (Jesus) by rebuking false teachers (Rev. 2:2-5). The church members of Ephesus "Abandoned the love they first had" (Rev. 2:4) for Christ. The word "Abandoned" also translates as depart, leave, divorce, and quit. God's love never stopped or gave up on the church of Ephesus; however, its members had removed themselves from Him, in the same way, the writer of Hebrews warns (Heb. 13:5).

Interestingly, the writer of Hebrews warns about the things of this world drawing people away from God, like the devil tried to do with Jesus. However, in the letter to the church of Ephesus, Jesus warns that the fight against false teachers can do the same when He is not given priority.

Today, there are those claiming to have a 'Deliverance ministry' majoring in rebuking and casting out the devil, whom themselves may not be saved. This should not come as a surprise, for Jesus warned that on judgement day, many will say, "Lord Lord, did we not cast out demons in Your name, and [He] will declare to them, I never knew you, depart from Me" (Matt. 7:22-23). Jesus' warning applies to the religious, trusting in their works, bringing us back to Jude, where he, too, warns that anything less than trusting in Jesus is destined to fail. Again, Jude provides six examples of this, with a seventh being the false teachers.

Regarding the above, some might say, "What about the authority of the believer?" arguing that Jesus gave the church all authority over the devil (Matt. 10:1, 28:18-20, Mk. 16:17). First and foremost, it is essential to note that the believer only has authority when they are submitted to the authority of Christ. As stated above, Christians do not have the authority to rebuke the devil. Instead, believers have the authority to proclaim Christ, lead people to Him, and disciple them in Him. Believers also have the authority to rebuke false teachers (Tit. 2:15). The business of casting out devils (Matt. 10:1, 16:17) relates to saving and discipling (Matt. 28:18-20). It does not relate to rebuking, binding, and loosing. Binding and loosing the devil is not supported in scripture, instead binding, and loosing refers to delivering, or damning a person's soul, depending on whether they receive or reject the gospel of Jesus Christ (Matt. 16:19, 18:18). In sum, the authority of the believer comes from Christ, through His word (scripture), which is His "Sword" (Eph. 6:17).

Through Jesus Christ, we have authority on this earth to proclaim His name, the only name by which we are being saved (Jude 21, Acts 4:12). This revelation prompts the doxology for Jude and others, mainly seen through the book of Revelation. Jesus Christ keeps those who keep themselves and keeps those who do not. Anyone failing to keep themselves by remaining within their proper place (Jude 6) is kept by God for judgement (Jude 6, 13), which is the "Eternal fire" (Jude 7). For those keeping themselves in the love of God (Jude 21), Jesus keeps them from stumbling (Jude 24). Nowhere else in scripture are these words found; an adjoining verse is given by Paul (Rom. 16:25). However, the book of Maccabees provides a closer declaration:

"On which the Lord of all most gloriously revealed His mercy and rescued them all together and unharmed" (3 Mac. 6:39). The connecting word is "Unharmed," referring to God's judgement, not this world. Many faithful followers of Jesus Christ have suffered terribly for His name's sake as promised, they would be (Jn. 16:33) and will be in the coming tribulation (Rev. 6:9-11, 13:10, 14:13, 20:4).

Again, the promise is to those "Keeping themselves in the love of God" (Jude 21), suggesting that those who do not can and will stumble and therefore be harmed. Paul provides evidence for those once saved, stumbling, and therefore are cut off (Rom. 11:11, 17, 19-21), warning the church, what God did to Israel, He will do to you too, if you behave in the same way (Rom. 11:22). The reason Israel was broken off was "Unbelief" (Rom. 11:20), also used by Jude as one of his apostate examples (Jude 5) with an application to those doubting (Jude 22). Unbelief caused the Israelites to go outside of the love of God, not looking to Him but to themselves. Those being saved keep themselves in the love of God, while the damned help themselves to the things of this world (Jude 12). The attitude of the false teachers might remind the reader of another saying often attributed to the Bible, "God helps those who help themselves." Nowhere in the Bible will you find a verse saying that. However, you will find evidence for the statement: "The Lord keeps those who keep themselves" (Jude 21, 24).

The promise to the ones keeping themselves from stumbling does not mean they will never stumble; instead, they will not suffer the judgement. James says, "We stumble in many ways" (Jam. 3:2), yet Peter says, we will never fail, providing we be diligent to make our election sure (2 Pet. 1:10). Again, the responsibility is on the believer to respond to what God has already done through His Son, Christ Jesus.

As mentioned above, the meaning behind not stumbling refers to being blameless, not faultless. When Jesus presents His faithful followers before

God, they are "Blameless" (Jude 24), as if they have never fallen. The blameless are without blemish; they have not been soiled by the things of this world nor blemished by the false teachers. In sum, they can stand before God because they have not fallen. Being without blemish is rooted in the Old Testament (Exod. 29:1, 38, Lev. 1:3, Num. 6:14, Ps. 15:2, Ezek. 43:22) and is carried over to the New Testament (Heb. 9:14, 1 Pet. 1:19, cf. Eph. 1:4, 5:27, Col. 1:22, 1 Thess. 3:13).

When the blameless believer stands before God on that day of judgement, instead of fear, they shall have joy (Jude 24). The reference is eschatological and has been prophesied several times throughout the entire Bible. The prophet Isaiah says it this way: "It will be said on that day, "Behold, this is our God; we have waited for Him, that He might save us. This is the LORD; we have waited for Him; let us be glad and rejoice in His salvation" (Isa. 25:9). And again, "I will greatly rejoice in the LORD; my soul shall exult in my God, for He has clothed me with the garments of salvation; He has covered me with the robe of righteousness, as a bridegroom decks Himself like a priest with a beautiful headdress, and as a bride adorns herself with her jewels" (Isa. 61:10).

Those who have shared the sufferings of Christ on this earth, also share in His joy in heaven, and on earth during the millennium, and thereafter (1 Pet. 4:13, Rev. 19:7, Enoch 5:10). Polycarp, John's disciple, said it this way, "Where the Lord will permit us to gather ourselves together, as we are able, in gladness and joy, and to celebrate the birth-day of his martyrdom for the commemoration of those that have already fought in the contest, and for the training and preparation of those that shall do so hereafter" (Martyrdom of Polycarp, 18:3).

Those standing before God on that day will experience His glory and not fall. Anyone less than "Perfect" coming face to face with God will die (Exod. 33:18-23), which is why John writes in the book of Revelation, "For the great day of their wrath has come, and who can stand?" (Rev. 6:17). The answer is, none, outside of Christ.

Today, people talk about the Shekinah glory of God, 'prophesying' its return, accompanying a great end time revival before the church is raptured. The verses often used to support this statement are found in the book of Acts, chapter two (Acts. 2:17-21). Haggai is also used (Hag. 2:6-9). Neither of the passages offer anything of what the so-called prophets claim. The book of Acts prophecy will be fulfilled during the tribulation, and Haggai's prophecy will be fulfilled in the millennium. The Shekinah glory of God will not be experienced again, this side of Christ's return. On that day, those professing, "The only God, our Savior" (Jude 25), looking for Him, living for Him, and keeping themselves in His love (Jude 21); therefore, being unblemished, they (alone) will have great joy. As for the blemished, who blaspheme Jesus, they will experience indescribable terror, which has been reserved for them (Jude 13), even before they were born (Jude 4).

The reference to "The only God" (Jude 25) is critical to salvation. It refers to the Trinity, the Father (Jude 21, 25), the Son (Jude 1, 4, 14, 17, 21, 24-25), and the Holy Spirit (Jude 19-20). Anyone denying the Triune God has no hope of being saved. The Trinity refers to one God, revealed through three 'Persons', as defined by the Council of Nicaea (325 A.D.), "God manifested in three 'Persons', coequal, consubstantial, and coeternal." The early church fathers taught the Trinity, such as Ignatius, Mathetes, Theophilus, Justin Martyr, Irenaeus, Tertullian, and Origen, to name a few.

Today, over three hundred Christian cults deny the doctrine of the Trinity. The Jehovah's Witnesses, Mormons, Christian Science, Scientology, and the Christadelphians, are some better known. Interestingly, a popular Pentecostal preacher, William Branham, rejected the doctrine of the Trinity in 1958. Up until then, he accepted and taught the three in one Godhead. Branham's teachings are also known as 'Branhamism'. His followers are known as 'Branhamites', who believed that 'brother Branhan' was the final prophet, fulfilling the Malachi prophecy (Mal. 4:5). Branham was also associated with 'The Latter Rain Movement' that claimed that God would pour out His glory, reaping an end time harvest. The verse misused to support their view is from the book of Joel (Joel 2:23) and Haggai (Hag. 2:9). Joel's verse falls into the context given by Peter in the book of Acts (Acts 2:17-21). Branham endorsed the teachings of the Oneness Pentecostals, who also denied the Trinity.

Like the false teacher of Jude's letter, Branham went outside the teachings of scripture, teaching 'extra-biblical revelation'. Branham died in a car accident in 1966. Interestingly, on his tombstone are the seven churches addressed by Jesus in the book of Revelation (Rev. 2-3), linked to a saint suggesting the timeframe of their prophetic fulfillment. Branham is rightly linked to the church of Laodicea, albeit the intent was not meant to be adverse.

- Ephesian Age–Paul
- Smyrnaean Age–Irenaeus
- Pergamean Age–Martin of Tours
- Thyatirean Age–Columba
- Sardisean Age–Martin Luther
- Philadelphian Age–John Wesley
- Laodicean Age–William Branham

Branham saw himself as the angel of the church of Laodicea; however, failing to realise the angel of the church refers to its pastor (Rev. 1:20, 3:14). A literal angel would not be told to "Repent, or else be spewed out" (Rev. 3:16, 19). It could be argued that Branham did not repent and therefore was spewed out. Another interesting inscription on Branham's tomb is John Wesley's link to the church of Philadelphia. Unlike Branham, John Wesley affirmed the doctrine of the Trinity by saying, "In the three Divine Persons we acknowledge a distinction established upon Scripture authority; but, holding the unity of substance in the Godhead, we protest against tritheism, or the notion of three Gods, and confine our worship to the one Supreme." And "To God the Father, God the Son, and God the Holy Ghost, who yet are not three Gods, but One, revered by all His host."

Again, Jude's purpose in pointing to the "Only God" and "Savior" (Jude 25) is to debunk the false teachers who have denied the deity of Jesus Christ (Jude 4). Denying the doctrine of the Trinity is no different. Not only do the false teachers deny Christ, but they also reject His authority (Jude 8) and judgement (Jude 18). Jude counters their claim of "No judgement" by quoting Enoch (Enoch 1:9, Jude 14-15). Again, when Jesus returns, that day will be equally terrifying for the false teachers as it will be joyful for those keeping themselves in the love of God. That really sums up Jude's message: "Stay clear of the false teachers lest they blemish you; instead, stay close to Jesus, who can present you unblemished (blameless) before God on judgement day."

Since Jude's letter points to the day Jesus judges the wicked and the righteous, the reference to Jesus' "Glory, majesty, dominion, and authority" (Jude 25) directly points to His return and applies to the millennial kingdom. While Jesus has all authority "Before all time and now, and forever" (Jude 25), He has given Satan rule over this world (Jn. 12:33, 14:30, 2 Cor. 4:4), ending on His return (Rev. 20:1-3). Anyone subscribing to Dominionism (The Seven Mountain Mandate), otherwise known as 'Kingdom Now Theology', which incorporates replacement theology, overlooks that Satan is the god of this world. Therefore, dominionists play into Satan's hands by helping themselves to the promises given to the nation of Israel and claiming for themselves the prosperity and power of this world. Again, the authority of the believer relates to proclaiming the gospel, not possessing this world.

In conclusion, God keeps those who keep themselves and those who help themselves. God keeps the first group, who are waiting for Jesus, from judgement, and keeps the second for judgement, which is awaiting them.

CONCLUSION & INTRODUCTION
Jude & John

As the letter of Jude ends, the letter of First John begins. Jude concludes by pointing to the event of Jesus' return (Jude 21), where He will present the believer blameless before God (Jude 24), resulting in great joy (Jude 24). The joy will be shared by God and the faithful followers of Christ who have remained, "Hating even the garment stained by the flesh" (Jude 23).

The flesh is stained by worldliness, promoted by the false teachers (Jude 19). While Jude does not instruct the church to avoid the false teachers, he does rebuke the church members for allowing the "Hidden reefs" (Jude 12) to "Creep in" (Jude 4) and participate in the "Love feast" (Jude 12), blemishing some, causing them to doubt and sin (Jude 22-23). After warning the church of the danger the false teachers present, Jude redirects them to Christ, and His return (Jude 12), proclaiming that there will be "Great joy" (Jude 24) on that day for those "Keeping themselves in the love of God" (Jude 21). John starts how Jude ends, testifying of, and proclaiming eternal life (1 Jn. 1:2) for those who are in fellowship with the apostles, the Father-God, and the Son (1 Jn. 3b). John says, "We are writing these things so that our joy may be complete" (1 Jn. 1:4). However, only those walking in the light (1 Jn. 1:5-10), hating the things of this world (1 Jn. 2:15-17) will share in John and Jude's proclaimed coming, and eternal joy.

The promise is conditional, based on whether the believer "Abides." John makes the condition clear, saying, "Let what you heard from the beginning abide in you. If what you heard from the beginning abides in you, then you too will abide in the Son and in the Father. And this is the promise that he made to us—eternal life" (1 Jn. 2:24-25). Knowing the danger at hand, John goes on to say, "I write these things to you about those who are trying to deceive you" (1 Jn. 2:26). The deceivers were preaching a perverted version of grace, stating, "You can do whatever you like, and it will be all right" (cf. Jude 4). In other words, there is no sin or no consequence for sin. Every person contributing to the Bible says otherwise; all have sinned and continue to wrestle against the sinful nature this side of Christ. Those who deny sin deny the redemptive work of the cross.

Consequently, both John and Jude warn their readers: "Do not be led astray (2 Jn. 2:26) by those who claim to be 'Christian' and are not." Both John and Jude remind their readers of what they already know (Jude 4, 17, 1 Jn. 1:1-4, 2:7, 12-14, 21, 24), yet have been distracted by the empty promises from the false teachers (2 Pet. 2:19), who deliberately set out to deceive (2 Jn. 2:26), narrowing in on those with "Unsteady souls" (2 Pet. 2:14).

As mentioned in the introduction of the letter of Jude, the same Gnostic cult of false teachers are troubling the churches that Jude, Peter, and John are addressing. The word 'Gnostic' refers to those relying on extra-biblical revelation and, often, mystical knowledge (Jude 8). These "Dreamers" (Jude 8) are false teachers who plagued the early church, and the modern church no longer belong to the ecclesiastical (2 Pet. 2:15, 1 Jn. 2:19). They have come out of the church (spiritually), as will the antichrist (1 Jn. 2:18-19), due to not remaining under scriptural authority (Jude 8), by going ahead of the teachings of Christ, and the apostles (2 Jn. 1:9). Specifically, they deny Christ, His deity, the Trinity, sin, and God's redemptive work.

Due to the increase of false teaching within the church, being a significant end-time sign (Matt. 24:10-12, 24-26, 1 Tim. 4:1, 2 Tim. 4:3, 2 Thess. 2:1-12, 2 Pet. 3:3, Jude 18), John says, "It is the last hour" (1 Jn. 2:18). Again, the two primary false doctrines the apostates are promoting are, 1). Jesus is not God (Jude 4, 2 Pet. 2:1, 1 Jn. 2:22-23), and 2). Sin has no power and therefore, no consequence (Jude 4, 2 Pet. 2:19, 1 Jn. 2:3-4, 26). To further distract and deceive, the false teachers promote the things (love) of this world (2 Pet. 2:3, Jude 16, cf. 1 Jn. 2:15-17). Those falling in love with the things of this world are in danger of departing from God (cf. 2 Tim. 4:10), which is why John says that only the abiding believer is saved (1 Jn. 2:24-25). Only those who remain in the truth (that which they heard from the beginning (1 Jn. 1:1-4), will receive the promise of eternal life (1 Jn. 2:25). Only those who overcome the world by obeying the commandments are born of God (1 Jn. 5:1-5).

Critical to this point is the word "Abide," which John uses sixteen times in his first letter (1 John) and another nine times in the gospel of John. The gospels of Matthew, Mark, and Luke do not contain this word. Within the gospel of John, there is the "Abiding" condition of salvation (Jn. 8:31, 15:6, 7, 10, cf. 1 Jn. 2:24-25). Regarding John's letter, the key verse says, "Let what you heard from the beginning abide in you. If what you heard from the beginning abides in you, then you too will abide in the Son and in the Father" (1 Jn. 2:24). That critical verse (1 Jn. 2:24) should be compared to another: "Everyone who goes on ahead and does not abide in the teaching of Christ, does not have God. Whoever abides in the teaching has both the Father and the Son" (2 Jn. 1:9). To reiterate, John makes it clear, that it is only when the truth abides in us that we have the assurance of eternal life (cf. 2 Jn. 1:2).

The Greek word for "Abide" is "Meno," also translating, "Remain, stay, persist, last, continue to live, and wait." In the context of John's letter, the word "Abiding" applies to walking (remaining) in the "Light" (1 Jn. 1:5-3:10) and

"Love" (of God) (1 Jn. 3:11-5:17), waiting for Jesus' return (Jude 21). Again, only those who keep these commandments, have eternal life (1 Jn. 5:18-20).

John's letter applies three key themes, life (eternal), Light/Truth (gospel), and Love. To express the importance of these themes, John uses a technique theologically known as "Amplification." The amplification technique essentially says the same thing over and over in slightly different ways, using different words. John does this in this letter (1 John), adding a little more to a repeated statement. In sum, John says, "If you want to have eternal life, you must remain in the light (truth) and the love of God." Jude said something similar: "Keep yourselves in the love of God, waiting for the mercy of our Lord Jesus Christ that leads to eternal life" (Jude 21). Those who do not remain in the truth and love of God forfeit eternal life (2 Jn. 8). The message therefore is, do not stray!

The warning against straying is repeated many times throughout scripture due to its danger and reality. For example, the book of Hebrews contains five warnings about apostasy in somewhat of a chiastic structure.

The warnings are as follows:

A Do not drift away (Heb, 2:1-4)
    B Take care (Heb. Chapters 3-4)
        C Warning about apostasy (Heb. 5:11-6:20)
    -B Hold fast (Heb.10:19-39)
-A Endure (Heb. 121:1-29)

Like Jude's letter, John's also has a chiastic structure:

A The manifestation of God in the flesh (1 John 1:1-4)
  B To deny sin makes God a liar (1 John 1:5-2:2)
    C Love one another (1 John 2:3-11)
      D Victory over the world (1 John 2:12-17)

      E The antichrist (1 John 2:18-27)
        F The believer's confidence (1 John 2:29-29)
          G Future state of the believer (1 John 3:1-3)
            H Righteousness and sin (1 John 3:4-10)
          -G Future state revealed (1 John 3:11-18)
        -F The believer's confidence (1 John 3:19-24)
      -E False prophets (1 John 4:1-3)
    -D Victory over the world (1 John 4:4-6)
    -C Love one another (1 John 4:7-5:5)
  -B Deny Jesus, make God a liar (1 John 5:6-12)
-A The manifestation of God in the flesh (1 John 5:13-21)

The focal point of John's letter is the practice of "Righteousness and/or sin" (1 Jn. 3:4-10), contrasting God against the devil. Those who practice sin are of Satan, and those who practice righteousness are of God. Whatever someone "Practices" is the evidence of whether they belong to God or not. The Greek word for 'Practice' is 'Praxis', which also translates as 'Action' and 'Activity'. In other words, "You will recognise someone by their fruit" (actions and activities)" (Matt. 7:16). Recognising whether someone is of God or not requires 'Judgement'. John instructs the church to judge anyone claiming to be a Christian by saying, "Test the spirits" (1 Jn. 4:1-6). Paul confirms the required judgement of those within the church (1 Cor. 5:12), stating that believers do not judge the world due to the world already being under judgement. The judgement, therefore, applies to whether a confessing Christian is of God by abiding by Christ and His word.

As mentioned above, the word "Abide" is seen sixteen times in John's letter and another nine times within his gospel. Chapter fifteen of John's gospel (Jn. 15) contains six of the nine references. In fact, the framework for the letter of First John is found within the gospel of John, chapters thirteen to seventeen, providing conclusive evidence of which John wrote the letters (John, 1, 2 & 3); the same John who wrote the gospel.

The said chapters of John are Jesus' last words before being arrested and crucified, fitting what John says: "It is the last hour" comment (1 Jn. 2:18). Similarly, Jesus' words: "Hour had come to depart out of the world" (Jn 13:1). With Jesus' departure, His disciples will need support and protection, for the devil was at work, and had already gained one of Jesus' followers (Jn. 13:2).

While at the supper (love feast), the devil entered the heart of Judas (Jn. 13:2, 27). Jesus loved His disciples, but Judas did not love Him back; Peter also fell for a time and was restored (Jn. 21:15-18).

Like Jesus' departure from the earth, the church will also depart after being tested (Rev. 3:10-11). However, many will fall away beforehand (cf. 2 Thess. 2:3) due to their love for Jesus growing cold (Matt. 24:12). This was the case for the church of Ephesus (Rev. 2:1-7), and was the concern for Peter, Jude, and John, hence the statement: "Keep yourself in the love of God" (Jude 21). Jude's proclamation implies that a person, once loving God, can grow cold towards Him. John agrees, saying, "Watch yourselves, so you do not lose what we have worked for" (2 Jn. 8). The danger John warns of is from the false teachers, who deceive any not on guard (2 Jn. 7-11).

The common concern for the early and modern church is cooling and wandering hearts. Many come into the faith, yet few remain, particularly when things get difficult (Matt. 24:10-12, Jn. 16:33). As mentioned, in chapter thirteen, Jesus said His hour had come (Jn. 13:1). In chapter sixteen He warned that the hour for the persecution of the church would also come (Jn. 16:31), therefore, they needed to be ready. Jesus prepared His disciples by washing their feet, instructing them to do likewise for each other (Jn. 13:14-15). Jesus was teaching His followers to love and receive each other, to keep each other in the love of God.

The washing of feet symbolises Salvation (Jn. 13:8), revealing the continual need for repentance. When a person is clean (Jn. 13:10), they do not need to take a bath, but still, the feet need washing. A person's feet encounter this world, making them unclean. The symbolic meaning refers to washing what has been stained by sin. Again, Jude says, "Hate the garment stained by the flesh" (Jude 23). The flesh refers to sin. When someone comes to Christ, they are made clean; however, there is still a need to rewash, symbolic of required continual repentance. John, in his letter, reinforces that followers of Christ will still sin (1 Jn. 1:8-10). Nevertheless, because they know Christ (Jn. 17:25-26), they repent continually (1 Jn. 1:9). This is the doctrine of progressive sanctification. Sanctification refers to separation from this world, actively and progressively becoming more like Christ. In this world, the believer is never sinless, but rather they sin less due to an inward and ongoing daily transformation (2 Cor. 3:13, Col. 3:10). None, this side of glory reaches perfection, not even Paul did (Phil. 3:12) - albeit we aim for it, making ourselves a slave to righteousness (Rom. 6:17-18). Once more, John makes it clear that we will never be totally free from sin in this life (1 Jn. 1:8-10).

Again, following the feet-washing ritual, Jesus gave His disciples a new commandment, "Love one another" (Jn. 13:14-35). John's letter is known as the 'Love letter', using the word love twenty-six times, linking love towards the Father-God and each other. John says that unless a confessing Christian loves his brother (in Christ), they are not of God (1 Jn. 3:10, 14, 16, 26, 4:7, 11, 12, 20, 21, 5:1, 2). John concludes by saying, "By this, we know that we love the children of God when we love God and obey his commandments" (1 Jn. 5:2). Those who walk-in love have eternal Life (Jn. 14:2, 1 Jn. 1:2, 2:8b, 17, 28, 3:14, 5:11).

The next topic, linking John's gospel and his letters, is the deity of Jesus Christ and the only means of Salvation (Jn. 14:1-14, 20, 1 Jn. 1:1-4, 2:28, 5:20). Salvation is secured through Christ alone, for those, alone, keeping His commandments (Jn. 14:15, 21, 23, 24, 17:2, 3, 1 Jn. 2:3, 5, 25, 5:3, 20, cf. 2 Jn. 6). Luke supports John, with his record of Jesus saying, "Why do you call me 'Lord, Lord,' and not do what I tell you?" (Lu. 6:46). In other words, Jesus is not the Lord of sinners, although He will lord over them on judgement day.

Another direct link between the gospel of John and his letter is the reference to the Holy Spirit. For the one obeying Jesus' commandments, thereby abiding in Him, His Spirit remains (Jn. 14:17, 1 Jn. 2:27). Worldly people who fail to abide are devoid of the Spirit (Jude 19). Drawing, sealing, and securing the believer is the work of the "Helper, the Holy Spirit" (Jn. 14:25, 15:26, 1 Jn. 2:20, 27, cf. 5:7), who also gives the overcoming believer "Peace" (Jn. 14:27, 16:33, 1 Jn. 4:4, 5:4, 5) in a world at war (Jn. 16:33).

Due to the empowering Holy Spirit, the abiding believer walks in peace, as Jesus walked, and bears fruit (Jn. 15:4-5, 1 Jn. 2:6). The 'Fruit' is first and foremost 'Love', producing perfect fellowship with God and each other (Jn. 17:21, 25, 1 Jn. 1:3, 3:24, 4:12, 17, 5:20). Keeping the commandment of love results with "Joy" now (Jn. 15:11, 2 Jn. 12) and on judgement day (1 Jn. 1:4). On judgement day "Perfect love casts out fear" (1 Jn. 4:18). In the meantime, we have a job to do.

To help the believer get the job done: "Whatever [the believer] asks [for] in [Jesus] name, [He] will do" (Jn. 14:12-14, 5:16, 1 Jn. 3:22, 5:14-15). As you can imagine, John's record of Jesus saying, "He will do whatever a believer asks," is a favourite with charismatics. The immediate context is that Jesus is going to be crucified. During a time of fear and confusion, Jesus encourages His disciples to abide in Him, no matter what. Jesus also encourages His disciples by saying that He will not abandon them and that He is coming back for those who love Him (Jn. 14:25-29, 16:16, 1 Jn. 2:8). In the meantime, they are to continue His work (Jn. 14:12). The continued work is linked with the statement: "Ask for whatever in My name." This statement is not referring to health, wealth, and happiness, but instead whatever is required to fulfill the will of the Father (Lu. 22:42), that the "Father may be glorified in the Son" (Jn. 14:13). "Anything asked for" that does not fall within the category of "Jesus' name" (being His will, and mission) will not be granted (Jam. 4:3). Again, the will of God is for Christ to be proclaimed.

In sum, "Ask for anything in My name" refers to praying according to God's will to get the job done. It is not a formula to get whatever we want from the world. Remember, this world hates Christ, and His followers (Jn. 15:18-19, 1 Jn. 3:13). Christians are no longer of the world (Jn. 15:19, 1 Jn. 4:5): therefore they will be persecuted by it (Jn. 15:20).

In conclusion, the gospel of John, chapters thirteen to seventeen, provides the framework for the letter of First John, starting with Salvation, through Christ alone, who is God. John's message is that the hour has come when all must choose whom and what they will serve. In the same way, Satan entered the heart of Judas; his work is continued through the false teachers, preparing unsteady souls, "In this last hour" for the coming antichrist. Every person coming to the truth is reborn into a world at war. Once saved, then regular repentance will follow due to continual interaction, therefore contamination from the world.

Throughout this life, there will be a constant need to remain in the light and love of God as the world attempts to draw people away. Keeping the new commandment of love is aided by the Holy Spirit. Those abiding in the love of Christ, and loving others, will be hated and persecuted by the world. However, Jesus has overcome the world, and so will those who remain in Him. Those remaining will experience both joy, and hardship, now, yet joy only when Jesus returns. When Jesus returns, His perfect love casts out fear of judgement. In the meantime, the believer must remain busy doing whatever God has asked, asking in return for whatever is required to complete that task, starting with the empowering Holy Spirit (cf. Lu. 11:9-13). The number one task is to proclaim Christ while walking in God's light (truth) and love, which is the evidence of righteousness over sin (1 Jn. 3:4-10).

Where Jude ends, John continues, focusing on the nearness of Christ's return, evident by the number of false teachers troubling the church. Jude and John instruct the church to remain/abide in the love of God. Loving God, His truth, and others is the solution to the problem.

FIRST JOHN

ETERNAL LIFE

CHAPTER 1
The Word of Life

From the Beginning

As mentioned in the previous section, like Jude, John wrote to the churches across Asia Minor (Turkey) in the late first century, warning them not to be led astray.

Challenging Calvinism, if the church members could not be led astray, therefore, not lose salvation, as Calvinists believe, there would have been no reason for Jude and John to warn them of the danger. Peter does the same, stating that it would have been better not to have known the truth than to have known it and then fall away (2 Pet. 2:20-21 paraphrased). The writer of the book of Hebrews agrees, saying, "It is impossible to restore again to repentance those who have once been enlightened, who have tasted the heavenly gift and have shared in the Holy Spirit, and have tasted the goodness of the word of God and the power of the age to come if they then fall away since they are crucifying once again the Son of God to their own harm and holding Him up to contempt" (Heb. 6:4-6).

Congruent with Peter, the writer of the book of Hebrews goes on to say, "How much worse punishment, do you think, will be deserved by the one who has trampled underfoot the Son of God, and has profaned the blood of the covenant by which he was sanctified, and has outraged the Spirit of grace?" (Heb. 10:29). Like John, the writer of the book of Hebrews takes aim at the confessing Christian, practicing sin (Heb. 10:26-27), warning them of hellfire (Heb. 10:31).

Every author contributing to scripture, from the Old Testament to the New, warns about sin and apostasy. In the same way, a person can be once married and get divorced, a Christian can be in covenant with God, and due to spiritualty adultery, be cut off, like Israel was (Rom 11:11--25). The failing churches in the book of Revelation were warned of the same (Rev. 2-3). Again, this is the point and purpose of Jude and John's letter to the churches, warning them!

The main reason confessing Christians get into trouble and fall away is due to departing from the truth. For this reason, John, like Jude (Jude 5, 17), reminds them of what they heard from the beginning from those who witnessed the account (1 Jn. 1:1-2). The truth refers to God made manifest in Jesus Christ (1 Jn. 1:2), revealing who He is. His word reveals what He did and will do soon. Anyone denying or departing from those fundamental truths does not have fellowship with the believers nor God (1 Jn. 1:3). The truth and gospel of Jesus is "The Word of life" (1 Jn. 1:1b).

The Word of Life (1 Jn. 1:1b) refers to "That which was heard from the beginning" (1 Jn. 1:1a). The opening verse in the gospel of John starts similarly, "In the beginning was the Word, and the Word was with God, and the Word was God (Jn. 1:1). The origin of John's statement is found in Genesis: "In the beginning, God created the heaven and the earth" (Gen. 1:1). Drawing from Genesis, John makes a clear statement that Jesus is God, who existed before anything, and created everything (Jn. 1:1-4). The denial of Christ's deity was the most dangerous teaching that the Gnostics introduced (cf. Jude 4, 2 Pet. 2:1). To deny Christ is to reject Him, and therefore, His salvation work, without which no one can be saved (Acts 4:12, Jn. 14:6).

Although John's opening statement is rooted in Genesis, the immediate context refers to the revelation of God, incarnate in Jesus Christ, the Word of Life. The Word of Life is what the apostles "Heard, Saw and Touched" (1 Jn. 1:1), referring to the physical Jesus. Luke records something similar: Jesus invited the frightened disbelieving disciples to "Touch" Him (Lu. 24:36-41). John's record is repeated by Luke, who narrows in on Thomas, often called "Doubting Thomas" for his disbelief (Jn. 20:24-28). Only after Thomas had touched the resurrected Jesus did he believe (Jn. 20:25, 27-28). The rest of the disciples were no different from Thomas (Mk. 16:9-14). Only after the disciples had seen and touched Jesus did they believe. For their unbelief, Jesus rebuked them (Mk. 16:14).

John repeats his testimony and eyewitness account of Jesus in chapter four, saying, "We have seen and testify that the Father has sent his Son to be the Saviour of the world" (1 Jn. 4:14). The firsthand experience of the apostles gives the apostles immediate credibility over the false teachers, and therefore, the authority to discredit them. While the false teachers claimed superior knowledge and special revelation, what they heard was second, or third-hand information. The word that John proclaims is a firsthand experience of the resurrected Jesus.

Peter confirms John's testimony, sayings, "We ourselves heard this very voice borne from heaven, for we were with Him on the holy mountain" (2 Pet. 2:18). Unlike the false teachers, Peter and the apostles were not following men (2 Pet. 1:16). Peter states, "We have something more sure than a prophetic word, to which you will do well to pay attention as to a lamp shining in a dark place until the day dawns and the morning star rises in your hearts" (2 Pet. 1:19). Peter goes on to say, God inspired all written scripture (1 Pet. 1:20-21, paraphrased). In other words, his written testimony of Jesus Christ is Holy Spirit-inspired, whereas the testimony of those denying Christ is demonically inspired. (cf. 1 Tim. 4:1).

The testimony of the apostles was also confirmed by their disciples, starting with John's disciple, Polycarp, who said, "Now I beseech you all to obey the word of righteousness and to endure with all the endurance which you also saw before your eyes, not only in the blessed Ignatius, and Zosimus, and Rufus, but also in others among yourselves, and in Paul himself, and in the other Apostles" (Polycarp, Philippians 9:1). Like John, Polycarp was instructing the church (of Philippi) to remain obedient to the teachings of their apostles, and their disciples, including himself, enduring suffering, if necessary. The addressed church has witnessed the suffering of Ignatius, Zosimus, Rufus, Paul, and others, therefore, needing encouragement. Stand firm, and don't shrink back (cf. Heb. 10:38b).

In the year 107, Emperor Trajan visited Antioch and forced Christians to choose between death and apostasy. Ignatius, Zosimus, and Rufus would not deny Christ and thus were condemned to be put to death in Rome. All three were thrown to the wild beasts and died. According to the Martyrdom of Polycarp, he also died a martyr, bound and burned at the stake, then stabbed when the fire failed to consume his body in 155 A.D.

Sharing in the sufferings of Christ (1 Pet. 4:13), and His disciples, persecution for the early church members were very real and near. The threat of being fed to wild animals and being used for sport in the colosseum stuck on a spike, burned alive, or crucified was enough to cause many to renounce Christ and they pledged their allegiance to Caesar. Those who did were said to be unredeemable by many. The exception was that if a Christian who was about to be martyred forgave them, God would also. Christians who were about to be martyred were said to be close to God due to being so close to death. If a believer on death row forgave the traitor, it was considered that God had forgiven them also, but not everyone held this view. Some maintained that if the confessing Christian renounced Christ, they had failed the test (cf. Rev. 2:10), and were discommunicated; therefore, forever damned by committing the sin that leads to death (1 Jn. 5:16).

According to John, the sin that leads to death is the rejection of what was taught from the beginning, referring to Jesus Christ (1 Jn. 2:23), the Word of Life, and continual disobedience toward Him. As mentioned earlier, the book of Hebrews (Heb. 6:4-6) is also used to support the claim that an apostate person is without hope of redemption. The warning equally applies to those who have moved away from the original teaching by running ahead and not continuing in the teaching of Christ (2 Jn. 1:9).

Once again, on each occasion, the testimony of the eyewitnesses points back to the beginning. Ten times John refers to the beginning (1 Jn 1:1, 2:7, 13, 14, 24 [2×], 3:8, 11, 2 Jn 5, 6), highlighting the importance of what was seen, heard, and taught by them, being critical to salvation. If anything changes, everything changes. John makes it clear in chapter two of his letter that salvation is conditional on whether someone has heard and received the truth (Word of Life) in the first place and whether that truth (life) abides in them and they in it: "Let what you heard from the beginning abide in you. If what you heard from the beginning abides in you, then you will also abide in the Son and the Father. And this is the promise that he made to us—eternal life" (2 Jn. 24-25). The abiding truth is connected to believing and doing, as in loving others. John says if someone says they love God, whom they have not seen, yet hates their brother, whom they have seen, they are liars, and there is no truth in them (1 Jn. 4:20-21).

The importance of John and the apostles seeing the resurrected Christ, alongside five hundred others (1 Cor. 15:3-8), affords him the qualification of an apostle. To meet the qualification of an apostle, the individual first had to be called and be an eyewitness to Jesus' ministry, His teaching, the miracles, His death, and resurrection (Acts 10:39-40). Paul was the exception, who was later called and qualified (Acts 22:14-15, Gal. 1:1, 1 Cor. 9:1). The purpose of the apostles was to build the foundations of the church, teaching Christ, the Cornerstone (Eph. 2:19-20). Once the Bible was complete and canonised, through the letters from the apostles, the foundations were built.

Despite many claiming to be apostles today, they are not on the grounds that they have not seen Christ with the physical eye. While some may have apostolic ministries, they are not apostles. Anyone claiming to be an apostle, often bringing in new teaching, runs ahead of scripture (2 Jn. 1:9) and is, therefore, a deceiver (2 Jn. 1:7). Paul instructs the church that they are to learn from Him and the other eyewitnessing apostles, warning them not to "Go beyond what was written" (1 Cor. 4:6).

Again, the apostles were eyewitnesses to the ministry of Jesus; therefore, they could say, "That which was from the beginning" (1 Jn. 1:1), "We have seen it" (1 Jn. 1:2). Because the apostles had heard, seen, and touched Christ, they could testify of it, and proclaim to their hearers, eternal life (1 Jn. 1:2). To reiterate, eternal life only comes through the "Word of Life" (1 Jn. 1:1), being Jesus (Jn. 14:6, Acts 4:12). In the closing chapter of his letter, John writes, "And this is the testimony, that God gave us eternal life, and this life is in His Son. Whoever has the Son has life; whoever does not have the Son of God does not have life" (1 Jn. 5:11-12). John writes something similar in his gospel, "For God so loved the world, that he gave his only Son, that whoever believes in him should not perish but have eternal life. For God did not send his Son into the world to condemn the world, but in order that the world might be saved through him. Whoever believes in him is not condemned, but whoever does not believe is condemned already because he has not believed in the name of the only Son of God. And this is the judgment: the light has come into the world, and people loved the darkness rather than the light because their works were evil. For everyone who does wicked things hates the light and does not come to the light, lest his works should be exposed. But whoever does what is true comes to the light, so that it may be clearly seen that his works have been carried out in God" (Jn. 3:16-21).

Three times John says he, and the apostles, have "Seen" (1 Jn. 1:1, 2, 3), and twice he says that they "Proclaim" (1 Jn. 1:2, 3) to others, what they have seen, that they may have fellowship with them, and God (1 Jn. 1:3). Again, the reason John is writing to the church is to warn them. They, like Jude's readers, have let false teachers in. The false teachers primarily attack the deity of Christ and reject the apostles' authority. Therefore, John says, "If you want to have fellowship with us, you have to reject the false teachers (cf. 2 Jn. 1:11); you cannot have it both ways" (paraphrased). The motive for John's letter is that he wants his readers to enjoy the fellowship the apostles have with each other and Christ (1 Jn. 1:4).

The fellowship John speaks of relates to an intimate relationship, as referenced previously in his gospel (Jn. 17:3). Without fellowship, there is no eternal life. To repeat, the only way to have the fellowship John speaks of is through Jesus Christ, the Son of God. John refers to the "Son" of God nineteen times in his first letter (1 John), consistently applying that term to Jesus, relating it to His deity. John also writes the name "Jesus Christ" eight times, making the distinction between who has eternal life (1 Jn. 2:22, 5:1). John marks the difference between Jesus, as the Son (God), and His followers, by calling them "Children" (1 Jn. 3:1). Thirteen times John addresses the church as 'Children,' three times more in his second letter (2 Jn.), and once more in his third (3 Jn.). Those having fellowship with God are His children, contrary to the children of the devil (1 Jn. 3:10). John warns the church (children of God), saying, "Little Children, let no one deceive you. Whoever practices righteousness is righteous, as he is righteous. Whoever makes a practice of sinning is of the devil, for the devil has been sinning from the beginning. The reason the Son of God appeared was to destroy the works of the devil" (1 Jn. 3:7-8).

Again, the warning is, "Let no one deceive you," suggesting the child of God can still be deceived, by the deceivers (2 Jn. 7); therefore, they can lose what they have (2 Jn. 8), hence the words, "Watch yourselves" (2 Jn 8). Those remaining on guard will gain a full reward (2 Jn 8) and complete joy (1 Jn. 1:4). The joy John refers to is now and when Christ returns. John's joy relates to the children of God staying in the truth (2 Jn. 1:4, 3 Jn. 1:4). And, if they do, they will have great joy on judgement day (cf. Jude 1:24). If the children of God depart from the truth; therefore, fellowship with the apostles, and God, to have fellowship with the false teachers, John's joy over the apostate person will be lost. So, joy for John and the apostate person will be incomplete (1 Jn. 1:4).

In conclusion, John reminds his readers of the gospel, its origin, and the promise of eternal life obtained through the "Word of Life." Those alone, remaining in fellowship with God (1 Jn. 1:7), abiding until the end (2 Jn. 2:24-25), will have complete joy (eternal life). The "Word of Life" refers to Jesus, who is under attack by the Gnostic, claiming He is not the Son of God and not the only means to inherit eternal life. While the Gnostics claim to be Christians, having fellowship with God, they are not due to denying Christ's deity, the Trinity, and the power of sin. Another reason the Gnostics are not in fellowship with God is that they are not in fellowship with the apostles, who witnessed Jesus' ministry and wrote scripture. The same scripture the Gnostics have rejected and gone ahead of.

CHAPTER 2
Walking in the Light

Do Not Be Deceived

In the previous section, John challenges his readers by saying, "If you want to have fellowship with us, you cannot have fellowship with the false teachers (1 Jn. 1:3, paraphrased, cf. 2 Jn. 10). John, like Jude and Peter, state that anyone accepting the teaching of the Gnostics is in danger of hell (Jude 22-23, 2 Pet. 2:14, 20-21, 2 Jn. 10-11). Again, the primary problem with the Gnostics teaching is the denial of Jesus Christ, His deity (2 Pet. 2:1, Jude 4), and salvation work (1 Jn. 2:2). The denial of His return in the flesh is also damnable (2 Jn. 7). Associated with the rejection of Jesus Christ is dismissing the power of sin, and its consequences.

Peter, Jude, and John address the issues of 'Greasy grace', where false teachers claim, "Because we are under grace, sin has no power." Often, those making such claims do so to justify their sin (We can do whatever we like, and it will be all right). Wrong! Dead wrong! Three times Paul says, "Do not be deceived" (1 Cor. 6:9, 15:33, Gal. 6:7) regarding sin and keeping company with those who practice sin while confessing to being Christian. John also warns about keeping company with sinners (false teachers) who lead others astray (1 Jn. 2:16, 3:7). The false teachers lead others astray by downplaying the power of sin. James joins the conversation, saying, "Each person is tempted when lured and enticed by his desire. Then desire, when it has conceived, gives birth to sin, and sin, when it is fully grown, brings forth death. Do not be deceived, my beloved brothers" (Jam. 1:14-16a). While it is an individual desire that lures into sin, the Gnostics enticed unsteady souls (2 Pet. 2:14) with false words, promoting greed (2 Pet. 2:3) and freedom to sin (2 Pet. 2:18-19).

Unlike the false teachers, John, like Paul and James, warns the confessing followers of Christ about the danger of sin, again reminding his reader of the message they heard (1 Jn. 1:5) in the beginning (1 Jn 1:1, 2:7, 13, 14, 24 [2×], 3:8, 11, 2 Jn 5, 6),). The message proclaimed by the disciples differs from what the Gnostics taught for the abovementioned reasons. Paul says what they teach is a "Different gospel," promoted through a different spirit (not the Holy Spirit), presenting another Jesus (2 Cor. 11:4). Paul calls the Gnostics presenting another Jesus "Super apostles" (2 Cor. 11:5, 12:11), who behave similarly to some celebrity preachers and televangelists today, who never mention sin or warn of the consequences. While dismissing the power of sin, the false teachers are self-seeking peddlers of the gospel, who are greedy for gain (Rom. 16:18, 2 Cor. 2:17, 1 Tim. 5:6, Tit. 1:11, 2 Pet. 2:3, 14, Jude 16).

Remember again, the qualification of an apostle is to have eyewitnessed the life and ministry of Jesus Christ (Acts 10:39-41), which automatically disqualifies anyone claiming to be an apostle today. The same was true of the 'Super apostles' in the First Century. They were not apostles; Paul's term (super-apostles) referred to their self-appointed superior position. The super-apostles claimed superiority over Paul, saying that he and his message was weak. Paul admits, by comparison, he was not a slick speaker (2 Cor. 11:6), but his gospel, by contrast, had power (1 Cor. 4:19-20). The power Paul referred to is the power of the gospel, which points to Christ and deals with sin. While the false teachers practiced sin, genuine followers of Christ reframed from it by "Walking in the light [of Christ]" (1 Jn. 1:7) and practicing righteousness (1 Jn. 3:3-10).

The message proclaimed and heard from the beginning was that "God is light, and in Him, there is no darkness at all" (1 Jn. 1:5). Therefore, if a person wants to have fellowship (1 Jn. 3, 6, 7) with the apostles, and God, they must "Walk in the light" (1 Jn. 1:7). In God, there is no darkness (1 Jn. 5b); therefore, anyone who walks in darkness has no fellowship with the apostles, or God (1 Jn. 6b).

Three times John counters the false teachers by saying, "If we say we have fellowship with Him while we walk in darkness…" ; "If we say we have no sin…" ; "If we say we have not sinned…" (1 Jn. 6, 8, 10). John's counterargument implies conditional salvation. Confessing Christians are saved "If [they] walk in the light…" (1 Jn. 1:7), and "If [they] confess [their] sins" (1 Jn. 9). The condition applies to the continuation of "Walking in the light," and "Confessing sin."

The Gnostics, who once were walking in the light, having fellowship with the apostles, and therefore (supposedly) God, walked away (2 Pet. 2:15). They went out of the church, back into the world (1 Jn. 2:19, 2 Jn. 7). If anyone is in the church, it is because they have come out of the world (Jn. 15:19, 1 Jn. 2:15-17, cf. 2 Cor. 6:17, Rev. 18:4). The only way to go back into the world, is from the church. No one can return to the world when they have not come out of it. Instead, they would remain in the world.

On the other side of the road from the 'Greasy-grace' ditch is another where condemnation shipwrecks those struggling with sin. The confessing Christian is to walk in the light while hating the world (1 Jn. 2:15-17, cf. Matt 6:24, Phil. 3:18-19) and wrestling with the Adamic nature, despite their best efforts - because of the Adamic nature, all will sin. Paul deals with the Adamic nature in Romans, chapter six, saying that, "Our old self was crucified with [Jesus]" (Rom. 6:6, cf. Gal 5:24); therefore, we are to "Walk in newness of life" (Rom. 6:4b, cf. Gal. 5:16). The problem is the sin nature is hard to kill; therefore, there is a continual need to "Put on the Lord Jesus

Christ and make no provision for the flesh to gratify its desires" (Rom. 13:14). Despite his best efforts, not even Paul achieved sinless perfection; nevertheless he pressed on (Phil. 3:12-14, cf. Rom 7:15-25, Matt. 26:41).

As mentioned in the previous section, no believer in Christ is sinless, but instead, they will sin less when walking in the light. Those claiming perfection on this side of Christ's return, are deceived. Addressing those claiming to be perfect, Lactantius (285. A.D.) said, "If anyone teaches it is possible to be perfect [sinless]. Let him first prove by demonstrating it in his life. Then we will listen." Clement of Alexandria (192-202 A.D.), agreed, saying, "It is not possible to be completely sinless. Christian perfection is the attitude of striving to be more like Christ." Earlier, Irenaeus (178 A.D.) said, "Perfect knowledge cannot be attained in the present life" (and neither can be perfection).

According to God, those claiming that they do not sin are liars, and the truth is not in them (1 Jn. 1:8). However, there is a vast difference between those who practice sin and those who practice truth and righteousness, yet stumble. The Gnostics claimed to have no sin, period, or that sin no longer had power over them, and to prove it, they encouraged it. Paul addressed something similar, condemning sinful behaviour and those promoting it (Rom. 3:8, 6:1-4.15-19).

Those who practice sin while confessing to having fellowship with God are deceived, they are liars, and the truth is not in them (1 Jn. 1:8); they walk in darkness continually (1 Jn. 1:6a). They wander in darkness because they "Do not know and practice the truth" (1 Jn. 1:6b). In contrast, those walking in the truth, walk in the light: "But whoever does what is true comes to the light, so that it may be clearly seen that his works have been carried out in God" (Jn. 3:21). The context of John's statement (Jn. 3:21) contrasts those doing wicked things against those who do what is true: "For everyone who does wicked things hates the light and does not come to the light, lest his works should be exposed" (Jn. 3:20). In both instances there is free will to choose one or the other. As mentioned above, no one can have it both ways. Maintaining fellowship with darkness and those who walk in it disqualifies anyone from fellowship with light (1 Jn. 1:6, cf. 2 Cor. 6:14).

"Practicing the truth" (1 Jn. 1:6) by walking in it (Jn. 3:20) is the same as "Walking in the light" (1 Jn. 1:7). John's gospel (Jn. 3:19-21) provides the best explanation of what "Walking in the light" implies. In sum, it refers to walking in the light of the revelation of Christ. Those who reject, or change the gospel, walk in darkness. Anyone tampering with God's word is already under judgement (2 Pet. 3:16, cf. Rev. 22:19). While those walking in darkness are destined for destruction (Jn. 3:21), those walking in the light have fellowship with God; therefore, eternal life (1 Jn. 1:3, 7). "The blood of Jesus [God's Son] cleanses [those walking in the light] from all sin" (1 Jn. 1:7).

As mentioned above, walking in the light, and confessing sin are continuous activities for genuine believers. The verb of these verses (1 Jn. 1:7, 9) is present tense. Only those walking in the light have the cleansing blood of Jesus, saving them from the consequence of sin. Jude says, "Keep yourselves in the love of God, waiting for the mercy of the Lord Jesus Christ that leads to eternal life" (Jude 21). The blood of Christ cleanses (continuously) those (continuously) walking in the light.

The fact that cleansing is continuous implies sin is also, however, not practiced. John confirms this fact by saying, "If we say we have no sin, we deceive ourselves and the truth is not in us" (1 Jn. 1:8, cf. 10). Like the verb 'Walking' and 'Cleansing', the claim (I have no sin) is present and ongoing - therefore, present tense. Remember, John is talking to the church, claiming to have fellowship with God. John is not addressing the false teachers but rather responding to their false teaching. The Greek word "To have sin" refers to present sins (cf. Jn 9:41; 15:22, 24; 19:11), not to sins of the past, before confessing and committing to Christ. In the same way, sin is present and continual; deception is also for the one denying that they sin. The truth is not in them (1 Jn. 1:8). The claims of having fellowship with God when walking in darkness and having no sin are connected.

Following John's counterargument against the Gnostics' claim to have no sin, John says, "If we confess our sins, He (Jesus) is faithful to forgive us our sins and to cleanse us from all unrighteousness (1 Jn. 1:9). The sin cleansed is the same that Jesus' blood (continually) cleanses (1 Jn. 1:7). Again, the action is continuous due to ongoing sin. Note once more the conditional 'If'. Said in reverse, "If we do not confess our sin, it will not be forgiven and cleansed." John's challenge to the false teaching of the Gnostics is over their confession. The Gnostics confess to being in fellowship with God yet say they have no sin, while Christians who are in fellowship with God walk in the truth and acknowledge their sin. The sin problem draws the believer nearer to God, recognising the need for continuous cleansing. James agrees with John, telling believers to confess their sins when they stumble (Jam. 5:16). Earlier, James says all Christians stumble in many ways (Jam. 3:2). Anyone saying otherwise puts themselves at odds with God and His word.

In theological terms, the forgiveness of sin is the cancellation of debt. God's cleansing removes all unrighteousness. Nothing remains! John's reference to God being faithful and just is rooted in the Old Testament. Several times it is repeated that "The LORD, the LORD, a God merciful and gracious, slow to anger, and abounding in steadfast love and faithfulness, keeping steadfast love for thousands, forgiving iniquity and transgression and sin" (Exod. 34:6-7, cf. Num. 14:18, Deut. 7:9, 2 Chron 30:9, Ps. 86:15, 103:8, 145:8, Jon. 4:2, Nah. 1:3, Neh. 9:17, Joel 2:13, cf. Rom. 2:4, Jam. 5:11, 2 Pet. 3:9, 1 Jn. 1:9).

God's faithfulness towards His elect (1 Cor. 1:9) and His word (2 Tim. 2:13) provides a way of escape from temptation that leads to sin (1 Cor. 10:13, Jam. 1:14-16a). Those escaping from temptation and or being cleansed through repentance are presented "Blameless before the presence of His glory with great joy" (Jude 24). Remember again, genuine believers in Christ are 'Blameless', not 'Faultless'. However, the aim is not to sin (1 Jn. 2:1a). Anyone continually, deliberately, habitually sinning is not of God (1 Jn. 3:9-10). Those who strive to do what is right and walk righteously are of the Righteous One (1 Jn. 2:29, 3:7).

God's righteousness toward sinners has been an age-old problem for many, questioning how God could forgive evil people. For example, how could God forgive someone like Hitler? Paul addresses the question in his letter to the church of Rome (Rom. 3:21-26). Paul says, "There is no distinction. For all have sinned and fall short of the glory of God" (Rom. 3:22b-24). Anyone who believes in Christ, and confesses their sins, is saved. There is no distinction. Paul confirms this again in chapter ten (Rom. 10:8-13). While Paul's address refers to those in the world coming to Christ, John's refers to those in Christ. He includes himself and the apostles by saying, "We" (If we say, if we walk, if we confess).

After debunking the false teaching of the Gnostics, who claimed they had fellowship with God, even though they had none with the apostles, and that they had no sin, John moves to his third point. "If we say we have not sinned, we make Him a liar, and His word is not in us" (1 Jn. 1:10). Verse eight (1 Jn. 1:8) and ten (1 Jn. 1:10) are similar, the difference being, with the first we deceive ourselves if we say we have not sinned, and the next, we make God a liar. Again, the problem John is dealing with is the false teaching from the Gnostics, claiming that they have not sinned since confessing Christ. It is important to note that the Gnostics confessed to believing in Christ; however, they rejected His deity (2 Pet. 2:1, Jude 4) and authority (Jude 8), and they twisted scripture (2 Pet. 3:16).

The Gnostics make God a liar when saying they have not sinned because God's word states that all have sinned (Rom. 3:10-18, 22-23). Again, Paul's reference refers to that outside of Christ, but James and John address those in Christ (Jam. 3:2, 5:15, 1 Jn. 1:9, 2:1b). Anyone claiming that they have not sinned since confessing Christ makes God a liar. His word is not in them (1 Jn. 1:10). John reiterates that the Gnostics who claimed to have fellowship with God lie (1 Jn. 1:6) and make God a liar (1 Jn. 1:10). They do not practice the truth (1 Jn. 1:6), and the truth is not in them (1 Jn. 1:10). They are deceived in every way (1 Jn. 1:8).

In conclusion, the aim is to walk in the light and not sin; however, the reality is that all do sin and will continually stumble in many ways (Jam. 3:2) until Christ returns (1 Jn. 3:2). When we (all) sin, God has already made a way out (1 Jn. 1:9, 2:1). The blood of Christ cleanses those who confess their sins (1 Jn. 1:7, 9). As for those claiming to have no sin, therefore not confessing sin, there is no forgiveness and no fellowship with God; the "Word of Life is not in them (1 Jn. 1:1b, 10). They are deceived (1 Jn. 1:8), and they go about deceiving others (1 Jn. 2:26, 2 Jn 7). Therefore, John says, avoid them! (2 Jn. 10-11).

CHAPTER 3
By This We Know

If We Keep His Commandments

Following John's challenge to the church, stating, "If you want to have fellowship with us, and God, you cannot have fellowship with the false teachers; you cannot have it both ways" (paraphrased), John emphasises the issue of sin (1 Jn. 2:1, 2). While the Gnostics downplayed sin, and its power, John majors on it, writing the word sixteen times in his first letter.

The specific Gnostic cult John is dealing with is the one formed by Cerinthus, writing his own gospel (the gospel of Cerinthus, identical to the 2nd Century gospel of Ebionites). He teaches that God did not create the world, and that Jesus was a mere man, denying the virgin birth, and that the Spirit of Christ descended on Him at baptism. The Spirit, Christ, then departed before Jesus, and the man was crucified. This false teaching is also known as adoptionism, also taught by Christian Science today. Adoptionism claims that because Jesus was sinless, He was adopted by God. John crushes adoptionism by saying, "The Word became flesh and made his dwelling among us. We have seen His glory, the glory of the one and only Son, who came from the Father, full of grace and truth" (Jn. 1:14). John's opening verses in his letter are a repeat of his gospel: "That which was from the beginning, which we have heard, which we have seen with our eyes, which we looked upon and have touched with our hands, concerning the word of life — the life was made manifest, and we have seen it, and testify to it and proclaim to you the eternal life, which was with the Father and was made manifest to us — that which we have seen and heard we proclaim also to you, so that you too may have fellowship with us; and indeed our fellowship is with the Father and with his Son Jesus Christ" (1 Jn. 1:1-3).

For the reasons mentioned above, Cerinthus was John's archenemy who also taught that sensual pleasures would be gratified in the millennium, like food, drink, and sex. That perverted view of unlimited, unhindered sexual freedom is directly connected with the Gnostic teaching that Jude was contending against (Jude 4-7). Muslims arrive at a similar conclusion with the idea of having seventy-two virgins in heaven. "Everyone that God admits into the paradise will be married to 72 Houries (wives) who are beautiful and virgins, with whom they can have eternal physical satisfaction."

Alongside Cerinthus was Valentinus, who taught that a believer cannot lose salvation. This is because saving faith comes from the spirit, not the flesh, which is why he had no problem with sin. The teaching of Cerinthus and Valentinus spread fast, far, and wide, troubling the churches that Jude and John were addressing.

Connected to the above millennium heresy taught by Cerinthus was that the book of Revelation was symbolic and not literal. While the book contains many symbols, it is still literal. Cerinthus taught that the millennial dispensation was not literal, despite God, through John, making it clear that it is - mentioning it six times (Rev. 20:1-7). Directly stemming from Cerinthus' teaching, around 290 A.D., amillennialism became a widespread view among Christians. By the fourth century, amillennialism dominated the church, stating that the book of Revelation should not be read or studied by the everyday believer. That view remains until this day, evident by most Christians not touching it, including many pastors.

John wrote his letter (1 John) to refute the teachings of Cerinthus. Due to his and other false teachings plaguing the early church, John said, "Children, it is the last hour" (1 Jn. 2:18), warning that many antichrists have come, attempting to deceive, in preparation for the antichrist (1 Jn. 2:18-19, 26). The problem now with amillennialism is that it states there is no rapture, no seven-year tribulation, and no antichrist to come. If there is no literal coming antichrist, then there is also no literal return of Jesus Christ at the end of the tribulation to set up His Kingdom, which is damnable (2 Jn. 7). Amillennialism, therefore, teaches that the one-thousand-year reign, or the Messianic Kingdom, is spiritual, not literal, subscribing to 'Millennial now' theory. Revelation, chapters nineteen and twenty present some challenges for amillennialism, which they deal with by saying they are not chronological events.

Instead of being prophetic and futuristic, amillennialism states that John is recording what he saw take place (occurring in the past). Amillennialism teaches that Satan has already been bound and can no longer deceive nations; therefore, the world is to be dominated by Christians. The same is taught by Kingdom Now 'Theology' (Seven Mountain Mandate), Dominionist, or Reconstructionist. Incorporated in the Kingdom Now teaching is replacement theology, where Israel has been replaced by the church, which is why proponents claim the prosperity promises of Israel for themselves.

Another heresy taught through amillennialism is that sin has been fully dealt with. Today, some Word of Faith hyper-grace movements teach that sin, past, present, and future, is under the blood of Christ Jesus; therefore, it has no power over the believer. Similarly, the First Century Gnostics taught that the body sins, not the spirit, which is saved; therefore, there is no need to repent. The Valentinians taught something similar, stating that believers can never lose their salvation due to the spirit of the elect being predestined to be saved, not the flesh. Calvinism teaches the same drawing that doctrine from the Gnostic Valentinian cult. Refuting the Gnostic cults and modern teaching flowing from those origins, John categorically says that all have sinned, do sin, and will sin continually, this side of Christ returning. Therefore, continual confession of sin (repentance) is required.

In the previous section of this work, it was mentioned that John states that anyone claiming to have no sin is a liar (1 Jn. 1:6), they are deceived (1 Jn. 1:8), there is no truth in them (1 Jn. 7), and neither is God's word (1 Jn. 1:10). On that basis, they have no fellowship with the apostles, nor with God (1 Jn. 1:3, 6, 7). Despite the continual struggle against sin on this side of Christ's return, the apostle John urges his readers not to sin (1 Jn. 2:1a). However, he also states, should you fail (and you will), God has already made an atoning sacrifice (1 Jn. 2:1b).

The opening line, "My little children," of chapter two (1 Jn. 2:1) shifts focus from the Gnostic teachers to those in fellowship with the apostles and God. The evidence of John's 'children' having fellowship with the apostles is seen in the term, confirming intimacy (fellowship) and the acknowledgement of sin. John's statement, "So you may not sin" does not contradict his previous reference against the Gnostic who claimed to have no sin (1 Jn. 1:8, 10) due to the provision added for sin (1 Jn. 2:1b), like his previous statements (1 Jn. 1:7, 9). The statement confirms that John's children have Jesus Christ, whom the Gnostics deny. Because they have Jesus Christ, the Righteous One, and advocate with the Father, forgiveness of sin has already been obtained (1 Jn. 2:2b).

The word 'Advocate' is translated from the Greek word "Paraklētos", which is only seen in John's writings. Once John uses the word in his first letter, and again he uses it in his gospel (Jn 14:16, 16:7). In John's gospel, the word refers to the ministry of the Holy Spirit, whereas in his letter, it refers to the ministry of Jesus Christ (cf. Rom. 8:34). The most literal application of the word refers to a friend speaking on behalf of another who has been accused of something rather than a judge. In context, the believer's "Friend" is Jesus, the "Righteous One." Jesus is the believer's Friend, providing they do as He commanded (Jn. 15:14-15). Jesus is that one's friend, and so much more. He is the atoning sacrifice for sin (1 Jn. 2:2).

When meditating on Jesus, the advocate, Zechariah, chapter three should come to mind. Directly linked with the opening verse (Zech. 3:1) is another, found in the book of Revelation (Rev. 12:10), where John's vision and revelation reveal Satan, the accuser of the brethren, is hard at work. In Zechariah's vision, Satan accuses Joshua of being a sinner (Zech. 3:3), and the accusation is correct! Joshua is a sinner dressed in filthy rags (Zech. 3:4). Note the sitting of the passage; it is a court of law. Joshua is standing before the Judge (God), guilty of wearing filthy robes. However, his filthy robe is exchanged for a clean one, and he is also given a (white) stone, Joshua, the High Priest, and allowed to sit. While all the while, his accuser (Satan) is condemning him.

However, the Lord rebukes the accuser (Satan) (Zech. 3:2), and Michael, the archangel, voiced the same when contesting Satan over Moses' body (Jude 1:9). Over what God has chosen, Satan has no claim. In other words, you cannot curse what God has blessed (Num. 23:8). Like with John's charge to "Walk in the same way Jesus walked" God says, through Zechariah, "IF you walk in My ways...," On that day, by meeting the conditional "IF," Joshua (Israel, the Jews) will receive three millennial blessings, 1). They will rule God's house; 2). They will have charge over God's courts, and 3). They will have the right to access (Zech. 3:7). The "Stone" (Zech. 3:9) is symbolic of innocence (Rev. 2:17) and is given to the one who conquers and remains conquering by putting their faith in Jesus alone. Besides trusting in Jesus, repentance is the key to salvation and keeping it (cf. Zech. 1:3, 1 Jn. 1:9, 2:1), which is continual obedience (Zech.3:7). The one who is given the white stone is, only because they have the Cornerstone, Jesus.

Repentance and abiding faithfulness go hand in hand, which brings us back to the conditional "If" (Zech. 3:6). Contrary to what some suggest, repentance has nothing to do with worked-based salvation but is the evidence of salvation, bearing fruit (Matt. 3:8). Repentance is also the evidence of the Holy Spirit working within, which is likewise the evidence of salvation. The one who has the Spirit has Christ (1 Jn. 3:24, 4:13), who is the Servant, Branch, and the Stone. Being tested refers to undergoing a 'close examination'. Keeping verses one and four (standing) and eight (seated) in mind (Zech. 3:1, 4, 8), Zechariah narrows in on the examination using the reference of "Seven eyes" (Zech. 3:9). The seven eyes on the stone symbolise the Holy Spirit (Isa. 11:2; Rev. 5:6). In the following chapter, Zechariah picks up on the same again, "These seven are the eyes of the Lord, which range through the whole earth" (Zech. 4:10). Both references (Zech. 3:9, 4:10) symbolise God's worldwide scrutiny, where nothing is hidden, everything is thoroughly examined and fully exposed. The examination's first and last area determined whether the one being tested has the Stone, Jesus Christ? If the answer is yes, the Judge finds the defendant innocent (Zech. 3:4-5), they are acquitted, and the trial is over. If not, the defendant will be found guilty and then sentenced according to their works (cf. Rev. 19:11-15). The greatest sin anyone can commit is to reject, or not have, Jesus Christ, and therefore lack His Spirit who reveals Him (cf. Matt. 16:17).

Like the Jews of Zechariah's days, John's concern is that many claiming to be Christians do not have the Messiah, Jesus (cf. 1 Jn. 2:18) due to not "Walking in God's ways" (1 Jn. 2:6, cf. Zech. 3:7). Unless that changes, they will not have the Advocate on that day.

Jesus Christ represents the abiding believer, in sinless perfection, before the judgement seat, as the atoning sacrifice for sin (1 Jn. 4:10). As seen through Zechariah, chapter three, the words "Propitiation for our sins" (1 Jn. 2:2) refer to the removal of sin, and therefore God's anger towards sinners, through sacrifice, thereby appeasing God's wrath. While Jesus represents the believer before God, God sent Jesus for this purpose (1 Jn. 4:10, Jn. 3:16). The offer of divine representation has been extended to all: "For God so loved the world that He sent His Son" (Jn. 3:16). Jesus came as a living sacrifice, atoning for the sins of the whole world, that He might represent everyone before God, on the day of judgement (1 Jn. 2:2b). Equally, Satan is on a mission to deceive the whole world (Rev. 12:9). Regardless, because of Christ's creation (Rom. 1:20), the Law (Rom. 2:1, 16, 3:19) and redemptive work, the whole world is accountable before God, and therefore without excuse.

At this point in the biblical calendar, there are a few judgements to come, as prophesied through scripture. The first is the judgement seat of Jesus Christ (Rom. 14:10-12, 1 Cor. 3:10-15, 2 Cor. 5:9-11), applying to raptured Christians (1 Cor. 15:51-54, 1 Thess. 4:16, Rev. 3:10, 4:1). Believers caught up will then be changed, like Christ (1 Jn. 3:2), and rewarded (Matt. 5:12, Lu. 6:23, 1 Cor. 3:14, 2 Jn. 8, Rev. 22:12). Anyone looking, therefore living for Jesus, abiding until He returns (1 Jn. 2:28) will be removed from the earth before the wrath to come (Lu. 21:34-36, Rom. 5:9, 1 Thess. 1:10, 5:9, Rev 3:10, 4:1). Once the church has been removed the tribulation commences and the antichrist will be revealed (2 Thess. 2:7-8). The antichrist cannot be identified on this side of the rapture. John's reference to Jesus being the advocate first and foremost applies to the believer's judgement. After the rapture, there is one more chance for those left behind to get right with God. When Jesus returns to the earth after seven years of tribulations, He will then judge those who either survived the tribulation or died in it; some unto salvation (Rev. 20:4) and others to damnation (Joel 3:1-16. Zech. 12:10-13:1, Matt. 24:29-31, Rev. 1:7, 6:12-17, 11:18, 19:11-21, Rev. 20:5).

Following one thousand years of Messianic reign (Ps. 2:9, Isa. 11:14, 65:25, Dan. 7:13-14, Amos 9:13-15, Joel 3:16-18, Mic. 4:6-8), everyone who rejected Christ and His redemptive work, who are waiting in hades, will be resurrected (Dan. 12:2, Jn. 5:28-29, Acts 24:15) to face the Great White Throne Judgement (Rev. 20:11-15). At the final judgement, there is no advocate; instead, the One who stood for the believers in the previous judgements now judges the rebellious guilty, giving them a sentence of eternal damnation in the great lake of fire. At this point, the antichrist and the false prophet have already been in the lake of fire for one thousand years (Rev. 19:20-21, 20:10), debunking the false doctrine of instant annihilation. Anyone who takes the antichrist's mark (666) during the tribulation will also experience the same fate (Rev. 14:9-11), which is why the angel of God says, "Do not take the mark, endure to the end" (Rev. 14:12, paraphrased). Jesus said the same, applied to those left behind to endure the tribulation; they must endure until the end (Matt, 24:13). Again, it is not God's desire for any to suffer. The tribulation is designed to save some from hell. The lake of fire was created for Satan and his angels (Matt. 25:41), not for humanity. Nevertheless, humanity will go there if they follow Satan, his angels, and agents (false teachers).

Not only is Christ's atoning work afforded to those who are in fellowship with Him but to all. Peter confirms it by saying that God is "Not wishing that any should perish, but that all should reach repentance" (2 Pet. 3:9b). John, Paul, and Peter contradict Calvinism by saying God desires to save everyone (1 Jn. 4:14). However, He can only save those who come through Jesus Christ (1 Jn. 5:12-13), by obeying and abiding until the end. In other words, the whole world's sins are not atoned for; instead, the atonement for sin is available to all.

Those claiming to know God are tested by obedience, not confession alone. The test for those claiming to believe in God is whether they obey Him. The Greek word for believing (Pistis) involves belief, but it goes beyond human belief because it involves God's personal revelation that can only result from obedience. Belief, like faith, is an outworking response to something, connecting belief and action. To say someone is saved because they believe is false. John says if anyone claims to love God but hates their brother, they are a liar and therefore condemned (1 Jn. 4:20). As mentioned earlier, it was due to an escalation of false teaching that John wrote the letter of First and Second John. John knew that before Jesus returned for the church, His bride, many would fall away, motivating him to repeatedly say, you must "Abide." John uses the word "Abide" sixteen times due to the danger of falling away.

In addition to Paul's warnings of a great falling away in the last days (2 Thess. 2, 1 Tim. 4:1, 2 Tim. 3:1, 4:3), many early church fathers forewarned of the same. For example, the Ascension of Isaiah (somewhere around 70-175 A.D.) says this: "And afterward, on the eve of His approach, His disciples will forsake the teachings of the Twelve Apostles, and their faith, and their love and their purity. And there will be much contention on the eve of [His advent and] His approach. And in those days, many will love the office, though devoid of wisdom. And there will be many lawless elders and shepherds dealing wrongly by their own sheep, and they will ravage (them) owing to their not having holy shepherds. And many will change the honour of the garments of the saints for the garments of the covetous, and there will be much respect of persons in those days and lovers of the honour of this world. And there will be much slander and vainglory at the approach of the Lord, and the Holy Spirit will withdraw from many. And there will not be in those days many prophets, nor those who speak trustworthy words, save one here and there in divers places. This is on account of the spirit of error and fornication and of vainglory, and of covetousness, which shall be in those, who will be called servants of that One and in those who will receive that One. And there will be great hatred in the shepherds and elders towards each other. For there will be great jealousy in the last days; for everyone will say what is pleasing in his own eyes. And they will make of none effect the prophecy of the prophets which were before me, and these my visions also will they make of none effect, in order to speak after the impulse of their own hearts" (Ascension of Isaiah 3:21-31).

The warning said slightly differently: "When the Messiah's coming is at hand, His disciples will forsake the teaching of the twelve apostles." For this reason, John opens his letter by saying, "You have fellowship with God if you have fellowship with us" (paraphrased). The Gnostics did not have fellowship with the disciples due to rejecting their authority and teaching. The prophecy given through the Ascension of Isaiah warns that just before Jesus returns, few will remain. Jesus said the same (Lu. 18:8).

Alongside the Ascension of Isaiah are many more early church writings warning about apostasy, such as Hippolytus who says, in 'The End of the World 7' (210 A.D.), "The temples of God will be like houses (house churches), and there will be overturning of the churches everywhere." Hippolytus says that sin will fill the land (shortened sentence), promoted by those professing to be Christians. Shepherds will be like wolves; the priest will embrace falsehood, and the monks will lust after the things of this world."

In sum, in the last days (now), many will be deceived, believing they are saved when they are not, which is why John writes, eight times, the phrase, "By this, we will know" (1 Jn. 2:3, 5, 16, 19, 3:24, 4:6, 13, 5:2) referring to salvation. On each occasion, the evidence of a believer being saved is in obeying and abiding. Remember again, the Gnostics claimed to have fellowship with God while denying Christ and practicing sin. From verse three, John once again takes aim at the false teachers, countering them by saying, "And by this, we know that we have come to know Him (Jesus) if we keep His commandment" (1 Jn. 2:3). John continues, "Whoever says I know Him but does not keep His commandments is a liar, and the truth is not in him" (1 Jn. 2:4). On each occasion, John writes, "Whoever says" (1 Jn. 4, 5, 6), implies a negative and positive. Twenty-two times in the letter of First John, the word "Whoever" is seen. Eight times in chapter two alone (1 Jn. 2:5, 6, 9, 10, 11, 17, 23). Chapter three gives the chiastic conclusion: "Little children, let no one deceive you. Whoever practices righteousness is righteous, as he is righteous. Whoever makes a practice of sinning is of the devil, for the devil has been sinning from the beginning. The reason the Son of God appeared was to destroy the works of the devil" (1 Jn. 3:8-9). John follows up with, "By this it is evident who are the children of God, and who are the children of the devil: whoever does not practice righteousness is not of God, nor is the one who does not love his brother" (1 Jn. 3:10). Again, John's counterargument is designed to save the deceived, who have entertained false teachers, by saying, "Only those [those alone] who obey the commandments of Christ, keep His word, and walk in the same way, are saved" (1 Jn. 2:3, 5, paraphrased). Those that do (genuinely) "Know Him" (1 Jn. 2:3).

Knowing Christ does not refer to mere knowledge of Him. The false teachers had that and were condemned. Instead, knowing Jesus/God refers to having an intimate relationship, or not, with Him (2:4, 13, 14; 3:1, 16; 4:7, 8). The Greek word John uses is 'Ginōskō', which is also translated as 'Experience'. Experiencing God again applies to having a relationship with Him, resulting in eternal life (cf. Jn. 17:3). Those claiming to have a relationship with God, yet do not have fellowship (1 Jn. 1:4) with the apostles [by holding to their teaching], do not. They are liars, and the truth is not in them (1 Jn. 1:8, 2:4). As John progresses in his letter, he makes it very clear that 'Knowing' God relates to obeying and abiding actions, not knowledge alone. Ten times John writes the word "Commandment" in his First Letter and four times more in his Second, referring to loving one another (2:7 [3×], 8, 3:23 [2×], 4:21), "Walking as Jesus walked" (1 Jn. 2:6). Those who love one another, truly know God as opposed to those who do not.

The false teachers claimed to know God, yet they did not obey His commandments (1 Jn. 2:4). Like with the previous claims of having no sin (1 Jn. 1:8, 10), the claim of knowing God is in the present tense, meaning, ongoing. However, the continued disobedience of the false teachers disqualifies them from "Knowing" God, which is why John calls them "Liars."

"The truth is not in them" (1 Jn. 2:4). The reverse is just as valid. For those keeping the commandments, the love of God is perfected" (1 Jn. 2:5a). Perfected love of God is evidence that the confessing Christian is in Christ (1 Jn. 2:5b). Again, the words "Keep" and "Obey" are present tense (current and ongoing actions), while "Perfected" is perfect tense (completed). To obtain God's perfect love, the requirement is to maintain the present, keeping and obeying. As mentioned in the previous section, Paul revealed something similar in his letter to the church of Philippi, saying that he has not yet obtained perfection. Yet, he presses on to make it his own, moving forward toward the goal of the prize in Christ Jesus (Phil. 3:12, 14). Furthermore, Paul is careful not to become disqualified (1 Cor. 9:24-27).

Three more times, John uses the word "Perfect" in his letter (1 Jn. 4:12, 17, 18), implying that the believer's love for God is completed when the commandments are obeyed. Those claiming to love God, who do not keep and obey the commandments, are deceived. Keeping the commandments is the evidence of salvation, "This is how we know" (1 Jn. 2:5). By keeping the commandments, the confessing follower of Christ abides in Him (1 Jn. 2:6). Again, abiding referring to ongoing actions. They (alone) remain "In Him" (1 Jn. 2:5).

To be "In Him," one must "Abide in Him" (2:5, 6, 27, 28, 3:6, 24, 4:13, 15, 16, 5:20), "Walking as Jesus walked" (1 Jn. 2:6, cf. Zech. 3:7). Again, Paul says something similar in his letter to the church of Philippi, "Brothers, join in imitating me, and keep your eye on those who walk according to the examples you have in us" (Phil. 3:17, cf. 1 Cor. 4:16, 1 Thess. 1:6). In sum, John is saying that those who claim to know God and keep the commandments have assurance. In contrast, despite their deception, those claiming to know God while not keeping the commandments equally have proof that they are not saved. While deceived this side of judgement day, on that day, all will be revealed (1 Cor. 4:5, 2 Cor. 5:10, Rom. 14:10, Rev. 11:18, cf. Lu. 8:17, Matt. 7:21-23).

CHAPTER 4
An Old/New Commandment

The Darkness is Passing Away

As with the previous section (1 Jn. 2:1-6), this next one (1 Jn. 2:7-14) commences with an address to the "Beloved" (friend), shifting away from the false teachers. Six more times, John will address the "Beloved" in this letter (1 Jn. 2:7, 3:2, 21, 4:1, 7, 11). Thirteen times John refers to his reader as [my] "Children," clearing up any confusion as to whom he is writing to.

Remember again, as mentioned earlier, some claim that Christians do not have to repent once in Christ; therefore, "1 John 1:9" applies to those coming to faith, not in the faith. Anyone claiming that a believer does not need to repent, based on the letter of First John, has as much difficulty with plain English as they do with the original Greek. In the previous section, it was stated that the issue of sin is present, ongoing, and active, according to both the English and the Greek languages.

Those who "Walk in the same way [Jesus] walked" (1 Jn. 2:6) are the same who "Walk in the light" (1 Jn. 1:7) and confess their sins (1 Jn. 1:9). They do so continually and are therefore frequently "Cleansed" (1 Jn. 1:7, 9). As the believer "Walks" in this world, their feet are in constant need of washing (cf. Jn. 13:1-17). The Greek word "Walk" (Gk. Peripatei) also translates as "Live." While we live in the world, we are not of it (J. 17:11, 14-15). Believers are in Christ; therefore, they are to live in the light (1 Jn. 1:7) and as Jesus lived (1 Jn. 2:6).

In the previous section, John gave the church the evidence of knowing Christ, "If we keep [keep on keeping] His commandments" (1 Jn. 2:3), and "Walk [keep on walking] in the same way in which He walked" (1 Jn. 2:6), then we truly know Him. John repeats this conditional and required commandment by saying it is both a well-known old commandment and a new one (1 Jn. 2:7, 8). In fact, it is a commandment they had heard from the beginning (1 Jn. 1:1, 7, 2:24, 3:11). Unlike the false teaching of the Gnostics, the word of God has not and will not change.

Remember from the previous section that the word, "Believes" correlates with action, debunking the false claim that one must only believe to be saved. James also refutes that idea (Jam. 2:19-20). Continuous believing and obeying (works) are the requirements: "And this is His commandment, that we believe in the name of His Son Jesus Christ and love one another, just as He has commanded us. Whoever keeps His commandments abides in God, and God in him. And by this, we know that He abides in us, by the Spirit whom He has given us" (1 Jn. 3:23-24).

John reminds his readers of the message of obedience from the beginning, narrowing in on the old/new commandment of "Love." John further states, "Whoever loves his brother abides in the light" (1 Jn. 2:10). As for the one who does not, that one "Walks [lives] in darkness" (1 Jn. 2:11), all the while falsely believing they are saved (1 Jn. 1:6). Again, those who "Keep the commandments" are those who are genuinely committed, and therefore, they are heaven bound. On the contrary, those who do not keep the commandment

"Do not know where they are going" (1 Jn. 2:11). They do not know where they are going in this life or the next. They are hell bound (cf. Jude 13).

At first glance, the old and new commandments can appear contradictory, like sinning, hence the confusion. The new commandment is old. Jesus said, "A new commandment I give to you, that you love one another: just as I have loved you, you also are to love one another. By this all people will know that you are My disciples if you have love for one another" (Jn. 13:34-35, cf. 1 Jn. 2:7, 8, 3:11, 23, 4:21, 2 Jn. 5). The "New commandment" from Jesus was an "Old commandment" for John's readers. From the beginning, they were made aware of this commandment, "The word they [the apostles] have heard" (1 Jn. 2:7); they proclaimed what they had "Seen and heard" (1 Jn. 1:3).

Again, John states that he is "Writing" to the church (1 Jn. 2:8, cf. 1:4, 2:1, 7, 12, 13) to remind them of what they already know. The purpose is to refute the Gnostics' false teaching. John's following statement, "Which [thing] is true in Him and in you" (1 Jn. 2:8b), refers to the commandment of love that is seen in Christ and must also be seen in Christ-followers (Christians). If someone is to go by His name, they must also be the same in nature. The word "True" (1 Jn. 2:8) provides a clue that John is comparing the true and the false, truthfulness against untruthfulness, those who are genuine against those who are not. Recall again that the early church was plagued with false teachers, which is why John thought he was living in the last hour (1 Jn. 2:18). The modern church is worse.

Because what is true in Jesus is also true in His followers, they are the "Beloved" (1 Jn. 2:7, 3:2, 21, 4:1, 7, 11). The beloved has heard, received, and continually obeyed the message from the beginning. They are "Walking" (continuous action) in the light of the revelation of Jesus Christ, whom the apostles heard, saw, touched, and proclaimed (1 Jn. 1:1, 3). In contrast, those who do not obey the message heard from the beginning, "Walk [live] in darkness."

Five times John writes the word "Darkness" in his first letter (1 Jn. 1:5, 6, 2:8, 9, 11). The first reference: "This is the message we have heard from him and proclaim to you, that God is light, and in him is no darkness at all" (1 Jn. 1:5), makes it clear because there is no darkness in God, those who walk in darkness are not of Him. The second reference confirms it: "If we say we have fellowship with him while we walk in darkness, we lie and do not practice the truth" (1 Jn. 1:6).

On each occasion, the word "Darkness" refers to sinful behaviour, leading to damnation (1 Jn. 2:11). The result for the one walking in darkness is opposite to what Jude says about those "Keeping themselves in the love of God, waiting for the mercy of the Lord Jesus Christ which leads to eternal life" (Jude 21). The one walking in the light has the promise of eternal life while the other has eternal damnation that is reserved for them, and they for it (Jude 4, 13). As the "Darkness is passing away" (1 Jn. 2:8) so are they.

The "Darkness that is passing away" refers to this world, which is also passing away (1 Jn. 2:17, cf. 1 Cor. 7:31). The darkness is passing away because the light is shining. God is light (1 Jn. 1:5), and those who know Him walk in that light (1 Jn. 1:7), dispelling darkness (1 Jn. 2:8). The light of God refers to Jesus Christ (Jn. 1:4–9; cf. 8:12, 9:5, 12:35–36, 46). John, in his gospel, records the words of Jesus regarding light, which he repeats in his letter: "So Jesus said to them, "The light is among you for a little while longer. Walk while you have the light, lest darkness overtakes you. The one who walks in the darkness does not know where he is going. While you have the light, believe in the light, that you may become sons of light" (Jn. 12:35-36, 1 Jn. 2:11).

Another passage of interest regarding the light is found in John's gospel, chapter nine (Jn. 9), where Jesus heals a man who was born blind (Jn. 9:1, 19). The statement of interest is found in verse four, where Jesus says, "We must work the works of Him who sent Me while it is day; night is coming, when no one can work" (Jn. 9:4). Jesus explains what He means in the following verse, saying, "As long as I am in the world, I am the light of the world" (Jn. 9:5). In response to the miracle, some of the Pharisees said, "This man is not of God, for He does not keep the Sabbath" (Jn. 9:16). The Pharisees' denial of Jesus (cf. Acts 7:51) is repeated by the Gnostic (2 Pet. 2:1, Jude 4), and is the unpardonable sin (Mk. 3:29, cf. Heb. 10:29), leading unto [eternal] death (1 Jn. 5:16). For this reason, the Gnostics were predestined for destruction (Jude 4, 12, 13). Both the Pharisees and the Gnostics claimed to have knowledge (Gnostic means knowledge), even calling Jesus a sinner (Jn. 9:24). Consequently, they were guilty of the unpardonable sin (Jn. 9:41).

*Important note: If anyone is fearful that they have committed the unpardonable sin, the evidence they are afraid of it confirms they have not. Once that sin has been committed, the Holy Spirit will no longer convict, for He only convicts His own, and Satan will no longer condemn, for he only condemns God's children. Once a person has received Christ through the revelation of the Holy Spirit, they can no longer commit the unpardonable sin. They can, however, become apostates by not remaining in the light.

Within the chapter (Jn. 9), note the exchange from darkness to light/sight. The healing of the blind man is symbolic of those in sin being delivered from the darkness to light (Jn. 9:35-39). While the religious people who claim to be in the light are in darkness, only those acknowledging Jesus and their sin can come into the light. Again, the verse of interest (Jn. 9:4) states that there is limited time to dispel darkness by proclaiming Christ (the Light). Although Jesus' time on earth was fast running out, the work would continue through His disciples (Jn. 14:12), as already seen in the gospel of Matthew (Matt. 10) and Luke (Lu. 10:1-20). While Jesus was on the earth, the light shined most bright, but still, the light continues to shine through His followers. The first notable conclusion of the day/light is when Jesus died on the cross, and the disciples fled. The absence of Christ, and His testimony, is also the absence of light in this world. For those who have rejected Christ through the proclamation of the apostles (scripture), the night has already come. They are in darkness, and in darkness, they shall remain (1 Jn. 2:11).

In John's gospel, Jesus is the light that dispels darkness for the one walking in it. Unless a believer continually walks in that light, darkness will overcome them, which is why John encouraged his reader to "Abide" in the light (1 Jn. 2:10). In other words, in the same way, someone comes out of darkness (the world) into the light (the kingdom of God through the revelation of Christ), they can go back into the darkness by failing to abide. Only by continually walking in the light, the light remains to shine in and through the believer (1 Jn. 2:8b). Here, the church of Ephesus should be considered who had lost their first love, and therefore, they were in danger of having their candlestick (lamp/light) removed (Rev. 2:1-7).

Because the true light is shining, the darkness is passing away (1 Jn. 2:8), like sin, using the present tense, John states that light and darkness are present and ongoing until Christ returns. Darkness passing away refers to it coming to an end when Jesus returns. John's letter points to the eschatological judgement of the world (1 Jn. 2:8, 17), which should not be surprising considering that the same John wrote the book of Revelation.

When Jesus returns, the old is done away with and replaced with the new. Even now, there is truth to that statement. Paul writes, "From now on, therefore, we regard no one according to the flesh. Even though we once regarded Christ according to the flesh, we regard Him thus no longer. Therefore, if anyone is in Christ, he is a new creation. The old has passed away; behold, the new has come. All this is from God, who through Christ reconciled us to Himself and gave us the ministry of reconciliation; that is, in Christ, God was reconciling the world to Himself, not counting their trespasses against them, and entrusting to us the message of reconciliation. Therefore, we are ambassadors for Christ, God making His appeal through us. We implore you on behalf of Christ, to be reconciled to God. For our sake He made him to be sin who knew no sin, so that in Him we might become the righteousness of God" (2 Cor. 5:16-21).

While the believer is a new creation in Christ, they are still required to abide if they want to remain in Him. Again, not losing sight of why John wrote the letter, remember, he is refuting the false teachers and their claim to be in the light while hating fellow believers, which is why he says, "Whoever says he is in the light and hates his brother is still in darkness" (1 Jn. 2:9). Three times within chapter two (1 Jn. 2), John addresses the "Whoever's" confessing to being in Christ:

- "Whoever says, "I know Him" but does not keep his commandments is a liar, and the truth is not in him" (1 Jn. 2:4)
- "Whoever says he abides in Him ought to walk in the same way in which He walked" (1 Jn. 2:6)
- "Whoever says he is in the light and hates his brother is still in darkness" (1 Jn. 2:9)

While many claim to be in fellowship with God, the evidence suggests that they are not. In fact, according to Jesus, most claiming to be Christian are not (Matt. 7:21-23). Few of the many attempting to enter heaven do: "He went on his way through towns and villages, teaching, and journeying toward Jerusalem. And someone said to him, "Lord, will those who are saved be few?" And he said to them, 'Strive to enter through the narrow door. For many, I tell you, will seek to enter and will not be able. When once the master of the house has risen and shut the door, and you begin to stand outside and to knock at the door, saying, 'Lord, open to us,' then he will answer you, 'I do not know where you come from.' Then you will begin to say, 'We ate and drank in your presence, and you taught in our streets.' But he will say, 'I tell you; I do not know where you come from. Depart from me, all you workers of evil!' In that place there will be weeping and gnashing of teeth when you see

Abraham and Isaac and Jacob and all the prophets in the kingdom of God but you yourselves cast out" (Lu. 13:22-28).

Like many today, the Gnostics claimed to know God (1 Jn. 2:4), to live in Him (1 Jn. 2:6) and walk in the light (1 Jn. 2:9). However, they were in (continuous) darkness (1 Jn. 1:6, 2:11). The Gnostics were in continuous darkness due to their constant rejection of scriptural authority, and for their continual hatred for their Christian brothers, namely the apostles. The Gnostic rejected the apostles' authority, evidenced by their rejection of scriptural authority. For this reason, John states they do not know God, whom they say they have fellowship with, because they do not have fellowship with the apostles (1 Jn. 1:3). Those walking in the light love their brother, namely the apostles, and their teaching. As the light is already shining, love is growing, and sin is dispersing. Because the light is shining and love is growing, sin is dissipating, and therefore, "There is no cause for stumbling" (1 Jn. 2:10).

When walking in the light, nothing can cause that person to stumble, contrary to those walking in darkness, who do not know where they are going (1 Jn. 2:11). Therefore, everything causes them to stumble. When living in Christ (1 Jn. 2:5) and Christ in us (Gal. 2:20), then there is nothing within causing that one to sin. However, as mentioned previously, no one walks in perfect love; therefore, everyone still stumbles in many ways (cf. Jam. 3:2) and needs continual cleansing (1 Jn. 1:7, 9, 2:1).

The Greek word "Stumble" is "Skandalon," also meaning "Stain" (cf. Jude 23) and is where the English word "Scandal" comes from. The specific scandal in the context of John's letter refers to the denial of Jesus Christ's deity and return (1 Jn. 2:22, 4:3, 2 Jn. 2:7) and the denial of sin (1 Jn. 1:8, 10). The first scandal fits with the same Greek word used elsewhere, saying the same (Rom. 9:33, 1 Cor. 1:23, Gal. 5:11, 1 Pet. 2:8). Apart from denying Christ and scriptural authority, offense is another way causing believers to stumble, as Jesus warned His disciples, "Temptations to sin are sure to come, but woe to the one through whom they come!" (Lu. 17:1, cf. Matt. 13:41, Rom. 16:17). Using the same Greek word, "Skandalon," Jesus warned that Satan would bait His followers through others offending and trapping them in sin. For this reason, John says seven times, "Love your brother" (1 Jn. 2:10, 3:10, 14, 16, 17, 4:20, 21), which also means, forgive him.

Walking in the light and love of God is linked with walking in forgiveness, particularly towards those who have offended. This does not mean that Christians are to overlook the sins of the false teachers. John, for example, would not enter a bathhouse if Cerinthus was inside, and he certainly would not have greeted him in the street (2 Jn. 7, 9-10). Likewise, John's disciple, Polycarp, called Marcion Satan's firstborn. Marcion rejected the Old Testament. He also edited Luke's letters and some of Paul's.

Anyone failing to abide in the things as mentioned above, especially scriptural authority, by teaching the whole, unchanged counsel of God (Act. 20:27), will be plunged back into the world, where they will continually "Walk in darkness" (1 Jn. 2:11, cf. 2:9). The context regarding Paul's statement, "The whole counsel of God" refers to warning about the wolves (false teachers) coming into the church, twisting scripture to gain disciples (Act 20:26-31). Notice that Paul calls the false teachers "Wolves." Jesus did also (Matt. 7:15). Jesus and John also call the false teachers snakes (Matt. 3:7, 23:33). Some might say that is not very loving. Paul loved the church by warning them. Like Ezekiel, because he warned the church, Paul's hands were clean (Acts 20:16, Ezek. 3:17-19, 33:1-9), unlike many today who never mention sin. For Paul, the offense came because he preached the truth. Jesus experienced the same, and at one point, seventy-two disciples who went out doing miracles in His name (Lu. 10:1-12), left Him (Jn. 6:51-66). Note that these are the same disciples whom Jesus said, "Rejoice that your names are written in heaven" (Lu. 10:20). Clearly, they once were, but due to their apostasy, their names were later removed. The same warning was given to the worldly church of Sardis (Rev. 3:5b) unless they wake up and repent [come out of the darkness] (Rev. 3:3).

Most of Jesus' disciples left Him due to offense, and the disciples experienced the same, in the same way we should expect today. An example of this for the apostles is that after the Jerusalem Council (Acts 15), some of their disciples fell away due to offense, resulting from them not accepting the resolution of the Council. Tertullian names Ebion as one who fell away, taking others with him, forming a cult after his name (Ebionites). The Ebionites fled Jerusalem after the temple's destruction, spreading across Israel and the surrounding regions. After falling away, they still considered themselves Christians, albeit the Ebionites denied the divinity of Christ, twisting scripture to suit themselves. Eusebius warned about the Ebionites, saying that evil demons spawned their doctrines and that those who believe and follow them are not Christians. Ignatius warned not to speak to anyone teaching heresies, such as the Ebionites taught. The same would be true of cults, today, such as the Mormons, and Jehovah's Witnesses.

In sum, the rejection of Christ, and scriptural authority, stems from an offense that leads to blinding hatred, trapping those who have stumbled. Therefore, they no longer know where they are going. Evidently, the darkness can blind the once-saved believer to the point that they reject Jesus Christ. This is ultimately Satan's aim (2 Cor. 4:4), and it is the number one sign of the end times (2 Thess. 2), which, again, is why John said he was living in the last hour (1 Jn. 2:18). Time was running out. Hence the warning, "The light is among you for a little while longer. Walk while you have the light, lest darkness overtakes you. The one who walks in the darkness does not know where he is going" (Jn. 12:35, 1 Jn. 2:11). The warning is that the darkness can still overtake the one walking in the light. Therefore, "Abide!"

CHAPTER 5
Overcome

Do Not Love the World

Again, clearing up any confusion as to whom John is writing to, he repeats the statement, "I am writing to you" (1 Jn. 2:1, 7, 12), resaying it in verse thirteen, three times more (1 Jn. 2:13 [x3]), and verse fourteen twice more (1 Jn. 2:14 [x2]). Anyone claiming that John is not writing to Christians, stating that they do not need to repent (1 John 1:9"), could not have read the letter as John could not have clarified it any better.

The only other group that John addresses are the Gnostics, whom he condemns, calling them antichrists (2 Jn. 2:18-19) and false prophets (1 Jn. 4:1). As for the "Beloved" and "Little children," who acknowledge their sin, John says, "Your sins are forgiven" (1 Jn. 2:12a). Their sins are forgiven because they have confessed them: "If we confess our sins, He is faithful and just to forgive us our sins and cleanse us from all unrighteousness" (1 Jn. 1:9). Notice the conditional "If" - therefore the reverse must also be true: "If we do not confess our sins…"

Those who have and continue to confess their sins hold fast to the message from the beginning. Seven times John writes "From the beginning" (1 Jn. 1:1, 2:7, 13, 14, 24, 3:8, 11). Those holding to the original unchanging message confess their sins (plural), which have been and are being cleansed. Those, alone, have overcome the evil one (1 Jn. 2:13, 14). John writes to that overcoming group (1 Jn. 2:13-14).

Contrary to those confessing their sins, some of the Gnostics taught sinless perfection. For example, Tatian, who was once an Orthodox Christian, fell away and wrote his own gospel called the Diatessaron. After he apostatised, he founded the Gnostic cult called the Encratites, meaning "Self-perfected ones." The doctrine of the Encratites is like those today who claim Christians can be perfect by becoming sinless. Not according to John, and the early church fathers, while on this side of heaven. While on earth, followers of Christ will wrestle against the sinful nature. The evidence of salvation is seen in those striving to please God by walking in the light and love of God, which includes resisting sin and repenting of it when slipping. As mentioned in the second unit of this work, on John's first letter, Clement of Alexandria (192-202 A.D.) said, "It is not possible to be completely sinless. Christian perfection is the attitude of striving to be more like Christ."

Irenaeus agrees with John, calling the Encratitae hypocrites; likewise, Hippolytus said they were very prideful. They were prideful for believing they could obtain sinless perfection and hypocrites due to being sinful while claiming to be "Self-perfected." Self-perfection through abstinences (while absent of the cross) was the plan. Paul calls it a doctrine of demons (1 Tim. 4:1-4).

While the Encratites could not be accused of "Loving the world" (1 Jn. 2:15) due to their strict lifestyles, reframing from wine, meat, sex (none of which are biblical), believing that sinlessness was the result of self-control, their sins were not forgiven; therefore, they had not overcome (prevailed against, conquered) the evil one (1 Jn. 2:13, 14). Within this section of the letter (1 Jn. 2:12-17), John narrows in on two things, 1). Sins being forgiven, and 2). Not loving the world. The reference to the world is also associated with sin. Eighteen times, John writes the word "World" six times just in this passage

(1 Jn. 15 [x3], 16, 17 [x2]), using the Greek word "Kosmos," also translating as "Order."

In the following chapter, John states that the "World" does not know the believers, or Jesus (1 Jn. 3:1), because "The whole world lies in the power of the evil one" (1 Jn. 5:19), which is why it hates Christ, and His followers (1 Jn. 3:13). Those from the world, are listened to, and followed by those in the world (1 Jn. 4:5). Some, who were once in the church, have failed to remain to overcome, having since departed, and gone back into the world (1 Jn. 4:1). The surest way to go back into the world is denying the deity of Jesus Christ (1 Jn. 5:5), which is what Tatian did, and so many others. The next sure way to depart is to love the world, and sin, especially sexual sin, and idolatry.

Four of the seven churches addressed in the book of Revelation (chapters 2-3) were warned about this, where Jesus said, "Unless you repent, judgement will come" (paraphrased). Jesus further said, "The one (only that one) who overcomes/conquers [this world and the evil one] and remains to, will inherit the promised reward" (paraphrased). Only those (those alone). John agrees, saying, "Whoever does the will of God abide forever" (1 Jn. 2:17).

In John's affirmation (1 Jn. 2:12-14), twice he calls the believers "Children" (1 Jn. 2:12, 13), fathers (1 Jn. 2:13 [x2]), and young men (1 Jn. 2:13-14). John is not differentiating various maturity levels within the groups, as some suggest, although there are varying levels. As mentioned earlier, John refers to all his readers as "Children" thirteen times. Again, the term is one of affection, like "Beloved." The beloved are the believers who are in fellowship with John, and Jesus, because their sins are forgiven (1 Jn. 1:7, 9, 2:12). Their sins are forgiven because they have acknowledged and confessed them "On account of His name" (1 Jn. 2:12), unlike the Gnostics who say they have no sin or do not sin. However, the root cause of the Gnostics' being without forgiveness is their denial of Christ, for sins are only forgiven "On account of His name" (1 Jn. 2:12).

Without Christ and the shedding of His blood, there is no forgiveness of sin (Heb. 9:22). Congruent with the writer of the book of Hebrews, John says, "He is the propitiation for our sins, and not for ours only but also for the sins of the whole world" (1 Jn. 2:2). And "In this is love, not that we have loved God but that he loved us and sent his Son to be the propitiation for our sins" (1 Jn. 4:10).

Following the address to the "Children," which is all-inclusive, John addresses the "Fathers" (1 Jn. 2:13a). The address is not a reference to their superiority but age. Paul calls the older men "Fathers" when writing to Timothy (1 Tim. 5:1). Despite Timothy's youth (1 Tim. 4:12), he was the pastor and "Overseer of the church" (1 Tim. 3:1). Timothy was the "Ruler" of the church (1 Tim. 5:17) and therefore had greater responsibility, starting with teaching, and guarding sound biblical doctrine (2 Tim. 4:1-2a). Timothy was also instructed to rebuke those introducing false doctrine (2 Tim. 4:2b), which included older men. Because of the spread of false teaching, Paul said, "The time is coming when people will not endure sound teaching but having itching ears they accumulate for themselves teachers to suit their own passions" (2 Tim. 2:3).

*Pay careful attention to the following verse, "And they turn away from listening to the truth and wander off into myths" (2 Tim. 4:4). Clearly, Paul, like John, Peter, and Jude, was concerned about the false teachers stealing converts (cf. Acts 20:29-31). The ones turning away and wandering off once listened to the truth, debunking the idea of "Once saved, always saved."

Again, the reference to the "Fathers" is one of age, not necessarily spiritual maturity. Because the fathers were older and had been around longer, they had "Known" [Jesus] who is from the beginning (1 Jn. 2:1, cf. 1 Jn. 1:1, 23, 4:2). The reference, "From the beginning" points to the ministry of Jesus, specifically, His incarnation and resurrection, as mentioned in an earlier section. Remember, the "Word of Life" is God incarnate in Jesus Christ (1 Jn. 1:1-2).

Following the address to the older men (fathers), John includes the younger men (1 Jn. 2:13b), which refers to age. While the younger men may not have heard the message from the beginning, like the fathers, they still had "Overcome the evil one" (2 Jn. 2:13b, 14). They had done so because they were "Strong, and the word of God abides in [them]" (1Jn. 2:14c). Five times John uses the word "Evil" (1 Jn. 2:13, 14, 3:12, 5:18, 19), constantly referring to the devil (3:12 [cf. 3:8, 10], 5:18, 19). The younger men have "Overcome" the devil by remaining strong in the word of God. The word of God is the same as the word of life (1 Jn. 1:1b), referring to Jesus, whom the false teachers have rejected. The young men have "Kept His word" (1 Jn. 2:5); therefore, they have overcome the evil one who comes to steal and then destroy (Jn. 10:10, cf. Matt. 13:1-30). The church of Philadelphia was commended for doing the same and was only told to remain (Rev. 3:10-11). Providing they continued to overcome, God would make them pillars in the millennial temple (Rev. 3:12). Five times John writes the word "Overcome" (1 Jn. 2:13, 14, 4:4, 5:4, 5:5), twice referring to the devil (1 Jn. 2:13, 14), once of the antichrist spirit (1 Jn. 4:4), and twice more referring to the world (1 Jn. 5:4, 5). The overcoming references apply to the same thing, which is why John says, "Do not love the world" (1 Jn. 2:15).

Like the previous statements, John carefully puts together a counterargument against the false teachers, who say they have fellowship with God (1 Jn. 1:6) and are without sin (1 Jn. 1:8, 10). John now distinguishes between those who have overcome and those who have not. John does so by comparing the false teachers who have abandoned "That which was proclaimed from the beginning" (1 Jn. 1:1, 13) to those who have remained strong in the word of God. Because they have remained strong, God abides in them. Despite the false teachers' attempts to deceive followers of Christ (1 Jn. 2:26), they have remained strong by resisting them. But still, the warning remains: "Let what you heard from the beginning abide in you. If what you heard from the beginning abides in you, then you will also abide in the Son and the Father. And this is the promise that he made to us—eternal life" (1 Jn. 2:24).

Again, debunking Calvinism, if a person could not lose their salvation, there would be no point in trying to draw them away, for they would be eternally secure. On the other hand, if the person drawn away was never saved or called to be saved, why would Satan bother to deceive them when they already belong to him, whether in the church or not? On the contrary, those open to deception, due to not being strong, and abiding in the word, are in danger of losing what they have (2 Jn. 8). The Greek John uses regarding overcoming those who tried to deceive (1 Jn. 2:13-14) is in the aorist tense, meaning past; yet, the deceivers continue in their attempts (1 Jn. 2:26), which is present tense (ongoing and continuous). John affirms the church by saying the false teachers wanted to deceive them in the past but failed. Twice John says they have overcome the evil one (1 Jn. 2:13, 14), who operates through false teachers.

John concludes his affirmation by coming back to the "Fathers" (1 Jn. 2:14), repeating himself, "I write to you fathers because you know Him from the beginning" (1 Jn. 2:13a, 14a). Contrary to the false teachers, the church fathers have remained, holding fast to what was taught from the beginning. John addresses the young men, commending them for remaining strong in the word proclaimed from the start. False teachers have not deceived them into going back into the world by following something different. Remember, if anything changes, everything changes!

In sum, John addresses his children in the faith, regardless of age. He commends them for holding fast to Christ and sound doctrine, and therefore overcoming Satan, who is the god of this world (2 Cor. 4:4), and ruler over it

(Jn. 12:31), from the air (Eph. 2:2). Indeed, John says that "The whole world lies in the power of Satan" (1 Jn. 5:9).

Following the affirmation, John shifts from the aorist tense (past) to the present (ongoing), saying to those who have had their sins forgiven (1 Jn. 2:12), "Do not love the world" (1 Jn. 2:15). The second part of the address is a strong appeal (Do Not Go Back!). The false teacher did go back (1 Jn. 2:19, 4:1) and wanted others to follow them. The comparison from the previous section (1 Jn. 2:12-14) to the next (1 Jn. 2:15-17) is the love for God versus the love for the world.

The first part of John's reason for writing to the "Fathers," "Young men," and "Children" is to address the benefits, "Your sins are forgiven, You have overcome the evil one, You are strong The word of God abides in you," However, the second part states the opposite: "If anyone loves the world, the love of the Father is not in him" (1 Jn. 2:15). Therefore, their sins are not forgiven; they have not overcome the evil one, they are not strong, and because God does not abide in them, they will not live forever (1 Jn. 2:17).

The exhalation commenced with, "Do not love the world, or the things of the world," shifting from the aorist tense (past) to the present tense (ongoing action). While the "Little children" (1 Jn. 2:12) have overcome the evil one, the evil one can still overcome them, luring them through the things and the love of this world. The love of this world (1 Jn. 2:15), albeit still the Greek word "Agape," does not carry the same meaning as "loving one another" but rather refers to "Desiring" (1 Jn. 2:17).

The Greek word for "Desire" is "Epithymia" which also translates to "Craving" and "Lust". Regarding "Lust", Paul writes the following, "Finally, then, brothers, we ask and urge you in the Lord Jesus, that as you received from us how you ought to walk and to please God, just as you are doing, that you do so more and more. For you know what instructions we gave you through the Lord Jesus. For this is the will of God, your sanctification: that you abstain from sexual immorality; that each one of you know how to control his own body in holiness and honor, not in the passion of lust like the Gentiles who do not know God; that no one transgress and wrongs his brother in this matter, because the Lord is an avenger in all these things, as we told you beforehand and solemnly warned you. For God has not called us for impurity, but in holiness. Therefore, whoever disregards this, disregards not man but God, who gives his Holy Spirit to you" (1 Thess. 4:1-8).

While Paul warns his readers not to desire/lust after the things of this world, James rebukes those who are on friendly terms with it: "You adulterous people! Do you not know that friendship with the world is enmity with God? Therefore, whoever wishes to be a friend of the world makes himself an enemy of God" (Jam. 4:4). Like John, James warns that the things of this world can cause the person, once secure, to fall away. There is a big difference between loving the things of the world and having love for those perishing in the world (cf. Jn. 3:16, 1 Jn. 4:9).

Both John and James state that the love of this world will replace the love of God. Such was the case for Demas, for Paul said, "Demas, in love with this present world, has deserted me and gone to Thessalonica" (2 Tim. 4:10). Remember, Demas had been one of Paul's fellow workers in the ministry of the gospel. Demas left Paul in a time of need in exchange for what Satan was offering. According to the Ante-Nicene Fathers, Demas was fully overcome by the evil one due to the love of the things of this world and became a priest of idols; therefore, "The love of the Father was [no longer] in him" (1 Jn. 2:15). Like with John's opening statement, "If you want to have fellowship with us, you cannot have fellowship with them" (1 Jn. 1:1-6, paraphrased). Similarly, John says, if you love God, you will hate the world, and visa-versa. You cannot have it both ways. In business terms, this is called 'Opportunity cost', meaning that one opportunity will cost you the other. You cannot have both.

One opportunity will cost you the other because the two opportunities are different from one another. John explains, "For all that is in the world, the desires of the flesh, and the desires of the eyes, and pride and possessions" (1 Jn. 2:16a cf. Prov. 21:10,) further stating that those things "Are not from the Father" (1 Jn. 2:16b). Anyone desiring those things, do not have God (1 Jn. 2:15, 17). As mentioned above, the word 'Desire' refers to lust; therefore, the lust of the flesh and eyes refers to a sinful craving, including covetousness. Covetousness is addressed in the words "Pride in possessions," referring to materialism. John makes it clear in the following chapter that the love of materialism is the problem: "But if anyone has the world's goods and sees his brother in need, yet closes his heart against him, how does God's love abide in him?" (1 Jn. 3:17).

The "Desire of the eye and flesh" goes back to Eve in the garden, who "Saw that the tree was good for food, and that it was a delight to the eyes, and that the tree was to be desired to make one wise, she took of its fruit and ate, and she also gave some to her husband who was with her, and he ate" (Gen. 3:6). Eve's desire led to sin, resulting in the Fall. Without God's plan of redemption, humanity would have been lost. Eve who was once secure, lost what she had. Satan tempted Eve with the promise that she "Can be like God" (Gen. 3:5), which is also seen today in select charismatic churches through their false 'little gods' doctrine.

Eve's choice to disobey God came at a high cost, not just for her, but also for her family and humanity. Of course, God still provided a way out for Eve, and everyone else, before time began (1 Cor. 2:7, 2 Tim. 1:9, Tit. 1:2). Following Eve, Cain went further into sin. God warned Cain that sin was crouching at the door and that "Its desire is for him, but [he] must rule over it (Gen. 4:7). Instead of obeying God, Cain rose up against his brother Able and killed him (Gen. 4:8). As a result, God sent Cain out of His presence" (Gen. 4:16). John says, "We should not be like Cain, who was of the evil one and murdered his brother. And why did he murder him? Because his own deeds were evil and his brother's righteous" (1 Jn. 3:12). Jude agrees with John, saying, "Woe to them (the false teachers who have departed)! For they walked in the way of Cain and abandoned themselves for the sake of gain to Balaam's error and perished in Korah's rebellion" (Jude 11).

As a result of Eve's choice, the world came under a curse (Gen. 3:17, Isa. 24:6, Rom. 8:22) and is subsequently "Passing away" (1 Jn. 2:17) along with those loving it. The world is under a curse because of sin. However, there is coming a day when Jesus will reverse that curse, but not before He deals with the guilty: "On that day the Lord will punish the host of heaven, in heaven, and the kings of the earth, on the earth. They will be gathered together as prisoners in a pit; they will be shut up in a prison, and after many days they will be punished. Then the moon will be confounded and the sun ashamed, for the Lord of hosts reigns on Mount Zion and in Jerusalem, and his glory will be before his elders" (Isa. 24:21-23).

The reference to the "World passing away" (1 Jn. 2:17) is connected to John's earlier statement regarding, "The darkness is passing away" (1 Jn. 2:8). The world represents sin, as does darkness. Anyone desiring the things of the world will likewise pass away, "But the one who does the will of the Father abides forever" (1 Jn. 2:17). Doing the will of the Father is the opposite of the will of the world or Satan. Specifically, the "Desires of the flesh, eyes, and the pride of possessions." Jesus warned of the latter with the parable of the rich fool (Lu. 12:13-21).

Eschatologically, Jesus warned that those "Weighed down with dissipation and drunkenness and cares of this life," then "That day [will] come upon [them] suddenly like a trap," therefore, "Stay awake." Those remaining awake "Escape all the things that are going to take place" (Lu. 21:34-36). Jesus provides a similar warning to the church of Sardis (Rev. 3:1-7). The "Escape" refers to the rapture, as promised to the church of Philadelphia (Rev. 3:10-11), and the "All these things that are going to take place" refers to the tribulation. After seven years of tribulation, the order of this world will pass away. After the millennium, the world itself will pass away (2 Pet. 3). On that day, only those who have had their sins forgiven, who have overcome by remaining in Christ by rejecting the world, and the things of the world, they alone, will abide forever.

CHAPTER 6
Antichrist Warning

It is the Last Hour

Until now, John has been warning about the false teachers who deny Christ and say that they do not sin; while they say they are in fellowship with God. John makes it clear; they are not, and neither is anyone who follows them. For this reason, John says, "If you want to have fellowship with us, you cannot have fellowship with them" (1 Jn. 1:3, cf. 2 Jn. 10, paraphrased).

The false teachers draw disciples away from the faith, and over to themselves, by "Creeping in unnoticed" (Jude 4) and by twisting scripture (Acts 20:30). Jude calls them "Blemishes" or "Hidden reefs" (Jude 12). Paul calls them "Wolves" (Acts 20:29). Jesus prewarned about the same, saying, "Beware of false prophets, who come to you in sheep's clothing, but inwardly are ravenous wolves" (Matt. 7:15). Paul further warns that the wolves are conditioning, and preparing the deceived for the coming antichrist, whom God will send to test those remaining on the earth, following the rapture (2 Thess. 2). The antichrist is the subject in the following section of John's letter (1 Jn. 2:18-19).

Four times, John mentions the antichrist in his first letter (1 Jn. 2:18 [x2], 22, 4:3) and once more in his second (2 Jn. 7), connecting the false teachers, the deceivers, with the coming antichrist. Both have the same spirit (1 Jn. 4:3, 2 Jn. 7). Remember in the previous section where John encourages the beloved for overcoming the evil one (1 Jn. 2:13, 14), who is Satan. The antichrist is Satan's son of perdition (2 Thess. 2:3). The only other reference to a "Son of perdition" refers to Judas (Jn. 17:12). Again, the antichrist is Satan's son, and those with an antichrist spirit, like Judas, are also Satan's children (Jn. 6:70, 8:44, 1 Jn. 3:10).

Consider that Satan entered Judas while he was with Jesus (Jn. 13:27). The Spirit of God also enters the believer (Rom. 11:8-9, 1 Cor. 3:16, 2 Tim. 1:14, cf. 1 Jn. 2:27) following confession, repentance, and baptism (Acts 2:28). In sum, both God and Satan desire children, and actively seek to acquire them through those already belonging to either one. Both actively seek to draw disciples away from the other. Only those holding onto what they heard from the beginning remain in God (1 Jn. 1:1, 2:7, 24, 3:11) - these alone continue to overcome the evil one (1 Jn. 2:13-14). For this reason, John warns about the danger of deception, that there are those actively seeking to draw away (1 Jn. 2:26), whom John calls "Antichrists" (1 Jn. 18-19).

John warns against the antichrist, accompanied by the solution to overcome, and remains in an overcoming condition. First, the believer must remember what they heard from the beginning, which equips them to recognise the deceivers. The deceivers will offer something different from the original message. Remember again, the word "Gnostic" means "Knowledge," referring to "Extra-biblical knowledge." The Gnostics gained extra-biblical knowledge through false dreams, visions, and words (2 Pet. 2:3, Jude 8, cf. Jer. 27:9). The extra-biblical doctrines go ahead of the teachings of Christ and thereby are condemned (2 Jn. 9).

John's reference in verse twenty-seven (1 Jn. 2:27) counters the teaching of the Gnostics, suggesting that the beloved do not need them to teach them anything outside of what they have already heard from the beginning. Today, some charismatics misinterpret John's statement, "But the anointing that you received from Him abides in you, and you have no need that anyone should teach you. However, as His anointing teaches you about everything, and is true, and is no lie—just as it has taught you, abide in Him" (1 Jn. 2:27), suggesting that it applies to not needing anyone to teach them. Those claiming that the church does not need teachers do so by stating that the Holy Spirit is your only teacher. The same group teaching that is most in need of sound biblical teachers. They ignore sound biblical doctrine, misusing John's statement (1 Jn. 2:27) to defend themselves, saying, "I do not need anyone to teach me because I have the Holy Spirit as my teacher."

The statement (1 Jn. 2:27) refers to the teachings of the Gnostics, whom John is warning against, thereby pointing his reader back to what they "Heard from the beginning" - anything new should be treated as suspect. The "New Apostolic Reformation (N.A.R.) is an obvious concern; the clue is with the word "New." The "Emergent Church" and "Progressive Christianity" are also dead giveaways.

The Emergent Church, like progressive Christianity, focuses on ecumenicalism and cultural sensitivity, otherwise known as being seeker sensitive. Members of those movements hold to relativism, which maintains that there is no absolute truth, even extending to biblical doctrine. To achieve ecumenicalism, one must compromise. Ecumenical churches compromise on doctrine, like the church of Pergamum did (Rev. 2:12-17). Jesus warned the church of Pergamum that unless they repent, "[He] will come soon and war against them with the sword of [His] mouth" (Rev. 216). The specific false teaching of the church of Pergamum came from the Nicolaitan Gnostics (Rev. 2:15-16). The Nicolaitans practiced sexual sin, including homosexuality, and idolatry, tolerating ungodly things. Both Victorinus (285 A.D.A.D.) and Eusebius (325 A.D.) rebuked them, and Jesus said that He hated their works (Rev. 2:6).

There are many similarities between the early church-age Gnostics and modern movements. It does not take much digging to identify inconsistencies with the original biblical teaching in modern 'theology' and similarities with the doctrines of problematic Gnostics. For example, the late 'prophet' Bob Jones and disgraced 'evangelist' Todd Bentley were on Patricia King's television programme, promoting astral travel, claiming to have brought back the "Vanilla" (anointing) from the third heaven. Astral projection is forbidden by God (Ezek. 13:17-23). The idea of astral projection is nothing new, as Origen (230 A.D.) addressed it, saying, "[Astral projection] is but a trick of demons" (Against Celsus 3:31). Solomon said, "There is nothing new under the sun" (Eccl. 1:9), including astral projection.

Solomon indirectly references astral projection, saying, "Before the silver cord is snapped… the spirit returns to God" (Eccl. 12:6-7). Within the New Age (Gnostic) Movement, the silver cord is said to connect the spirit to the body; once broken, the spirit can no longer return. New Agers teach not to go too far or stay out of the body too long when astral traveling, lest the cord breaks and you cannot return.

As the Gnostics did, members of the N.A.R. also have a solid track record for producing false prophecies. Recent examples include, but are not limited to, COVID-19 being destroyed, a particular hurricane (one of many) dissipating before reaching land, Trump winning the election, and a host of other failed predictions, in the name of God. While Patricia King downplayed the failed prophecies, saying, "We are new at this," the penalty for prophesying falsely in the Old Testament was death (Deut. 18:20-22). In the New Testament, false prophets are to be rebuked, rejected, removed, and avoided because they are deceived, deceptive, and dangerous.

As mentioned, several times before, John is writing to the church (1 Jn. 2:1, 12, 18) who are in danger of being deceived (1 Jn. 2:26). The warning commences with John saying, "Children, it is the last hour" (1 Jn. 18, 19). The reference to the last hour is given due to the increase of false teaching plaguing the church, deceiving many and drawing them away from the original message. Those drawn away are in danger of hellfire (Jude 23).

While the term "Last hour" is unique to John's letter, other similar phrases are found in scripture, referring to the last days, confirming they will be difficult times (1 Tim. 4:1, 2 Tim 3:1, 4:3, 2 Pet 3:3, Jude 18). Paul expounds on the most significant end times sign in the last days in his second letter to the church of Thessalonica, which is apostasy (2 Thess. 2:3-4), confirmed by Jesus (Matt. 24). The word "Rebellion" (2 Thess. 2:3), comes from the Greek word "Apostasia," translating "Apostasy." The book of Hebrews contains the strongest warning about apostasy (Heb. 5:11-6:12). Regarding Paul's reference, Bible translations vary in their treatment of the word, translating it as "Rebellion" (N.I.V., N.L.T., ESV, ISV, G.N.T., M.S.B., N.S.R.V.), "Apostasy" (B.L.B., N.A.S.V., L.S.B., AB, C.S.B., H.S.C.B., N.A.B., WNT), "Falling away" (K.J.V., A.S.V., ERV, WBS, Y.L.T.), "Revolt" (A.B.P.E., D.R.B., G.W.T.), and "Departure" (L.S.V., G.B.G.B., C.B.C.B., T.B.T.B.).

The varying translations treat the Greek similarly, congruently stating that Paul is warning that in the last days, many churches and denominations will revolt by departing from sound biblical doctrine. Indeed, "[Most] people (confessing to being Christian in the last days), will not endure sound doctrine, but [instead will] have itching ears, they will accumulate for themselves (Gnostic) teachers to suit their passions" (2 Tim. 4:3).

John's warning about the last hour falls into the same category as Paul's, Peter's, and Jude's. It points towards and highlights the increase of false teachers (1 Jn. 2:18-19), who are sneaking in (2 Pet. 2:1, Jude 4), actively seeking to deceive (2 Jn. 2:26). The increase of false teachers suggests that the antichrist is close, whom they "Have heard is coming" (2 Jn. 2:18). The "Many antichrists" (false teachers) is the evidence that the one to come, is nearby. Again, five times John writes the word "Antichrist" (1 Jn 2:18 [x2], 22,

4:3, 2 Jn 7), which is not seen anywhere else in scripture, albeit Jesus said [in the end times] "False christs" would appear in His name (Matt. 24:24, Mk. 13:22). False christs are antichrists.

The original message that John's readers "Heard from the beginning" (1 Jn. 1:1, 5, 7) included a warning about the antichrist, whom they "Have heard was coming" (2 Jn. 8). Alongside John, Paul also warns about the coming antichrist, who is the "Strong delusion" (2 Thess. 2:11). John provides more information about him in the book of Revelation (Rev. 13, 17, and 19). Daniel provides a great deal of material about the coming antichrist (Dan. 7), comparing him to Antiochus (Dan. 8 and 11). Daniel, chapter nine is also significant regarding the time of the antichrist (Dan. 9:24-27). Chapter twelve also references the time appointed (Dan. 12:9, 11), as does the book of Revelation (Rev. 11:2-3, 12:6, 14, 13:5).

Discrediting false teaching, suggesting that the antichrist is a system - in the same way, those with the spirit of the antichrist (antichrists and false prophets) were men, the coming antichrist will also be a literal man. The antichrist is the false messiah, counterfeiting the Messiah; God incarnate in the man Jesus. To say that the antichrist is a system is like saying Jesus was a system.

Scripture has much to say about the coming antichrist, providing at least twenty-eight deeds and characteristics:

- He comes from among ten kings in the revived Roman Empire; his authority will have similarities to the ancient Babylonians, Persians, and Greeks (Dan. 7:24, Rev 13:2 / Dan. 7:7)
- He will subdue three kings (Dan. 7:8, 24)
- He is different from the other kings (Dan. 7:24)
- At first, he will appear to be insignificant, a "little horn" (Dan. 7:8)
- He will speak boastfully (Dan. 7:8; Rev 13:5)

- He will blaspheme God (Dan. 7:25; 11:36; Rev 13:5), slandering His Name, dwelling place, and departed Christians and Old Testament saints (Rev 13:6)
- He will persecute the saints (Dan. 7:25; Rev 13:7)
- He will change the calendar, perhaps to define a new era related to himself (Dan. 7:25)
- He will change the laws to suit himself (Dan. 7:25)
- No other earthly ruler will succeed him, but Jesus Christ alone (Dan. 7:26-27)
- He will confirm a covenant with "many," i.e., the Jewish people (Dan. 9:27). This covenant will likely involve the establishment of a Jewish Temple in Jerusalem (see Dan. 9:27; Matt 24:15)
- He will put an end to Jewish sacrifice and offerings after 3.5 years and will set up an abomination to God in the Temple (Dan. 9:27, Matt. 24:15)
- He will not answer to a higher earthly authority; "He will do as he pleases" (Dan. 11:36)
- He will show no regard for the religion of his ancestors (Dan. 11:37)
- He will not believe in any god [except himself] (Dan. 11:37)
- He will have "no regard for the desire of women": The fact that he has no regard for the one desired by women suggests he repudiates the messianic hope of Israel (Dan. 11:37)
- He will claim to be greater than any god (Dan. 11:37; 2 Thess. 2:4)
- He will claim to be God (2 Thess. 2:4)
- He will rule like a Roman "god" of war. His whole focus and attention will be on his military. He will conquer lands and distribute them (Dan. 11:39-44)
- His arrival on the world scene will be accompanied by miracles, signs, and wonders (2 Thess. 2:9)

- He will claim to be the Christ (Matt. 24:21-28)
- He will claim that Jesus did not come in the (flesh or that Jesus did not rise bodily from the grave) nor will He return in the flesh (2 Jn. 7)
- He will deny that Jesus is the Messiah (1 Jn. 2:22)
- He will be worshipped by many people (Rev. 13:8)
- He will destroy any competing religion, even the one that helps establish him (Rev. 17:16, 18)
- He will appear to survive a fatal injury (Rev. 11:7, 13:3, 12, 14 17:8, 11)
- His name will be related to the number six hundred and sixty-six— but not necessarily in a prominent fashion (Rev. 13:17-18)
- He will be empowered by the devil himself (2 Thess. 2:9, Rev. 13:2)

Again, from the list above, the coming antichrist is a literal man, not a system. John confirms, "They went out from us" (1 Jn. 2:19) - "They" are men, not a system. John refers to confessing 'Christians' departing from the truth. As mentioned earlier, Paul predicted that the departure from sound biblical doctrine is a significant end-time sign (2 Thess. 2:3, 1 Tim. 4:1, 2 Tim. 4:3). The false teachers departed because they never truly belonged to God, evident in their denial of Jesus (1 Jn. 2:22-23a) and attempt to lead others away (1 Jn. 2:26). While the false teachers may never have belonged to God (and that is debatable), those whom they were seeking to deceive, do! Hence the warning, "I write these things to you (church), about those who are trying to deceive you" (2 Jn. 2:26). John further warns the church not to "Shrink from Him in shame of His coming" (1 Jn. 2:28). The writer of the book of Hebrews says something similar, "For, yet a little while, and the coming One will come and will not delay; but My righteous one shall live by faith, and if he shrinks back, My soul has no pleasure in him" (Heb. 10:37-38).

Twice, within this section of John's letter (1 Jn. 2:18-27), John warns the church about the deceivers (1 Jn. 2:18-19, 26), and twice more he says, "But you have been anointed" (1 Jn. 2:20, 27). The anointing comes from the

"Holy One" (1 Jn. 2:20), who is Jesus Christ (Jn. 6:69), whom the Gnostics deny (Jn. 2:22—23a). The anointing is not the "Vanilla" whom Bob Jones and Todd Bentley claimed to bring back from the third heaven while astral traveling.

Those having the Holy One (Jesus) have and know the truth (1 Jn. 2:21), separating them from the deceived. This is how it is known, who belongs to God, and who does not. There is no need for further teaching about who Jesus Christ is for those who know Him (1 Jn. 2:21, 27). The revelation of Christ is a fulfilment of prophecy (Jn. 6:45), revealed by the Holy Spirit who now abides in the believer (1 Jn. 2:27) and continues to abide, providing the believer and receiver of the Holy Spirit continues to abide in what they heard from the beginning (1 Jn. 2:24). Again, that which was heard from the beginning refers to the message and gospel of Jesus Christ (1 Jn. 1:1-4).

Once more, for the reasons stated above, John does not need to write to the church about who Jesus is (1 Jn. 2:21). He does, however, still feel the need to write to them about the deceivers (1 Jn. 2:26), who spread lies about Jesus (1 Jn. 2:21b), aiming to draw some away (Acts 20:30). If drawn away, they, thereby, no longer abide, and therefore, no longer remain in God (1 Jn. 2:24). Jude confirms that the once abiding believer can become apostate, resulting from lies, where some were doubting, and others were sinning (Jude 22-23). Jude says, "Save them, snatch them out of the fire before it is too late!" (Jude 23, paraphrased).

John says anyone who changes the original message is a liar, and an antichrist (1 Jn. 2:22), which includes anyone adding to or taking away from the written word. Those who said they have fellowship with God (1 Jn. 1:5) did not because they changed the gospel (2 Jn 7) and because they denied the deity of Jesus Christ. Mainly because they denied Christ, they do not have fellowship with God, chiefly because they deny His Son (1 Jn. 2:22-23).

Dealing with the issue of denying Christ, in 325 A.D., the church elders met at Nicaea. The topic of concern was the Gnostic Arian cult, which claimed that Jesus was an angel created by God, like the Jehovah's Witnesses. The outcome of the Council, called First Nicaea, is the Nicene Creed. The (Original) Nicene Creed of 325 is as follows: "We believe in one God, the Father almighty, Maker of heaven and earth, and of all things visible and invisible. And in one Lord Jesus Christ, the Son of God, the only begotten, begotten of the Father before all ages. Light of Light, true God of true God, begotten not made, of one essence with the Father by whom all things were made, who for us men and for our salvation, came down from heaven, and was incarnate of the Holy Spirit and the Virgin Mary and became man. And He was crucified for us under Pontus Pilate and suffered and was buried. And the third day He rose again, according to the Scriptures; and ascended into heaven and sits at the right hand of the Father; and He shall come again with glory to judge the living and the dead; whose Kingdom shall have no end. And in the Holy Spirit. But as for those who say, there was when He was not, and, before being born He was not, and that He came into existence out of nothing, or who assert that the Son of God is from a different hypostasis or substance, or is created, or is subject to alteration or change – these the Catholic (Universal) Church anathematizes (denounce, or curse)."

Following the Second Ecumenical Council in Constantinople in 381 A.D.), the Creed was further supplemented due to an attack on the Holy Spirit. The Gnostic controversy was aimed at discrediting the doctrine of the Trinity. A modern application of this is seen through the Oneness Pentecostals, with whom William Branham was associated. Oneness theology states that there is only one God while denying the tri-unity of God. Oneness theology, or Jesus-only doctrine, does not recognise the distinct persons of the Godhead: Father, Son, and Holy Spirit. In the second century, the early church strongly contended against the view that God is a singular person who acted in different forms at different times. The Second Ecumenical Council in

Constantinople concluded with the following: "And [we believe] in the Holy Spirit, the Lord, the Giver of Life, who proceeds from the Father; who with the Father and the Son together is worshipped and glorified; who spoke by the prophets. In one Holy, Catholic, and Apostolic Church. I acknowledge one baptism for the remission of sins. I look for the resurrection of the dead, and the life of the world to come. Amen."

The conclusion of the Councils was known from the beginning; therefore, and to reiterate, John does not need to write to the church about what they already know. However, he does still go to great lengths, warning them that if anyone changes their confession regarding Jesus, who is the Christ, then they no longer belong to God (1 Jn. 4:2–3, 15, 5:1, 6–8). The Nicaea Council concluded by denouncing and cursing anyone who changes the gospel. Paul said something similar, "But even if we or an angel from heaven should preach to you a gospel contrary to the one we preached to you, let him be accursed. As we have said before, so now I say again: If anyone is preaching to you a gospel contrary to the one you received, let him be accursed" (Gal. 1:8-9).

Interestingly, Paul includes angels in his statement. Many cults have formed following angelic encounters, such as Islam, the Jehovah's Witnesses, Mormons, and the Seventh Day Adventists. Many more modern charismatic churches also claim angelic visitations, healings, and manifestations, including William Branham and Todd Bentley, as mentioned above. N.A.R. leaders Mike Bickel (of IHOP), who supported Todd Bentley, and Bill Johnson (Bethel) also major in angelic visitations, including angel feathers and gold dust falling from the sky. While they have not denied the Son, the early church fathers still would have rejected their angelic obsession and Gnostic practices, such as grave soaking, uncontrollable shaking, roaring, barking, howling, chirping, and 'Holy Ghost' laughing.

While John's statement in verse twenty-three (1 Jn. 2:23b) confirms that "Whoever confesses the Son has the Father also," there still must be sound doctrine and active obedience linked to that one's confession (cf. Matt. 7:21-23). Both belief and obedience are critical, which is why John says, "See that what you heard from the beginning remains in you" (1 Jn. 2:24a). Departure and disobedience will disqualify; but, John's focus is to guard his readers against the aim of the false teachers, who seek to pluck the seed sown out (cf. Matt. 13:1-9, Lu. 8:1-15).

Paul, like John, reminds the church of what they heard from the beginning (1 Cor. 15:1-11), confirming that they are only saved "If they hold fast to the word [Paul] preached to [them], otherwise they have believed in vain" (1 Cor. 15:1-2). Remember, the Greek application for the English-translated word "Believe" implies ongoing (obedient) action. Believing alone is not enough (Jam. 2:17-20). John agrees with Paul, saying, "If what you heard from the beginning abides in you, then you too will abide in the Son and in the Father" (1 Jn. 2:24). Those who abide inherit the promise of eternal life (1 Jn. 2:25, 27b).

John mentioned "Eternal life" six times in his first letter (1 Jn. 1:2, 2:25, 3:15, 5:11, 13, 20). Only those who have the Son have eternal life (1 Jn. 5:11, 13, 20, cf. Jn. 17:3). Jude says only those who are waiting for Jesus can expect to gain eternal life (Jude 21, paraphrased). Jesus said something similar, stating that only those looking for Him will be raptured (Lu. 21:34-36 paraphrased). Those confessing Christ have eternal life promised to them on this side of His return. However, eternal life is still to be fully realised (1 Jn. 2:25, Jude 21), which discredits the false Calvinistic doctrine, "Once saved, always saved." Remember, the Gnostic, Valentinus, introduced predestination, meaning some are saved regardless, while others are damned, regardless. The false teaching of Valentinus influenced Calvinism.

As mentioned several times already, the believers are the target of the Gnostics, who aim to draw them away from the original teaching, therefore, from Christ (1 Jn. 2:26). Any who change their confession are lost - are lost, eternally (Heb. 6:4-8). Nevertheless, again, John returns to his statement in verse twenty (1 Jn. 2:20), "But the anointing that you received from Him abides in you" (1 Jn. 27a). Providing "You abide in what you heard from the beginning. If you continue to abide in that, then you too will abide in Him" (1 Jn. 2:24, paraphrased). The promise is conditional and dependent on the receiver, not God. God promised never to leave or forsake those clinging to Him (Heb. 13:5b); yet, a confessing Christian can forsake God, lured away by the things of this world (Heb. 13:5a). Elsewhere, Jesus said, "I give them eternal life, and they will never perish, and no one will snatch them out of My hand. My Father, who has given them to Me, is greater than all, and no one is able to snatch them out of the Father's hand" (Jn. 10:28-29). John writes something similar in his first letter, saying, "For He who is in you is greater than he who is in the world" (1 Jn. 4:4). Again, the promise applies to the abiding believer clinging to God.

The "Anointing" of the "Holy One" (Jesus and the Holy Spirit) abides in the abiding believer. The believer must abide, which also debunks the false teaching that "The gifts and the calling of God are irrevocable" (Rom. 11:29). While the verse is correct, the application many charismatics give is incorrect. The verse refers to the salvation of the Jews. In the tribulation, following the rapture (Rom. 11:25), a remnant of Israel (Rom. 11:5) will have their temporally blinded eyes opened. Then, they shall call upon the name of Jesus (Rom. 11:26-27), whom they rejected, fulfilling prophecy (Matt. 23:39). Verses seventeen to twenty-four (Rom. 11:17-24) provides a warning to the church; if the church does what Israel did, she too will be treated in the same way. God's kindness is extended to those who continue to remain. The condition of God's continued kindness is on the provision that professing members of the church remain (Rom. 11:22).

Like John's conditional statement in chapter two (1 Jn. 2:24), he provides another in the following by saying, "Whoever keeps His commandments abides in God, and God in him. And by this, we know that He abides in us, by the Spirit whom He has given us" (1 Jn. 3:24). The abiding believer is known by their keeping of the commandments, provided in chapter one (1 Jn. 1:7-8). The condition of salvation is dependent upon abiding by what was heard from the beginning, which includes keeping the commandment of love. The Spirit remains with the abiding, law-keeping believer. The abiding Spirit is the evidence of salvation in the same way heresy, lawlessness, and lovelessness are evidence of damnation, even in the confessing Christian, such as it was with the Gnostics. The original word and the indwelling Holy Spirit are the believer's best defences against deception, albeit many deceived individuals claim to have both.

As mentioned earlier, John's following statement is that because the believer has the Holy Spirit, they do not need anyone else to teach them (1 Jn. 2:27). Again, as mentioned above, the statement refers to what they had heard from the beginning (1 Jn. 2:24), primarily regarding the doctrine of Christ, whom the Gnostic was denying (1 Jn. 2:22). John does not state that believers do not need teachers, period. Anyone claiming that they do not need teachers in Christ is the one most in need of them, for they (2 Pet. 2:14) are the primary target of the Gnostics, aiming to deceive (1 Jn. 2:26). Remember once more, the Gnostics claimed to have special revelation and superior knowledge, which was extra-biblical information, going ahead of the teachings of Christ (2 Jn. 2:7). Many charismatic Christians act similarly, promoting "New' revelation, promising (false) freedom (hyper-grace), and prosperity, leading the unsteady soul away from the apostle's teaching.

If John were saying his readers do not need anyone to teach them anything, he would not need to write the letter affirming what they already know and warning them about the false teachers. Furthermore, there would be no need for Christians of all ages to have the letter preserved for all time, teaching, and warning them. The preserved scripture teaches the believer "Everything" (1 Jn. 2:27b) they need to know about Jesus, as the Holy Spirit reveals Christ to those seeking to know Him.

John adds to his statement that the anointing and teaching of the Holy Spirit "Is true and is no lie" (1 Jn. 2:27), which counters the lying false teachers, who have no truth in them (1 Jn. 1:6, 10, 2:4, 11, 22). Earlier, John said, "You know it (the truth about Jesus), and because no lie is of the truth" (1 Jn. 2:21). Therefore, John says, "Just as it was taught you, abide in Him" (1 Jn. 2:27). While Jesus, and the Holy Spirit will remain in the abiding believer, those departing from sound biblical doctrine have no such assurance. If the believer remains, so does the anointing (Jesus and the Holy Spirit), which continues to teach and preserve. The foundation has been laid (1 Jn. 1:1, 2:7, 13, 14, 24, 3:11), the conditions have been made (2 Jn. 2:24, 3:24), and now, it is up to the believer to remain.

In conclusion, as this age draws closer to the return of Jesus, there will be an increase in false teachers, which is why John thought he was living in the last hour. John was troubled by an increasing number of false teachers coming out of the church, drawing others away. The false teachers targeted any not holding onto what they had heard from the beginning. They introduced all sorts of "New" things through dreams, visions, angelic visitations, and false words. They claimed to have divine revelation and superior knowledge, promising freedom, and prosperity. All the while, John says they are liars, void of the truth, Jesus, and the Spirit. Anyone who has fellowship with the false teachers cannot have fellowship with the apostles and, therefore, does not have fellowship with God the Father through Christ Jesus, His Son. In sum, the false teachers have the same spirit as the coming antichrist; therefore, those who follow them follow him - they are children of the devil and might as well have taken his mark (666) now (Rev. 13:16-18, 14:9-11).

CHAPTER 7
When He Appears

Do Not Shrink Back

The remaining section of chapter two in John's first letter reinforces the distinction between God's children and the devil's children. This concept is developed further in chapter three (1 Jn. 3:4-10) and is the chiastic point of the letter. The distinction between those belonging to God, or Satan, hinges on the conditional "If" (1 Jn. 2:29). Previously, John said, "If what you heard from the beginning abides in you, then you too will abide in the Son and in the Father" (1 Jn. 2:24, cf. Jn. 8:31, 15:7, 10). The closing verse of the previous section also provides a conditional statement: "But the anointing that you received from Him abides in you, and you have no need that anyone should teach you. But as His anointing teaches you about everything, and is true, and is no lie—just as it has taught you, abide in Him" (1 Jn. 2:27). The condition for Christ abiding in the believer is that the believer continues to abide in Him.

As stated several times earlier, the Gnostics came out of the church (1 Jn. 2:19, 4:1, 2 Jn. 7), failing to abide, and were condemned. Peter confirms that the Gnostics were once on the right path (2 Pet. 2:15), further stating that it would have been better not to have known the truth, then realise it and then fall away (2 Pet. 2:20-21, paraphrased). The early church fathers confirmed the same, stating that the Gnostics were once confessing Christians, who departed the way, and led others astray. As mentioned many times, for this reason, John, Jude, and Peter write their letters, warning the church against the false teachers, aiming to deceive (1 Jn. 2:26).

As the previous section encouraged the believer to remain in Christ, the following does likewise, once again addressing the church as "Little children" (1 Jn. 2:28, 3:7), whom John is writing to, warning about deceivers (1 Jn. 2:26, 3:7). John continues with his conditional statements by saying, "Abide in Him, so that when He appears, we may have confidence and not shrink from Him in shame at His coming. If you know that He is righteous, you may be sure that everyone who practices righteousness has been born of Him" (1 Jn. 2:28-29). Within the statement, there are two more conditions, adding to the previous: the first is, "[Do] not shrink back," and the next is: "If you know..." A third condition is to "Abide in Him." Only those abiding will stand confidently before Jesus when He appears.

Those abiding in Christ, having not shrunk back, are the same who have continued in what they have heard from the beginning and have continued to follow the commandments of Christ. The faithful follower of Christ also commits to holiness, "Purifying himself as Christ is pure" (1 Jn. 3:3). On the contrary, "Whoever makes a practice of sinning, also practice lawlessness" (1 Jn. 3:4), they are of the devil (1 Jn. 3:8). "No one born of God makes a practice of sinning" (1 Jn. 3:9). The evidence of whether a confessing Christian belongs to God is faithfulness, love and holiness over faithlessness, and lovelessness, and lawlessness, (1 Jn. 3:10).

The call to continued (ongoing and active) obedience is seen in the opening words, "Abide (remain) in Him" (1 Jn. 2:28). As stated earlier, John praised the church for knowing God and overcoming the evil one (1 Jn. 2:12-14), yet still warns them, "Do not love the world" (1 Jn. 2:15), and do not be deceived

(1 Jn. 2:26). John repeats the warning in the following chapter, verse seven, saying, "Little children, let no one deceive you" (1 Jn. 3:7). In other words, John's reader was still able to be deceived, therefore overcome, and drawn away from what they had heard from the beginning, and back into sin. For this reason, John says, "Whoever makes a practice of sinning is of the devil" (1 Jn. 3:8). Anyone confessing to having fellowship with God while deliberately practicing sin is deceived.

The one (alone) who continues in Christ has the assurance of eternal life. When Jesus appears, that one, only, will not shrink back, as one ashamed (1 Jn. 2:28), and will be transformed, as Christ is (1 Jn. 3:2). When Jesus appears, the abiding believer will not be ashamed and will have no cause to fear punishment, for the perfect (abiding) love of God drives out all fear (1 Jn. 4:17-18).

As previously mentioned, John's letter is eschatological, pointing to the return of Jesus Christ (1 Jn. 28, 3:2). Peter has the same focus (1 Pet. 5:5, 2 Pet. 1:16, 3:4, 12), as does Jude (Jude 14-15, 21, 24). John's six references to "Eternal life" (1 Jn. 1:2, 2:25, 3:15, 5:11, 13, 20) also confirm his mind is fixed on the next appearing of Jesus Christ, which he believes is very soon, within the "Hour" (1 Jn. 2:18).

The return of Jesus Christ is a significant theme throughout the New Testament. Paul mentioned it (Rom. 5:9, 1 Cor. 15:23, 51-52 1 Thess. 1:10, 2:19 3:13, 4:15-17, 5:9, 23 2 Thess. 2:1, 8, Tit. 2:13) as did James (Jas. 5:7, 8). There are many more references pointing to the Second Coming, such as in the gospel of Matthew (Matt 24:3, 27, 37, 39), Mark (Mk. 13:3-13, 24-27), Luke (Lu. 12:35-48, 14:12-24, 17:20-37, 21:25-28, 34-36) and the book of Revelation (Rev. 1:1, 3, 7, 8, 6:12-17, 14:17-20, 16:17-21, 19:11-21, 21:5-7, 22:7,10, 20), to list a few.

The difference between most of the gospel (Matthew, Mark, and Luke) references and Paul's is the distinction between the rapture and the Second

Coming. Most of the gospel references, and the book of Revelation, refer to the Second Coming of Jesus Christ, not the rapture. The gospel of Luke has two references for the rapture (Lu. 12:25-40, 21:34-36). At the same time, the book of Revelation contains two more (Rev. 3:10, 4:1) and another applying to the Two Witnesses at the end of the tribulation (Rev. 11:12). The rapture and the Second Coming of Christ are two separate events. John's references in his first letter address the church (1 Jn. 2:28, 3:2); therefore, the rapture is intended. Paul's references also mostly point to the rapture. Paul confirms that the church will not suffer the wrath (tribulation) to come (Rom. 5:9, 1 Thess. 1:10, 5:9).

Contrary to many falsely claiming that the rapture is a recent invention created by John Darby in the 1800s, popularised by Tim LaHaye, the early church fathers taught about it. For example, John's disciple Polycarp, taught his disciple, Irenaeus (170 A.D.), who said, "When in the end that church will suddenly be caught up from this, it is said, "There will be tribulation such as not been since the beginning, nor will be" (Against Heresies 5:29). Tertullian (207 A.D.) agrees with Irenaeus, saying, "He [Paul] says those who remain unto the coming of Christ, along with the dead in Christ, will rise first, being "Caught up in the clouds to meet the Lord in the air…" (Against Marcion 5:16). The Shephard of Herman (150 A.D.) describes a dream and gives the interpretation of it. The dream revealed that the church was escaping the great tribulation. The writer warns the church to prepare herself and, with whole heart, turn to the Lord in repentance; then shall she be able to escape the coming tribulation. For those prepared, the tribulation will be as nothing (Shepherd of Hermas 2:2-6). The record reveals that the early church maintained a pretribulation position.

Likewise, Cyprian (250 A.D.) agrees, stating that before the antichrist is revealed, the church will have an early departure, taken away and delivered from the shipwrecks, and disaster that is imminent. Cyprian encourages the church to greet the day, which assigns each one to his home (in heaven), which snatches the church and sets her free from the snare of this world (Treatises of Cyprian 21-26). Cyprian also says, "The antichrist is coming, but above him comes Christ also" (Epistle 55). Ephraim (373 A.D.) concurs, saying, "Because all saints and the elect of the Lord are gathered together before the tribulation which is about to come and be taken to the Lord..." (On the Last Times 2).

As confirmed by the above early church fathers, John's readers can be confident of being "Caught up" when Jesus returns for His bride, the church, providing that they continue to abide in Him. If not, then when Jesus returns, they will shrink back in shame (2 Jn. 2:28), and they will be consumed with fear (1 Jn. 4:17-18). Anyone who does not fear God on this side of the tribulation will be given an opportunity to fear Him during the tribulation (Rev. 14:6-7).

The tribulation will last seven years (Dan. 9:24-27, 12:9, 11, Rev. 11:2-3, 12:6, 14, 13:5), concluding with Christ's Second Coming. As mentioned above, the gospels and the book of Revelation references to Christ's return primarily refer to the event following the seven-year tribulation. Remember again; John is dealing with those who are denying Christ, and His return in the flesh (2 Jn. 7), like Peter (2 Pet. 3:3), and Jude (Jude 18), reminding them that He will appear (1 Jn. 2:28, 3:2), in the same way, He did the first time (1 Jn. 1:1-4), thereby, warning the faithful to remain. Luke's gospel warns: "But watch yourselves lest your hearts be weighed down with dissipation and drunkenness and cares of this life, and that day will come upon you suddenly like a trap. For it will come upon all who dwell on the face of the whole earth. But stay awake at all times, praying that you may have strength to escape all these things that are going to take place, and to stand before the Son of Man" (Lu. 21:34-36).

The "Day coming upon [the world] like a trap" refers to the tribulation; therefore, Jesus is stating that the one watching themselves (their deeds and doctrines) can escape it. In the book of Revelation, Jesus confirms that the church, which is holding onto His word, will escape the tribulation, saying, "Because you have kept My word about patient endurance, I will keep you from the hour of trial that is coming on the whole world, to try those who dwell on the earth. I am coming soon. Hold fast to what you have, so that no one may seize your crown" (Rev. 3:10-11).

Only those holding onto sound biblical doctrine can have "Confidence" (1 Jn. 2:28) when Jesus appears. The believer's confidence relates to the judgement (1 Jn. 4:17). If the believer is removed at Christ's appearance, they have been judged righteous. If they have been left behind, they have been judged wicked and unworthy. Again, the promise relates to those who have remained in the original word (1 Jn. 2:24) and have kept the commandments (1 Jn. 3:24). Those who do both have confidence that they know God and walk righteously, the latter being the evidence that they know God (1 Jn. 3:10) and are known by Him (1 Jn. 3:1-2).

As mentioned above, the conditional evidence is connected to verse twenty-nine: "If you know that He is righteous, you may be sure that everyone who practices righteousness has been born of Him (1 Jn. 2:29). Those who walk in the light, and the love of God, are His, while those who practice sinning, belong to the devil (1 Jn. 3:8). Only those walking in the light (truth) and love, are Born of God." Nine times John uses the phrase Born of God (2:29, 3:9 [x2], 4:7, 5:1 [x2], 4, 18 [x2]). John's gospel, chapter three, introduces the born-again condition, for without, "No one can see the kingdom of God" (Jn. 3:1-15). Jesus concludes His discussion with Nicodemus by saying, "Whoever believes in [Me] may have eternal life" (Jn. 3:15). Remember once more, believing is active and ongoing obedience: "Everyone who thus hopes in [Jesus] purifies himself as He is pure" (1 Jn. 3:3). Salvation is a two-way street! God did the work; however, His children must respond and remain.

John reminds his reader that it is due to the kindness of God that they should be called His children (1 Jn. 3:1). Something similar is found in his gospel: "But to all who did receive Him, who believed in His name, He gave the right to become children of God, who were born, not of blood nor of the will of the flesh nor of the will of man, but of God" (Jn. 1:12-13). Those Born of God are Born of the Spirit (Jn. 3:6). John includes himself by using the words "Us" and "We," concluding with, "And so we are (born again)" (1 Jn. 3:1). John's declaration is purposed to remind his reader not to throw away what they have, encouraging faithfulness and endurance. Something similar is seen in the book of Hebrews, following a reminder of what the reader has already endured in order to inherit the promise (Heb 10:32-39). The author gives similar conditions to John, encouraging them to "Hold fast" to their confession without wavering (Heb. 10:23). Like John, the author of Hebrews focuses on the return of Christ (Heb. 10:25b), with a warning against sinning deliberately, threatening worse punishment for the one who knows the truth, and turns away (Heb. 10:26-31).

The author of the book of Hebrews confirms that life as a believer is not easy (Heb. 10:32-24), like John, who also confirms, the world "Does not know us" because "It does not know God (1 Jn. 3:1). Indeed, the "World hates you" (1 Jn. 3:13) because it hates Jesus since the whole world lies in the power of the evil one" (1 Jn. 5:19). The evil one (Satan) aims to discredit Jesus, and the apostle's testimony (1 Jn. 2:22–23, 4:2–3), and by doing so, destroy anyone caught in his web of deception. For this reason, John twice reminds his reader that Jesus is returning, applying a reward for those remaining and punishment for those departing.

John repeats that Jesus will (soon) appear (1 Jn. 2:28, 3:2, cf. 1 Jn 2:18), and when He does, "We shall be like Him." No doubt, John refers to the believer receiving a glorified body (1 Cor. 15:49, 51-52, Phil. 3:21), like Christ. Those departing and or continuing in sin (1 Jn. 3:8) will also receive a glorified body when resurrected for the purpose of everlasting torment (Dan. 12:2, Jn.

5:28-29, Acts 24:15). The tribulation will be the last opportunity afforded to those left behind, to avoid the everlasting fiery judgement.

Following the removal of the church, countless millions of confessing 'Christians' will be left behind to endure seven years of tribulation; again, the purpose of the tribulation is for salvation. The tribulation is God's last attempt to reach humanity before being cast into hell, alive and forever. Those left behind are the same who will shrink back in shame. If they do not repent during the tribulation, their shame will be many times more following Christ's second coming (Dan. 12:2).

While John says the evidence of those belonging to God is their keeping of the original word (1 Jn. 2:24), the commandments (1 Jn. 3:24), and pursuing purity (1 Jn. 3:10). The additional evidence will be with those removed before the tribulation commences, separating them from the ones left behind. The promise to escape the tribulation is given to the faithful church of Philadelphia on the condition that they continue to hold fast to God's word (Rev. 3:10-11). On the other hand, Thyatira's unfaithful church was warned that, unless her members repent, they will be cast into the great tribulation. Every 'church' left behind will then know that God searches the mind and heart, giving each as their works deserve (Rev. 2:22-23). Again, many confessing 'Christians' will wake up in the tribulation, as the church of Sardis was also forewarned (Rev. 3:3). To the church of Sardis, Jesus warned, "If you will not wake up, I will come like a thief, and you will not know at what hour I will come against you" (Rev. 3:3).

Jesus coming like a "Thief in the night" is rapture talk (Matt. 24:43, 1 Thess. 5:2), customary of a Galilean wedding where the Groom (Jesus) would/will come for his bride (the church) at an hour she would not know. The day and the hour are unknown; therefore, the bride must be ready at all times (Matt. 24:36, 42, 44, 50). The parable of the Ten Virgins, where five foolish virgins were shut out of the marriage feast, follows the warning to be ready

(Matt. 25:1-13) and concludes with: "Watch therefore, for you know neither the day nor the hour" (Matt. 25:13). The marriage feast commences in heaven, lasting seven years following the marriage ceremony. When the bride (church) meets Jesus in the air, she is married to Him and will, thereby, be "Like Him" (1 Jn. 3:2).

To reiterate, the majority missing the rapture, being left behind, will include millions of deceived churchgoers who believed they were in fellowship with God when they were not; however, they will have one more opportunity to get right with Him. Although the same spirit of the antichrist whom they loved and were deceived by this side of the tribulation will be more convincing on the other side, conditioning and preparing the masses for the antichrist to come (1 Jn. 2:28-19, 4:1-3, 2 Jn. 7). Indeed, God sends the antichrist (strong delusion) to condemn those (left behind) who did not believe the truth but had pleasure in unrighteousness (2 Thess. 2:11), which includes the false teachers John was addressing, and any who follow them.

In contrast to those who do what is right (1 Jn. 2:29), keeping themselves pure (1 Jn. 3:3), John addresses the false teachers and those following them, who "Make a practice of sinning" (1 Jn. 3:4, 8, 9), which are those who "Keep sinning" (1 Jn. 3:6, 9). These are the lawless ones, practicing "Lawlessness" (1 Jn. 3:4). The Greek word for "Lawless" is "Anomia," contextually referring to anyone ignoring the law or commandments. These people say they have no sin, are deceived, and make God a liar (1 Jn. 1:8, 10). Jesus uses the same word to describe the outcome of those believing they were born of God when they were not (Matt 7:23; 13:41; 23:28). As previously mentioned, the most dangerous position to be in is to believe you are right with God when you are not. In this late hour, those deceived will soon wake up in the great tribulation (Matt. 24:21).

For the above-mentioned reason, John goes to great trouble to make it very clear who are the children of God and who are not:

Children of God	Children of Satan
Everyone who thus hopes in Him purifies himself (v. 3)	Everyone who makes a practice of sinning also practises lawlessness (v. 4)
No one who abides in Him keeps sinning (v. 6)	No one who keeps sinning has either seen Him or known Him (v. 6)
Whoever practices righteousness is righteous (v. 7)	Whoever makes a practice of sin is of the devil (v. 8)
No one born of God makes a practice of sinning (v. 9)	Whoever does not practice righteousness is not of God, [they are children of the devil] nor is the one who does not love his brother (v. 10).

The "Children of the devil" (1 Jn. 3:10) are the same John warned about in the previous section (1 Jn. 2:18-19) and the next chapter (1 Jn. 4:1-3), who have the spirit of the antichrist. They are first and foremost antichrist because they deny Jesus, and because they deny Him, they disobey and lead others astray. In the book of Acts, Paul rebuked Elymas, the magician, also known as Bar-Jesus, who claimed to be a prophet of God yet opposed those seeking to turn away from sin. Paul called him the "Son of the devil" and an "Enemy of righteousness," saying that he was "Full of deceit and villainy" (Acts 13:10). Similarly, John's disciple, Polycarp (69-156 A.D.), called Gnostic Marcion (85-160 A.D.) "Satan's firstborn," when he ran into him in Rome, for editing scripture and producing his own gospel. Like the other Gnostics who had defected from the faith, Marcion was the son of the bishop of Sinope, in Pontus, on the southern shore of the Black Sea. According to Irenaeus, Marcion's teacher was Cerdo, who was a follower of Simon Magus (cf. Acts 8:9-24), "A certain Cerdo, originating from the Simonians, came to Rome under Hyginus ... and taught that the one who was proclaimed as

God by the Law and the Prophets is not the Father of our Lord Jesus Christ" (Against Heresies, 1, 27, 1). Marcion was also condemned as a heretic in the writings of many other church fathers, including Justin Martyr, Irenaeus, Tertullian, Hippolytus, and Epiphanius.

Irenaeus regarded the memory of Polycarp as a link to the apostolic past. In his letter to Florinus, a fellow student of Polycarp who had become a Roman presbyter and later lapsed into heresy, Irenaeus relates how and when he became a Christian, "I remember well the place in which the holy Polycarp sat and spoke. I remember the discourses he delivered to the people and how he described his relations with John, the apostle, and others who had been with the Lord; how he recited the sayings of Christ and the miracles he wrought; how he received his teachings from eyewitnesses who had seen the Word of Life, agreeing in every way with the Scriptures" (Fragments 2, cf. 1 Jn. 1:1-4).

Like Paul, and Polycarp, John's reference to the "Children of the devil" (1 Jn. 3:10) is primarily aimed at the "False prophets" (1 Jn. 4:1), who say they have fellowship with God and do not (1 Jn. 1:6). They are children of the devil producing more of the same kind, even twice the child of hell that they are (Matt. 23:15). This is why John says, "If you want to have fellowship with us, you cannot have fellowship with them" (1 Jn. 1:3, paraphrased, cf. 2 Jn. 10-11). Again, only those in fellowship with the apostles have Jesus and eternal life (1 Jn. 1:2, 2:25, 5:11, 13, 20).

The giver of eternal life is Jesus Christ, alone, who took away the sins of the world (1 Jn. 3:5) and destroyed the works of the devil (1 Jn. 3:8b). For this reason, He appeared the first time. John writes the word "Appeared" three times" (1 Jn. 3:2, 5, 8). Twice more, the word "Appears" (1 Jn. 2:28, 3:2), which is connected to the phrase, "At His coming" (1 Jn. 2:28). Jesus appeared two thousand years ago to take away the sins of the world (Jn. 1:29, 1 Jn. 3:5), and destroy the works of the devil (1 Jn. 3:8b). This same

Jesus whom John first introduced (1 Jn. 1:1-4) will soon reappear to remove the sinless (cleansed) from the world (1 Jn. 2:28, 3:2), separating the saved, from the unsaved. Only the unsaved are left behind to endure the tribulation. After the tribulation, Jesus will cast the antichrist and the false prophet into the lake of fire (Rev. 19:20) and Satan into the bottomless pit (Rev. 20:1-3).

As mentioned above, the false teachers, having the antichrist spirit, condition and prepare their victims for the antichrist to come by denying Christ, drawing them into sin, and away from salvation. However, Jesus came to take away sins and destroy the devil's works. When Jesus next appears, He will remove His bride and then deal with the unrepentant sins of those left behind. This was the warning to the church of Sardis (Rev. 3:3). The coming tribulation is God's chosen way to deal with sin, as it was for Israel and Judah (Lam. 3:5), as God forewarned, "When you are in tribulation, and all these things come upon you in the latter days, you will return to the Lord your God and obey His voice" (Deut. 4:30).

As mentioned, the purpose of the tribulation is salvation. The Deuteronomy warning is like that of the book of Hebrews (Heb. 10:19-39), instructing Israel to "Take care, lest [they] forget the covenant with the Lord [their] God" (Deut. 4:23), "For the Lord your God is a consuming fire, a jealous God" (Deut. 4:4:24, cf. Heb. 10:27, 31). During the tribulation, those who have forsaken God, will "Seek Him, and find Him, if [they] seek Him with all [their] heart and all [their] soul" (Deut. 4:29). The section concludes with, "For the Lord your God is a merciful God. He will not leave you or destroy you or forget the covenant with your fathers that he swore to them" (Deut. 4:31). The verse (Deut. 4:31) should remind the readers of another, in the book of Hebrews: "Keep your life free from love of money, and be content with what you have, for he has said, "I will never leave you nor forsake you" (Heb. 13:5). Note, God will not leave the abiding believer; however, that person can still leave (apostatise) Him.

The Greek word for "apostasy" (apostasia) and the words for "Writ of divorce" (apostasion) come from the same root. Marriage is used by God, likened to apostasy. The book of Jeremiah provides around fifty references to apostasy. The word is used several times in Jeremiah, chapter three, where it becomes a description of (generic) Israel: Israel is "Apostasy Israel," the example of apostasy (Jer. 3:6, 8, 11, 12). Israel's backsliding is set in a marital context; the wife of God has played the whore (Jer. 3:1, 20-21). As a result, God also threatens to serve Judah with a "Writ of divorce" (Jer. 3:9), as He has already done for Israel (Jer. 3:8; cf. Deut. 24:1-4).

Apostasy, thus, is marital infidelity, followed by an end to the marriage with a divorce certificate. Nevertheless, God is still calling Israel back (Jer. 3:12-18, 22), and she does return to God in the tribulation (Rom. 11:25-32). During the tribulation, Israel will call on the name of Jesus (Matt. 23:39) and be saved (Jer. 3:23, Rom. 11:26-27), and after that, she will inherit the promise (Jer. 3:18).

The difference between Israel, and those coming to repentance through Christ Jesus, is that Israel never inherited salvation through the finished work of the cross. After coming to repentance, anyone denying Christ runs the risk of being eternally cut off (Heb. 6:4-8, 10:26-31). John calls this "The sin unto death" (1 Jn. 5:16-17). Those who have "Tasted the goodness of God" and since departed cannot return due to the cost of their salvation. Jesus, the Son of God, died on the cross and shed His blood. That was the cost (cf. Heb. 2)! His blood cleanses (1 Jn. 1:7, 2:1b) those repenting of sin (1 Jn. 1:9). The blood of Christ takes sin away (1 Jn. 3:5, cf. 2:12, 4:10).

As mentioned above, Peter confirms the writer of the book of Hebrews, saying it would be better that an apostate never knew the truth than to realise it and depart (2 Pet. 2:20-21). The Apocalypse of Peter repeats the same, in reference to a vision of those suffering in hell. Peter writes, "And yet others near unto them (idolaters in hell), men, and women, burning and turning themselves about and roasted as in a pan. And these were they who forsook the way of God" (3 Pet. 34). While The Apocalypse of Peter (3 Peter) is Apocrypha, it was considered canon by the early church, up until 325 A.D., where the Council of Nicaea ruled against it, as inspired text. Despite the Council of Nicaea's ruling, historical records show that Eusebius (4th Century) quoted The Apocalypse of Peter, as did Macarius Magnes, and Sozomen (5th Century), Methodius, bishop of Olympus in Lycia (6th Century), and The Armenian annalist Mkhitan (13th Century).

Falling away from the faith is to reject, and trample underfoot, the atoning blood of Christ through the finished work of the cross (Heb. 10:29). Jesus Christ, the Son of God, was the required sacrifice for sin (1 Jn. 2:2, 4:10) because "In Him there is no sin" (1 Jn. 3:5b). Therefore, those in Him (alone) no longer sin (1 Jn. 2:1, 3:6), instead, they (continually) purify themselves, as Jesus is pure (1 Jn. 3:3). Followers of Christ, actively pursue righteousness (1 Jn. 3:7), contrary to the deceived, who practice lawlessness (1 Jn. 3:4). By actively pursuing righteousness, the believer remains in God (2:6, 24, 28, 3:6, 24, 4:12, 13, 15, 16). Remember, John's purpose for writing the letter is to counterargue the false teachers who say they have fellowship with God; they say they walk in the light and have no sin, yet they do not remain. John reinforced the statement with, "No one who abides in Him keeps on sinning, no one who keeps on sinning has either seen Him or known Him" (1 Jn. 3:6). While John says the Gnostics have not known God, they say that they do (1 Jn. 1:6).

Again, John warns the church, saying, "Little children, let no one deceive you" (1 Jn. 3:7, cf. 2:26). The Gnostics, who claim to know God (1 Jn. 1:6), also claim to have no sin (1 Jn. 8, 10), all while, are children of the devil (1 Jn. 3:8, 10). They are children of the devil because they deny Christ, dismiss the authority of scripture, willfully sin, and lead others into sin. For the reason of sin, Jesus appeared "To destroy the works of the devil" (1 Jn. 3:8b). If any continue in sin, they work against the work of Christ.

The verse, "The devil has been sinning from the beginning" (1 Jn. 3:8b), refers to his original rebellion against God (Isa. 14:13-14), also in the Garden (Gen. 3), and outside the Garden (Gen. 4:6), through the corruption of God's creative design (Gen. 6), in the wilderness (Matt. 4:1-11), before the cross (Matt. 16:23), at the Last Supper (Jn. 13:27), and continuing through the false teachers, leading to the antichrist (1 Jn. 2:18-19). The devil's primary aim is to prevent and undo what God has already done, "Take away sins" (1 Jn. 3:5). Only those who "Confess" Christ, and their sins, are cleansed (1 Jn. 1:7, 9, 2:1b).

Because the work of the devil is ongoing and active, through the false teachers, John warns the church, "Not to be deceived by them" (1 Jn. 2:26, 3:7). Satan's weapon of choice to get the church off track is the world, which is why John says, "Do not love the world" (1 Jn. 2:15). Satan tried the same tactic on Jesus (Matt. 4:9), and failed. However, he was successful with Eve (Gen. 3:6), Judas (Jn. 16:6) and Demas (2 Tim. 4:10), among the Gnostics, and countless millions more.

Again, John states that those who are born of God do not sin and cannot keep on sinning (1 Jn. 3:9), which is not to say they do not sin (1 Jn. 19, 2:1), but rather, they cannot practice sin as the false teachers do. Sin is not active and ongoing in the lives of those following Christ. Those born of God do not work against the finished work of the cross because "God's seed abides in [them]" (1 Jn. 3:9). While some say they are of God, not all are, evident by their works (1 Jn. 3:10), confirming that, instead, the seed of Satan abides in them. The "Seed" of God and Satan is in context with being "Born of" (1 Jn. 3:9) either one, implying spiritual sperm. Those born of another are their "Children," which is why John calls the church "Children" (1 Jn. 3:7) and the false teachers "Children of the devil" (1 Jn. 3:8, 10).

Because there is no sin in Christ (1 Jn. 3:5b), there is no sin in his followers. That is, there is no condemning sin (1 Jn. 2:1) because it has been and is continually being confessed (1 Jn. 1:9), and therefore cleansed (1 Jn. 1:7). This is how it is known who the children of God are, and the children of the devil (1 Jn. 3:10). While the children of God are being prepared for Christ's appearing, the children of the devil are also being prepared for the antichrist. Both are 'Marked' even now, identifying who belongs to whom.

In conclusion, when Jesus next appears, He will separate His children from the rest. Those left behind will initially 'Shrink back', having then a choice to make; either repent, lay down their lives and follow Christ, enduring (abiding) to the end, or continue as a child of the devil and then join him in hell (Matt. 25:41). Those failing to follow Christ during the tribulation, will 'Shrink' back further when He returns (Rev. 6:14-17), and again later when He resurrects them from hell (Dan. 12:2), for the final judgement (Rev. 20:11-15). Only those in Christ can have confidence in His appearing (1 Jn. 28), having no fear of judgement (1 Jn. 4:17-18).

For the reasons mentioned above, on both sides of the tribulation, followers of Christ are told to stay awake (Matt. 24:42, 44, Mk. 13:34, 35, 37, Lu. 21:36, Rev. 16:15). Remember, the church of Sardis, who were once awake, were told to wake up due to falling asleep. Falling asleep refers to the spiritual condition of apostasy. Hence the warning to remain (abide).

CHAPTER 8
Love

By this We Shall Know

In the previous section, John clearly states which "Children" belong to God and those to the devil. Chapter three (vv. 4-10) is the critical point of John's letter, narrowing in on the practice of sin. Whoever makes a practice of sin practices lawlessness (1 Jn. 3:4); they follow the devil (1 Jn. 4:8); so, they are his children (1 Jn. 3:10). Those who are born of God (1 Jn. 2:29, 3:9), purify themselves (1 Jn. 3:3) - they resist sin (1 Jn. 3:6), and they cannot keep on sinning (1 Jn. 3:9); thus, they abide in Christ (1 Jn. 3:9); they (alone) are His children (1 Jn. 3:1, 2, 10).

The following section builds on the last; in fact, the entire letter continues to add another layer, one after the next, reinforcing the point that not all who call themselves God's children are. The point is strengthened with the words, "By this, we know." Three times within this section of the letter (1 Jn. 3:11-24), the words are seen (1 Jn. 3:16, 19, 24). The phrase is seen eight times throughout the letter (1 Jn. 2:3, 5, 3:16, 19, 24, 4:6, 13, 5:2), proving whether someone belongs to God. Those belonging to God are those who:

   a.   Keep His commandments (1 Jn. 2:3, 5, 3:24, 5:2)

b. Lay down their lives and possessions for others, as Jesus did for them (1 Jn. 3:16-18)
   c. Have the assurance of the heart (1 Jn. 3:19)
   d. Listen to the apostles, obey what was written, and do not follow the world (1 Jn. 4:6)
   e. Abide in Christ (1 Jn. 4:13)

On the contrary, the children of the devil are so because they do not do any of the above. The primary reason is that they do not keep the commandments (1 Jn. 2:3, 5, 3:24, 5:2), which they heard from the beginning (1 Jn. 3:11), being the commandment of love (1 Jn. 2:7-8). John writes the word "Love" twenty-six times in his first letter, five more times in his second, and twice more in his third. Within the first letter, the love John refers to chiefly relates to God loving His children and His children loving Him and His followers; the two are interconnected.

Negatively, John also warns about having love for the world, and things in the world (1 Jn. 2:15). The love of the world will take the abiding believer away from God, as seen with Demas (2 Tim. 4:10). The Gnostics, who came out of the church (1 Jn. 2:19, 4:1), also loved worldliness (1 Jn. 2:15-17). The evidence that the Gnostics are children of the devil is because they love the world and because the world loves them (1 Jn. 4:5).

As mentioned above, John majors on the theme of love throughout his first letter, concluding the last section by saying the children of the devil do not love their brother (1 Jn. 3:10b), comparing them with Cain, who murdered his brother, Able (1 Jn. 3:12). John develops his argument further by saying, "Everyone who hates his brother is a murderer, and you know that no murderer has eternal life abiding in him" (1 Jn. 3:15). John commences this section (1 Jn. 3:11-24) with the words, "For this is the message you have heard from the beginning" (1 Jn. 3:11). Seven times John writes the words, "From the beginning" (1 Jn. 1:1, 2:7, 13, 14, 24, 3:8, 11). The phrase refers to:

a. Jesus (1 Jn. 1:1, 2:13, 14, 24)
b. Love (1 Jn. 2:7, 3:11), and
c. The devil (1 Jn. 3:8)

The message the church has heard from the beginning is that its members must have love for one another, which is the evidence that Christ's followers have eternal life (1 Jn. 3:14, 4:12) because they know (1 Jn. 4:8) and love God (1 Jn. 4:20-21). Regardless of a person's confession regarding Christ (1 Jn. 3:23), if they hate their brother, they do not have eternal life (1 Jn. 3:15). Instead, John compares them to Cain (1 Jn. 3:12, Gen. 4:1-25).

The reason Cain murdered his brother Able was because "His own deeds were evil and his brother's righteous" (1 Jn. 3:12). The "Deeds" refer to Cain and Abel's sacrifice. God accepted Abel's offering and rejected Cain's. The writer of the book of Hebrews provides more information on the topic, saying, "By faith Abel offered to God a more acceptable sacrifice than Cain, through which he was commended as righteous, God commending him by accepting his gifts. And through his faith, though he died, he still speaks" (Heb. 11:4).

In the same way, Cain hated his brother Able for his faith in God and righteous deeds. John says, "Do not be surprised, brothers, that the world hates you" (1 Jn. 3:14). The world hates God's children, the true church, because the world has the "seed of Satan," contrary to "God's seed" (1 Jn. 3:9). John's statement regarding the world hating the true church is probably drawn from his gospel, chapter fifteen (Jn. 15:1-25). The passage is broken up into three parts, 1). Abiding in Christ (Jn. 15:1-8); 2). Loving one another (Jn. 15:12-17); and 3). The hatred of the world towards God's children (Jn. 15:18-25). Because the world hates God's children, those abiding in Christ can expect trouble in this life (Jn. 16:32-33).

The trial John's readers face in his first letter comes from the Gnostics, who were once among them (1 Jn. 2:19, 4:1). Those whom the Gnostics are not able to deceive (1 Jn. 2:26, 3:7), they hate (1 Jn. 3:13). Remember, the Gnostics have the same spirit as the antichrist (1 Jn. 2:18-19, 4:1-3), and will therefore act similarly (cf. Rev. 13:6, 10, 15). Those with the antichrist spirit "Are from the world; therefore, they speak from the world, and the world listens to them" (1 Jn. 4:5). John's statement (1 Jn. 4:5) equips the child of God, providing evidence of whether a 'church' is of God, or not, by comparing what the world loves or hates. If the world loves the church, there is a high level of confidence that that church does not belong to God. Joel Osteen, for example, is said to be voted by the world America's most popular preacher. Such endorsements come from Oprah Winfrey, who also said, "There cannot possibly be just one way to God." Oprah also came out of the church and now claims to be a spiritual person. While Joel appears to be very loving, not wanting to condemn anyone, he sits on the fence on critical doctrines, such as sin, judgement, and hell, to name a few, which is one of the reasons the world loves him.

The reason for mentioning Osteen is to show that an appearance of love may not qualify to be the same as what John has in mind. Remember, the Gnostic claimed to be in fellowship with God, yet are from the world, and the world listens to them (1 Jn. 4:5). The world's hatred primarily comes from the false teachers, as it did for Jesus. Remember, the religious Pharisees were the ones who called for Christ to be crucified, not Rome (Matt. 27:24-25).

Another reason the world hates the children of God is that they have passed out of death into life because [they] love the brothers (1 Jn. 3:14a). In the book of Revelation, chapter thirteen, John sees the coming antichrist cursing God, and those dwelling with Him in heaven (Rev. 13:6), revealing his hatred for both. The saints dwelling with God have passed from death to life. The occurrence commenced this side of eternity as a process of sanctification, which leads to eternal life (Jude 21). Those alone who (have ongoing) love for their brothers have the hope of eternal life. However, "Whoever does not love abides in death" (1 Jn. 3:14b). As mentioned above, John adds, "Everyone who hates his brother is a murderer, and you know that no murderer has eternal life abiding in him" (1 Jn 3:15). Again, John has in mind the future judgement of God that hangs over the necks of the Gnostics, like a guillotine, ready to fall (1 Jn. 3:14b).

The phrase "Passed from life to death" is also seen in John's gospel (Jn. 5:24), referring to escaping God's judgement. John mentions something similar further along in his first letter, saying, "We may have confidence for the day of judgement, because as He is, so are we in this world" (1 Jn. 4:17). We are as Jesus is, due to receiving His finished work on the cross, through that redemptive work. Anyone who believes (with active and ongoing obedience) on Him has the confidence of eternal life. John's statement does not mean that Christians are the same as Jesus, being 'little gods' as some charismatics teach, but instead, they have His Spirit and, therefore, eternal life abiding in them, even while in this world.

Being "As He is" requires the believer to do what He did. As Christ laid down His life for the church, the church is expected to do the same for Him and one another (1 Jn. 3:16). Here, John probably draws from chapter ten of his gospel (Jn. 10:1-18), where Jesus said, He was the (only) door, and that if anyone enters by Him, that person will be saved (Jn. 10:9). John adds that Jesus is the Good Shephard who lays down His life for the sheep (Jn. 10:11, 15, 17, 18), making a comparison with the hired hands who only seek to serve themselves (Jn. 10:12-13). As mentioned above, anyone confessing Christ has eternal life. Jesus said, "My sheep hear My voice, and I know them, and they follow Me. I give them eternal life, and they will never perish, and no one will snatch them out of My hand" (Jn. 10:27-28). No one abiding can be snatched away from Jesus; however, the once-abiding believer can depart.

As mentioned above, as Christ laid down His life for the church, the church is expected to do the same for Him and one another (1 Jn. 3:16-18, Jn. 15:12-14). Specifically, John is referring to material needs, being worldly possessions (1 Jn. 3:17-18), which is again why John says, "Do not love the world or the things of the world" (1 Jn. 2:18). In other words, do not pursue the world, or withhold the things of the world from others in need (1 Jn. 3:17). John adds, concerning the one who does not have pity, therefore, does not help a brother in need, "How does God's love abide in him?" (1 Jn. 3:17). Said another way: anyone withholding from another in need, cannot claim to be abiding in the love of God.

The one denying their brother's needs (1 Jn. 3:17) is contextually linked to the one hating their brother (1 Jn. 3:15, cf. 4:20). God loves and pity's His children; the same should be seen in those confessing to know Him.

Verses nineteen to twenty are the main verses within the passage, within the somewhat creative chiastic structure, as per the following:

A - Love one another (1 John 3:11)
    B - Obey God's commands (1 John 3:12)
        C - Practice righteousness (1 John 3:13-14)
            D - Be not deceived by false prophets (1 John 3:15)
                E - Love for others demonstrated by having a pure heart before God (1 John 3:19-20)
            D' - Be not deceived by false prophets (1 John 3:21-22)
        C' - Practice righteousness (1 John 3:23)
    B' - Obey God's commands (1 John 3:24)
A' - Love one another (1 John 3:16)

At first glance, verses nineteen to twenty (1 Jn. 3:19-20) do not fit within the passage. On each side of verses nineteen to twenty, John focuses on love (1 Jn. 3:11-18 & 3:23-34), expressed outwardly, yet within the passage, there are two seemingly, obscure verses (1 Jn. 3:19-20), focusing on the heart, or inner conscious. The immediate connection is with the words "By this, we shall know" (1 Jn. 3:19).

As mentioned above, John has already used this phrase three times (1 Jn. 2:3, 5, 3:16), and on each occasion, he talks of love. John now connects the believers with their love for God and one another, which is related to their sacrifice and generosity (1 Jn. 3:17). In the previous verses (1 Jn. 3:17-18), John instructs his readers not to withhold from others who are in need. James says something similar, "If a brother or sister is poorly clothed and lacking in daily food, and one of you says to them, "Go in peace, be warmed, and filled," without giving them the things needed for the body, what good is that?" (Jam. 2:15-16, cf. Deut. 15:7-9).

John's readers will know they are in the truth when their hearts and words are actively aligned. Not only do genuine believers meet the needs of others when made known, but they look for needs to be met. The kind of love John is talking about is active and on display; however, not in the same way as the Pharisees, who announced every good work. Jesus said, "Thus when you give to the needy, sound no trumpet before you, as the hypocrites do in the synagogues and in the streets, that they may be praised by others. Truly, I say to you, they have received their reward" (Matt. 6:2). Today's equivalent would be taking a selfie when doing something good and posting it on a social media page. The person who promotes themselves with every good work has the wrong motive; therefore, their heart is not right before God. The heart must be guarded against improper motives and hard-heartedness.

If a child of God refuses to meet a legitimate need, their hearts will condemn them, and their stinginess will not go unnoticed by God (1 Jn. 3:20). However, "God is greater than our hearts" (1 Jn. 3:20b), meaning that He will override His children's natural stinginess, prompting them to act; this is how they shall know they are of the truth, having reassured hearts before

God (1 Jn. 3:19). Those having pure, uncondemned hearts, will also have their prayers answered (1 Jn. 3:21-22).

God answers the prayers of those who meet the needs of others. The reverse is also true. An example of this is when I would provide financial support to another brother when asked. Every time a request was made, it was met, until one day when that brother did not meet the needs of another within his Christian community. From that time onwards, I no longer met his needs but instead supported the one he did not. My love for that brother never changed; however, my response to his request did.

John continues his address to the church with the word, "Beloved" (1 Jn. 3:21). John uses this word six times (1 Jn. 2:7, 3:2, 21, 4:1, 7, 11), again, clearing up any confusion as to whom he is writing the letter. Those within the church, who have uncondemned hearts, not only have the confidence of their right standing before God, through Christ Jesus (1 Jn. 3:21) but also have confidence that God will hear and answer their prayers (1 Jn. 3:22). Once again, verses twenty-one and twenty-two (1 Jn. 3:21-22) are conditional statements. Said in reverse, if anyone's heart condemns them, they will not have confidence before God, nor in their prayers. The lack of confidence should remind the reader of a previous statement, "Abide in Him, so that when He appears we may have confidence and not shrink from Him in shame at His coming" (1 Jn. 2:28). As with verses twenty-one and twenty-two (1 Jn. 3:21-22), verse twenty-eight (1 Jn. 2:28) is conditional. Only those who abide will have confidence on His appearing, and the rest will shrink back in shame.

While the previous reference of having confidence relates to a future event, being Christ's return (1 Jn. 2:29, 3:2), John's following reference relates to the time in between. On this side of Christ's return, leading up to that event, the beloved can expect God to hear them and answer their prayers. Again, the phrase, "Whatever we ask we receive from Him because we keep His commandments and do what pleases Him" (1 Jn. 3:22), is conditional. Only those who keep the commandments of God can expect Him to answer their prayers. John repeats this statement in chapter five of his first letter (1 Jn. 5:15). However, the original is found in his gospel (Jn. 14:13-14, 15:7, 16).

As you can imagine, the promise of God doing whatever the believer asks in Jesus' name has been misused and abused by the Word of Faith Movement, which claims that God will give them whatever they desire whenever they ask. Scripture makes no such promise but instead says God will grant whatever is within His will (1 Jn. 5:14). Again, charismatics falsely claim that it is God's will for every Christian to be healthy, wealthy, and happy, overlooking that Jesus said the world would hate His followers (Jn. 15:18-27, 1 Jn. 3:13), and in this world, His followers will have trouble (Jn. 16:32-33).

Additional references regarding prayer are found in Matthew and Mark's gospels. In the gospel, according to Matthew, Jesus said, "Ask, and it will be given to you" (Matt. 7:7), following the Lord's prayer (Matt. 6:9-15). And again, in Mark's gospel, Jesus said, "Truly, I say to you, whoever says to this mountain, 'Be taken up and thrown into the sea,' and does not doubt in his heart, but believes that what he says will come to pass, it will be done for him. Therefore, I tell you, whatever you ask in prayer, believe that you have received it, and it will be yours" (Mk. 11:23-24). The account recorded in Mark's gospel is a favourite with charismatics, who claim they can cast a literal mountain into the sea if they have enough faith. The application is also seen where some attempt, and fail, to have power over storms and "Blow COVID away."

Charismatics major in misinterpreting the Bible due to ignoring context. The account in Mark's gospel relates to the cursing of the fig tree (Mk. 11:12-14, 20-25), which incorporates verses twenty-three and twenty-four (Mk. 11:23-24). The reason Jesus cursed the fig tree was because of its fruitlessness. While the tree looked healthy, it was barren, symbolising Israel. Churches and confessing Christians can be the same, appearing healthy (lots of leaves, being programmes and good works) at first glance, yet fruitless. In context, the "Mountain" is Israel's unbelief, unfaithfulness, and fruitlessness. Hence, perhaps Jesus was saying to His disciples, who were going into the world to proclaim His name, "Say" to those mountains of unbelief and fruitlessness be removed, even cast into the sea (Mk. 11:23). And "Ask" that God would do it for you (Mk. 11:24). Interpretations vary, nevertheless, the contextual application is a far cry from anything the charismatics claim, whether it be a literal mountain or a symbolic one, it is never a mountain of debt being taken up and thrown into the sea, or something else along those self-serving lines.

As with Mark's account (Mk. 11:23-34), John's reference to "Asking and receiving" is contextually bound. It does not suggest that believers have a license to "Command God" as the charismatics do. The statement is not an open cheque book, assuring the believer, "Whatever they ask, they receive from Jesus" (1 Jn. 3:22). In context, the statement refers to the confidence God's children have in God, His Love, mercy, and kindness (1 Jn. 3:1-2, 16), for the one striving to please Him (1 Jn. 3:22b). Chapter five (1 Jn. 5:14-15) provides more, saying, "If we ask anything according to His will, He hears us" (1 Jn. 5:14). The critical words are "According to His will." Therefore, the conditions for prayers being answered and desires received are obedience and the request being in accordance with Jesus' will.

Interestingly, within the chiastic structure, D warns against false teachers (1 Jn. 3:15), as does D' (1 Jn. 3:21-22), indirectly, when considering those who claim that God says His children can command and demand anything, and God must do it. Remember, John is counterarguing the false teachers who misrepresent God by twisting scripture.

The way charismatics treat God and handle scripture is very concerning, based on Paul's warning, found in the second letter to Timothy. Paul says, "But understand this, that in the last days there will come times of difficulty.

For people will be lovers of self, lovers of money, proud, arrogant, abusive, disobedient to their parents, ungrateful, unholy, heartless, unappeasable, slanderous, without self-control, brutal, not loving good, treacherous, reckless, swollen with conceit, lovers of pleasure rather than lovers of God, having the appearance of godliness, but denying its power. Avoid such people" (2 Tim. 3:1-5). Paul's warning is aimed at the church, in the last days, who are predicted to be lovers of money, proud and arrogant, having an appearance of godliness, etc. Commanding of God, the way Word of Faith members does, fits Paul's predicted description of the church in the end times.

John wraps the section up (1 Jn. 3:23-24) in the same way he commenced "Love one another" and "Obey God's commands." Those who do, they alone can have confidence in salvation and answered prayer. The chiastic point is: How the child of God treats others is how God will treat them. As the beloved gives to others when asked, God will also give to them. When the child of God withholds, the Holy Spirit will convict them, "By this, we know that He (Christ) abides in us, by the Spirit whom He has given us" (1 Jn. 3:24). The abiding Spirit is the evidence that a person has Christ, in whom they say that they believe (1 Jn. 3:23). If the Spirit does not convict, when in sin, that in itself is evidence that Jesus does not abide in that person. "This is how we know" (1 Jn. 3:16-17, 19, 24).

While some say that they "Believe in the name of the Son Jesus Christ" (1 Jn. 3:23), their lack of love for others disqualifies them from truly "Knowing" (experiencing) Him. John points to the command that a person must "Believe" to have eternal life. The command is active and includes action. Belief without action (fruit) is the same as the cursed fig tree bearing no fruit. The expected fruit, contextually, is love (1 Jn. 3:11-24). Therefore, "Whoever keeps His commandments (of love) abides in Him and He in them." Once more, the statement is conditional. God continues to abide in the abiding, obedient believer. The reverse is also true.

In conclusion, as with the previous section, John is marking those who belong to God and those who do not by focusing on love. If the confessing Christian truly is of God, the fruit of love will be evident in their life. As Jesus laid down His life for others (1 Jn. 3:16), His disciples will lay down their lives also, which includes material goods (1 Jn. 3:17). The laying down of materialism proves that a person loves God more than the world (1 Jn. 2:15).

CHAPTER 9
Test the Spirits

Every Spirit that does not Confess Jesus is Not from God

John focuses on how "We know that we are in the truth" (1 Jn. 3:19) and that "The Spirit abides in us" in the preceding verse (1 Jn. 3:24). If someone in Christ fails to provide for his or her Christian sibling when asked and able to do so, their hearts will condemn them (1 Jn. 3:17, 20), and the Spirit will convict them (1 Jn 3:24), "This is how we know Christ abides in us." The opposite is also true; if we lack conviction, we can clearly see that Christ does not reside within us.

While many claim to be in fellowship with God, not all are (1 Jn. 1:6), and not all remain of those who were once in fellowship with God (1 Jn. 2:24). Remember, the Gnostic came out of the church (2 Jn. 2:18, 4:1), once confessing Christ, and now denying Him (1 Jn. 4:3). The false prophets continue to associate themselves with the church while denying the deity of Christ (1 Pet. 2:1, Jude 4, 1 Jn. 2:2), the Trinity (cf. Matt. 3:16-17, 2 Cor. 3:14, 1 Jn. 5:7), and His return in the flesh (2 Jn. 7); all of which reject that salvation is through Jesus Christ, alone (Jn. 14:6, Acts 4:12). Peter says, "But false prophets also arose among the people, just as there will be false teachers among you, who will secretly bring in destructive heresies, even denying the Master who bought them, bringing upon themselves swift destruction" (2 Pet. 2:1).

The false doctrines as mentioned above are "Doctrines of demons" and are predicted to increase in the latter times, causing some to depart from the faith (1 Tim. 4:1). Elsewhere, Paul said a significant end time sign is the great falling away from sound biblical doctrine (2 Thess. 2:3, 2 Tim. 4:3). Jesus also said, the number one sign of the end times is deception (Matt. 24:5, 11, 23-26). The danger is the deceived remain within the church (cf. Matt. 7:15, Acts 20:29-30) and on the fringe, seeking to draw others away (1 Jn. 2:26, 3:7, 2 Jn. 7). Both Peter and Jude state that the false teachers are even at the love feast, blemishing/defiling and shipwrecking some (1 Pet. 2:13, Jude 12). For this reason, John says, "Test the spirits" (1 Jn. 4:1).

Once more, John commences this section of his letter (1 Jn. 4:1-6) with the word "Beloved" or "Dear friends," again confirming to whom the letter is written - the church. As said several times, anyone claiming that John is writing to the world, suggesting that those in Christ no longer need to repent (1 Jn. 1:9), could not possibly have read the letter. Those holding to that position are closely aligned with the Gnostics, who say they have not sinned (1 Jn. 8, 10).

John's "Beloved" is the beloved of God who is told to "Test the spirits to see whether they are from God" (1 Jn. 4:1b). Leading into this statement, John first says, "Do not believe every spirit" (1 Jn. 4:1a). In sum, not everyone claiming to be a Christian actually is, therefore not everyone claiming to speak for God, does, hence, "Many false prophets have gone into the world" (1 Jn. 4:1c), these are those with the "Spirit of the antichrist" (1 Jn. 4:3b, 2:18-19).

First and foremost, the spirit of the antichrist rejects the deity of Jesus Christ; therefore, John instructs the beloved to test anyone claiming to be in fellowship with God by asking them, "Who do you say Jesus is?" This is the litmus test; if anyone does not confess Jesus is from God - they have the spirit of the antichrist (1 Jn. 4:3b). John continues by saying, "By this, you know the Spirit of God" (1 Jn. 4:2a). John provides two conclusions to the question: "Who do you say Jesus is?" The first: "Every spirit that confesses that Jesus Christ has come in the flesh is from God" (1 Jn. 4:2b). The second: "Every spirit that does not confess Jesus is not from God" (1 Jn. 4:3a).

The "spirit" refers to people's inner being, claiming to know and be in fellowship with God. In context, it does not refer to demons, as some suggest, thereby 'demanding them to confess Christ' during exorcisms. The "spirit" denying that Jesus Christ came in the flesh the first time (1 Jn. 4:2b, cf. 3:5, 8) also rejects that He will return in the flesh (2 Jn. 7). The first statement has the second in mind (cf. 1 Jn. 28-29, 3:2, 2 Jn. 7). By denying Christ's first appearing, they also reject the work of the cross, and future judgement (cf. 2 Pet. 3:3, Jude 18). Anyone denying the appearance and deity of Christ and His return cannot claim to know God, for they have "The spirit of error" (1 Jn. 4:6) and "The spirit of the antichrist" (1 Jn. 4:3b). They must be tested, accepted, or rejected based on their confession.

In the same way, followers of Christ are to test the spirits; God will also test them. Deuteronomy, chapter thirteen, provides such a test, saying: "If a prophet or a dreamer of dreams arises among you and gives you a sign or a wonder, and the sign or wonder that he tells you comes to pass, and if he says, 'Let us go after other gods,' which you have not known, 'and let us serve them,' you shall not listen to the words of that prophet or that dreamer of dreams. For the Lord your God is testing you, to know whether you love the Lord your God with all your heart and with all your soul. You shall walk after the Lord your God and fear him and keep his commandments and obey His voice, and you shall serve Him and hold fast to Him. But that prophet or that dreamer of dreams shall be put to death because he has taught rebellion against the Lord your God, who brought you out of the land of Egypt and redeemed you out of the house of slavery, to make you leave the way in which the Lord your God commanded you to walk. So, you shall purge the evil from your midst. "If your brother, the son of your mother, or your son or your daughter or the wife you embrace[or your friend who is as your own soul entices you secretly, saying, 'Let us go and serve other gods,' which neither you nor your fathers have known, some of the gods of the peoples who are around you, whether near you or far off from you, from the one end of the earth to the other, you shall not yield to him or listen to him, nor shall your eye pity him, nor shall you spare him, nor shall you conceal him. But you shall kill him. Your hand shall be first against him to put him to death, and afterward the hand of all the people. You shall stone him to death with stones because he sought to draw you away from the Lord your God, who brought you out of the land of Egypt, out of the house of slavery. And all Israel shall hear and fear and never again do any such wickedness as this among you" (Deut. 13:1-11).

The Deuteronomy passage reveals the seriousness of the matter, whereas even if a family member attempts to entice someone away from God, it will be at the cost of their lives. The false prophets claimed to be in the family of God yet were set on enticing those with unsteady souls away from the truth (2 Pet. 2:14), using false words (2 Pet. 2:3), promising false freedom (2 Pet. 2:19). Moses warns, even if a false prophet operates in signs and wonders (Deut. 13:1-2), yet denies God, do not follow him.

False signs and wonders are also significant end-time signs leading many astray (Matt. 24:24, Mk. 13:22, 2 Thess. 2:9, Rev. 13:13, 16:14). During the tribulation, the antichrist will operate with lying signs and wonders (2 Thess. 2:9, Rev. 13:13), and demons will also (Rev. 16:14). Those with an antichrist spirit will do the same (Matt. 24:24, Mk. 13:22) leading up to the tribulation, and throughout, preparing and conditioning their victims for the antichrist to come. Those with the spirit of the antichrist are already operating in the church (1 Jn. 2:18-19, 4:1) and the world (1 Jn. 4:5). The evidence for the spirit of the antichrist being in the church is that John thought he was living in the "Last hour" (1 Jn. 2:18). John says, "The spirit which you heard was coming, and now is in the world already" (1 Jn. 4:3). The antichrist presented a threat to the early church, as it does the modern one; however, more so in the latter due to the limited time remaining.

Following the warning, again, John addresses his reader as "Little children" (1 Jn. 4:4), succeeding the initial address using the word "Beloved" (1 Jn. 4:1). Again, seven times, John uses the phrase "Little children" (1 Jn. 2:1, 12, 28, 3:7, 18, 4:4, 5:21). Thirteen times, John uses the word "Children," and six times the word "Beloved" (1 Jn. 2:7, 3:2, 21, 4:1, 7, 11). As mentioned earlier, and several times before, there is no mistaking to whom John is writing the letter.

John uses the intimate address to remind the readers of what they already know (cf. 1 Jn. 2:21); "[They] are from God" (1 Jn. 4:4). John's readers are from God due to overcoming the false prophets, the spirit of the antichrist (1 Jn. 4:4b, 2:13b, 14b), who is still trying to deceive them (1 Jn. 2:26, 3:7). John's readers have overcome, and continue to overcome the evil one through tribulation, as Jesus did (Jn. 16:33). They have overcome by abiding in the original teaching, by remaining in fellowship with the apostles. They have overcome by confessing Christ and their sins and by walking in God's light (truth) and love. However, it is not by their efforts alone that they have overcome, but by the strength of the "Greater One" within (1 Jn. 4:4b). Remember, Jesus came "To destroy the works (ongoing) of the devil" (1 Jn. 3:8). The indwelling Spirit (1 Jn. 3:24) continues the work Christ began (Phil. 1:6).

Worth mentioning here is that 1 John 4:4b is a verse well known to charismatics. They often quote the verse in prayer when attempting to overcome, and rule over the devil, sometimes cursing and even 'binding' him, which should never be done (cf. Jude 8-10). They also quote the verse in positive affirmation when wanting to overcome worldly opposition, and they have the verse printed on cups, t-shirts, hats, flags, and banners. Unsurprisingly, the contextual meaning has nothing to do with what charismatics claim. The verse has nothing to do with binding the devil, overcoming physical or verbal opposition, or securing and preserving success. Instead, as mentioned above, the implied meaning is that the beloved (1 Jn. 4:4a) has overcome deception, namely, false doctrine, the spirit of the antichrist, and Satan (the evil one) himself.

There is a great danger in liberal preaching, for John says, those who abandon, and twist God's truth, are of this world (1 Jn. 4:5). The correlation is seen in chapter two (1 Jn. 2:15-17). Verse five, "We are from God" (1 Jn. 4:5), is the defining verse between God's children and those who are not. The evidence of who belongs to God and do not is in "Knowing and listening to (keeping, preserving) the truth" (1 Jn. 4:6b). The opposite is pointed out in the latter part of the verse, "Whoever is not from God does not listen to us" (1 Jn. 4:6c), which is why they are not in fellowship with us (the apostles), and therefore not in fellowship with God" (1 Jn. 1:6, paraphrased).

Those who listen to God, and keep His commands, abide in Him, and His Spirit abides in them. The abiding Spirit is "Greater" than the one (false teachers, antichrist, Satan) who is in the world (1 Jn. 4:4b). The Holy Spirit secures the believer against the spirit of the antichrist. While the spirit of the antichrist is strong, there is no greater power than God. The importance of abiding, therefore, is twofold, 1). To remain secure in Christ, 2). Thereby, remaining to have ongoing protection against deception ("The ongoing works of the devil"). Anyone outside of Christ is without protection against deception; hence "The god of this world has blinded the minds of unbelievers" (2 Cor. 4:4).

Because they (the false prophets) are from the world (1 Jn. 4:5a), their minds are blinded by the god of this world (2 Cor. 4:4), ç As mentioned in the previous section, another indicator of who belongs to whom is, who is listening. If the world is listening and celebrating a church or 'preacher,' then that is evidence that they are not listening to God or are of Him. Instead of representing God, and proclaiming His message, from the beginning, the false prophets speak from a worldly viewpoint. Their belief that Jesus Christ comes from the god of this world (Satan) makes them, in fact, his ministers (2 Cor. 11:13-15).

In contrast to those who are from the world, John affirms his reader by saying, "You are from God" (1 Jn. 4:4), and then, "We are from God" (1 Jn. 4:6). On both accounts, John says, we are not from the world! God's children listen to God, and His messengers, the apostles, while the children of the devil listen to Satan and his messengers. Therefore, the obvious question should be: What are you listening to? Who are you listening to? And where does the message originate from? Those who know God will listen to those from God (the apostles, scripture). Those who do not know God will not listen to God's ministers and messengers but instead, they listen to worldly 'preachers' otherwise known as false teachers and prophets (1 Jn. 4:6). No matter how well the minister of God presents the gospel, the world will not listen to him, in the same way, they did not listen to Jesus, even though Jesus ran rings around the best preachers of the day, the scribes, and Pharisees.

As the passage starts, it ends, "By this, we know" (1 Jn. 4:2, & 6), providing a clue of the chiastic structure. The chiastic arrangement of the passage (1 Jn. 4:1-6) is as follows:

A. Beloved do not believe every spirit but test the spirits to see whether they are from God, for many false prophets have gone out into the world. (1 Jn. 4:1)
> B. By this, you know the Spirit of God: every spirit that confesses that Jesus Christ has come in the flesh is from God (1 Jn. 4:2)
>> C. and every spirit that does not confess Jesus is not from God. This is the spirit of the antichrist, which you heard was coming and now is in the world already. (1 Jn. 4:3)

C'. Whoever is not from God does not listen to us. By this, we know the Spirit of truth and the spirit of error. (1 Jn. 4:6)

B'. Little children, you are from God and have overcome them, for he who is in you is greater than he who is in the world. (1 Jn. 4:4)

A'. They are from the world; therefore, they speak from the world, and the world listens to them. (1 Jn. 4:5)

In this chiasm, John instructs the church to "Test the spirits," saying, "By this, we know" whether they are from God. The test is through their confession regarding Jesus Christ. Whoever cannot testify that Jesus Christ came in the flesh, and will also return in the flesh, does not have Him. Whoever does testify correctly regarding Jesus Christ has Him and, thereby, has overcome the spirit of the world proclaimed through the false prophets. John's readers can know which spirit/Spirit they are listening to by comparing the message to the original, "What they have heard from the beginning" (1 Jn. 1:1, 2:7, 24, 3:11).

In conclusion, the contrast between God's children and the devils is once more the critical point of this section. Twice more within the passage (1 Jn. 4:1-6), the words, "By this, you/we know," are seen (1 Jn. 4:2, 6), relating to confession and listening. Nine times John uses the phrase (1 Jn. 2:3, 5, 16, 19, 24, 4:2, 6, 13, 5:2). The fundamental way a believer knows they belong to God is by abiding in the original message, relating to light (truth), love, and life, through Christ, alone.

CHAPTER 10
God is Love

Perfect Love Drives out Fear

Leading into this section (1 Jn. 4:7-21), John warns about those who have the spirit of the antichrist (1 Jn. 4:3) and, therefore, the spirit of error (1 Jn. 4:6). These are the same who love the world and its goods (1 Jn. 2:15-17) moreover their 'brother,' who is in need (1 Jn. 3:17). While withholding, they are without conviction (1 Jn. 3:20), because they are without the Spirit of God (Rom. 8:9b, Jude 19). They are, in fact, an enemy of God (Jam. 4:4) because they love the world and the things of it (1 Jn. 4:15). They speak from the world, and the world listens to them and loves them back (1 Jn. 4:5).

As seen in the previous section, the critical point was to warn that not everyone who claims to know God actually does:

> C. And every spirit that does not confess Jesus is not from God. This is the spirit of the antichrist, which you heard was coming and now is in the world already. (1 Jn. 4:3)
> C.' Whoever is not from God does not listen to us. By this, we know the Spirit of truth and the spirit of error. (1 Jn. 4:6)

Therefore, John instructs his reader to "Test the Spirit" (1 Jn. 4:1) by asking them, "Who do you say Jesus Christ is?" This is the litmus test, the fastest, most straightforward, and cleanest way to determine whether a confessing Christian is born of God. Remember, John majors on this critical point: Who is of God, and who is not. Five times John writes the words, "Born of God" (1 Jn. 3:9, 4:7, 5:1, 4, 18), which is conditional, based on abiding in the original message of "Light" (truth) and "Love." Only those who remain inherit eternal life. Six times John writes the words, "Eternal Life" (1 Jn. 1:2, 2:25, 3:15, 5:11, 13, 20).

Twice, John says, "I write these things to you" (1 Jn. 2:26, 5:20), warning about deceivers (1 Jn. 2:26) and encouraging the beloved that they have eternal life, "I write these things to you who believe in the name of the Son of God, that you may know that you have eternal life" (1 Jn. 5:20). Nine times, John says, "This is how you/we know" that you/we have God, and therefore eternal life. Only those abiding in Christ have eternal life and will have no fear on the day of Judgement (1 Jn. 4:17).

Like the previous section, verses seven to twenty-one (1 Jn. 4:7-21) contain a chiastic structure. Remember, the chiastic form is a literary device in which the author arranges his words, phrases, or ideas in a symmetrical pattern, with the main point of view in the centre. In this section (1 John 4:7-21), John uses a chiastic structure to reinforce the main point of the passage, which is the perfect love of God that drives out fear (1 Jn. 4:17). The passage can be broken down into the following:

A. Introduction (4:7-8)
    B. Love comes from God (4:9-10)
        C. God is love (4:11-12)
            D. Believing in the love of God (4:13-16)
                E. Loving one another (4:17-18)
                    F. Perfect love drives out fear (4:18)

> E' Loving one another (4:19-20)
> D' Believing in the love of God (4:21)
> C' God is love (4:8)
> B' Love comes from God (4:7)
> A' Conclusion (4:21)

The passage starts and ends with the conclusion that God is love and that love comes from God. The passage also emphasises the importance of believing in the love of God and loving one another and how perfect love drives out fear. Essentially, this passage returns to one previous (1 Jn. 3:11-24) after straying to the last (1 Jn. 4:1-6).

Again, John commences by addressing his audience as "Dear Friends" (1 Jn. 4:7), repeating his instruction to "Love one another" (1 Jn. 3:11, 23, 4:7). Twice more in this section, John will instruct the church to love one another (1 Jn. 4:11, 12). Verse twelve is conditional, stating that "If we love one another, [then] God abides in us and His perfected love in us" (1 Jn. 4:12). The word "Perfected" refers to completion and is connected to the critical verse of the passage, regarding judgement (1 Jn. 4:17).

As mentioned above, John distinguishes between those who are "Born of God" and those who are not. In the previous section (1 Jn. 3:11-24), John states that those who have the Spirit belong to God (1 Jn. 3:24). One of the ways a person can know whether they have the Holy Spirit is through conviction (1 Jn. 3:20). In this section, John continues, providing more evidence of whether someone is born of God by saying, "Whoever loves has been born of God, and knows God" (1 Jn. 4:7). Verse eight is the reverse (1 Jn. 4:8), "This is how we know." A person lacking love also lacks knowledge, regardless of their claims. The Gnostics claimed to have superior knowledge yet were ignorant of the truth about God, "The truth was not in [them]" (1 Jn. 1:8, 2:4).

The "Love of God" (1 Jn. 4:7) is only known by those born of Him. The statement is repeated in reverse in the following verse, "God is Love" (1 Jn. 4:8) and explained in the next verses (1 Jn. 4:9-10, 14), expanding on those previous (1 Jn. 2:2, 3:5, 8, 16). Essentially, John's statement regarding God's love points to the saving work of Christ through the cross. Through the cross, Jesus atoned for the sin of humanity (1 Jn. 4:10), that is, for the whole world (1 Jn. 2:2, 4:9, 14).

While God sent Jesus to atone for the sins of the whole world, John narrows in on those who have received Him, with the words, "Among us" (1 Jn. 4:9a), who "Might live through Him" (1 Jn. 4:9b). Living through Christ applies to eternal life by walking in the light (truth), practicing righteousness (1 Jn. 3:7), and walking in love (1 Jn. 3:16, 4:7). These things lead to eternal life (1 Jn. 5:11, 13, 20, cf. Jude 21). However, no matter how well anyone does with the conditions mentioned above leading to eternal life, without Jesus, none qualify. Indeed, John takes it a step further, saying, "Not that we loved God, but He loved us" (1 Jn. 4:10). The statement implies that none were even looking to God, never mind living for and through Him (cf. Rom. 3:9-18, cf. Ps. 53:1-3). Paul provides more on the subject in his letters to the church of Rome, saying, "For while we were still weak, at the right time, Christ died for the ungodly. For one will scarcely die for a righteous person—though perhaps for a good person, one would dare even to die— but God shows His love for us in that while we were still sinners, Christ died for us. Since, therefore, we have now been justified by His blood, much more shall we be saved by Him from the wrath of God. For if while we were enemies, we were reconciled to God by the death of His Son, much more, now that we are reconciled, shall we be saved by His life" (Rom. 5:6-10).

Paul, like John, narrows in on being saved through Christ's life; therefore, the believer is to "Live through Him" (1 Jn. 4:9), leading to eternal life. Both Paul and John focus on judgement. Paul says that God, through His Son, has "Saved [the beloved] from the wrath to come" Rom. 5:10), while John says that the beloved "May have confidence on the day of judgement" (1 Jn. 4:17). On both counts, Jesus came to secure eternal life for all who confess His name, snatching them out of hell's fire (Jude 23).

With the above revelation of God's love, John repeats verse seven (1 Jn. 4:7) in verse eleven (1 Jn. 4:11), each time starting with the word "Beloved," purposely exposing the loveless Gnostics. While they say they have fellowship with God (1 Jn. 1:6), the evidence is that they do not. Instead, they are compared to Cain, who hated his brother (1 Jn. 3:12). Contrary to the Gnostics, loving others in response to God's love is a sign that God lives within (1 Jn. 4:12b), albeit no one has ever seen Him (1 Jn. 4:12a). The love of God expressed to one another is evidence of the unseen God. John confirms this in verse twenty, saying, "If anyone says, 'I love God,' and hates his brother, he is a liar; for he who does not love his brother whom he has seen cannot love God whom he has not seen" (1 Jn. 4:20). As mentioned previously, loving one another is the old and new commandment (1 Jn. 2:7-8, 4:21). Anyone failing to keep the commandment, and yet confesses to know God, is a liar, and the truth is not in them (1 Jn. 2:4). The evidence of not keeping the commandment is to withhold from the requesting brother in need (1 Jn. 3:17).

On the one hand, John confirms that the Gnostics do not know or have God; on the other, he settles any doubts that the beloved might have for themselves. They have God! Verse thirteen confirms it, saying, "By this, we know that we abide in Him and He in us, because He has given us His Spirit" (1 Jn. 4:13, cf. 3:24). It is the Spirit within that convicts and counsels, contextually of Christ, and walking in love (1 Jn. 3:20), displayed through sacrifice (1 Jn. 3:17).

It is through the work of the Triune God that the beloved is perfected in their response to Him and through Him towards others. Four times John uses the word "Perfect" (1 Jn. 2:5, 4:12, 17, 18), meaning completed through an ongoing process of sanctification (separation from the world). The evidence of being separated from the world is seen through giving the things of the world up and sharing worldly possessions with others in need.

John's use of the word "Perfected" in verse twelve (1 Jn. 4:12) refers to the ongoing love walk; when and where love is evidence, it is also known "That we abide in Him and Him in us" (1 Jn. 4:13). However, the first and foremost evidence that a person has Christ is through their confession of Him (1 Jn. 4:2-3, 15), and of their sin (1 Jn. 1:9, 2:1-2). Again, good works without Christ amount to nothing.

Once more, John clearly informs his reader who has Christ and who does not. John goes to great lengths to qualify and disqualify anyone confessing to being in fellowship with God because the Gnostics have brought deceptive heresies into the church. The following chart provides self-checking evidence of who belongs to God. To simplify, those who confess Christ, hold fast to His Word (scripture), and walk in love towards others, have the Spirit and are born of God. Anyone who does not meet these criteria is not born of God and therefore does not have His Spirit.

This is how you/we know. Whoever:

Confesses Christ	Keeps His Word	Listens To the Apostles	Keeps His (love) Commandments	Loves Others	Has the Holy Spirit
1 Jn. 4:2	1 Jn. 2:5	1 Jn. 4:6	1 Jn 2:3	1 Jn. 3:16	1 Jn. 4:13
			1 Jn. 3:24	1 Jn 3:19	
			1 Jn. 5:2		

Upon confessing Christ, the believer has the Spirit, who teaches and enables that person to abide in the original word and to walk in love. The relationship takes two willing participants - God, who calls, and the believer, who answers that call, and God who seals, and the believer who remains. The partnership is revealed in verse fifteen, where John says, "God abides in him, and he in God" (1 Jn. 4:15). Verse sixteen also says, "Whoever abides in love abides in God, and God abides in him." It takes two willing participants to form the relationship and one to break it, just like any marriage. While only one remains committed to the relationship, and the other walks away, it ends in divorce. Remember, from the Greek word for "Apostasy" also comes "Writ of divorce." Only those who remain, remain to have the Spirit of truth, which continually testifies about Jesus Christ, resulting in eternal life.

Verse fourteen confirms that verse thirteen (1 Jn. 4:13) refers to the Spirit given to those who "Testify that the Father has sent His Son to be Savior of the world" (1 Jn. 4:14). The confessing, word, and commandment abiding believer can have confidence that the Spirit of truth remains within. Everyone else has the spirit of error (1 Jn. 4:6).

It is the Spirit of Truth who testifies of Jesus Christ: "Whoever confesses that Jesus is the Son of God, God abides in him, and he in God" (1 Jn. 4:15). The role of the Spirit is to testify about Christ (1 Jn. 4:14), to teach about Christ (1 Jn. 2:27), to reveal the love of God towards sinners (1 Jn. 2:2, 3:5, 16, 4:14), and to convict and strengthen the believer in Christ (1 Jn. 3:20). John repeats his opening statement (1 Jn. 1:1-3) in verse fourteen (1 Jn. 4:14), now including everyone who has confessed Christ, "The Savior of the world" (1 Jn. 4:14), that one also has the abiding Spirit.

The importance of the phrase "Savior of the world" points back to the cross and the need for continual repentance. The Gnostics said they had no sin (1 Jn. 1:8, 10) and therefore rejected the redeeming work of the cross. For this reason, they had no hope. Another critical point being made about the "Savior of the world" is the love of God: "God is love" (1 Jn. 4:16). Because of God's love for humanity, He sent Jesus to atone for sin (Jn. 3:16, 1 Jn. 3:16) to deliver humankind from His wrath (Rom. 5:9). Only those confessing and abiding in Christ can have the confidence to stand before God on the day of judgement (1 Jn. 4:17).

Slightly digressing, but worth mentioning is that in verse seventeen (1 Jn. 4:17) there is another well-known and misquoted verse by charismatics. As already stated, the passage is about "Love," mentioned an incredible twenty-seven times within the context of just fifteen verses (1 Jn. 4:7-21). Within John's first letter, twenty-six verses mention the word love; some verses contain the word multiple times. With that in mind, verse seventeen alludes to the return of Christ, as introduced in chapter two (1 Jn. 2:28). When Jesus returns, believers will be judged by their love, or lack of, for one another. On that day, where there is little love, there will be little confidence.

Another misquoted half verse is the latter part of seventeen (1 Jn. 4:17b). The expression, "As He is, also are we in this world," keeping with the context, can only suggest, "As He loved, so do/must we." The interpretation is far from what charismatics claim, known as the doctrine of "little gods". The application used with that ideology revolves around self-empowerment, gain, and divine identity. These things give the genuine believer no confidence on the day of judgement. The believer's confidence does not stem from worldly power, position, and possession but from love in and through Christ Jesus.

The Word of Faith doctrine of God's elect being "little gods" comes from Psalm eighty-two (Ps. 82:6) and John's gospel (Jn. 10:34). The confusion is with the Hebrew word "Elohim," correctly translated as "God/s." However, Asaph, the writer, is not saying humans are "gods," as the charismatics falsely claim, but rather, some live like gods, or can represent God. Therefore, living like gods is what Asaph is saying, and even then, even the most remarkable men still die (82:7) and are then judged by God (Ps. 82:8). As for representing God, Moses was said to have done that, but in no way does the Bible say that he was a god (Ex. 7:1). Jesus quotes Asaph (Ps. 82:6) when confronted by the Pharisees (Jn. 10:22-39). There, Jesus reminded them that God said men are gods (Jn. 10:34), referring to their status in the world. Jesus rebukes the Pharisees by saying, how much more may the One whom God has chosen and sent be called "God" if those who hold a position of divine appointment can be referred to as "gods?" (Jn. 10:34–36).

Another Psalm misquoted, claiming that humankind is referred to as "little gods," is written by David (Ps. 8), and is a prophecy of Jesus Christ. There, verses five and six (Ps. 8:5-6) have been misunderstood by charismatics claiming that God, through David, is saying His children are "little gods," stating that the Hebrew word "Elohim" refers to humanity. However, the book of Hebrews clears up any confusion, quoting David (Ps. 8:5, Heb. 2:6-8) when pointing to Jesus, the "Son of Man" (Ps. 8:4, Heb. 2:6), who "For a little while" He was made lower than the angels (Heb. 2:7). In verse nine, the Hebrews writer says, "But we see Him who for a little while was made lower than the angels, namely Jesus, crowned with glory and honor because of the suffering of death, so that by the grace of God He might taste death for everyone" (Heb. 2:9). The purpose for Jesus to become a little lower than angels for a little while is salvation. To claim that the mentioned verses (Ps. 8:5-6) refer to humanity is blasphemy. To support the allegation of blasphemy Kenneth Copeland openly says, "When I read in the Bible 'I AM,' I just smile and say, I am too." Copeland is joined by many other high-ranking Word of Faith 'ministers,' claiming the same.

Following is verse eighteen (1 Jn. 4:18), which is another misquoted half-verse within the charismatic camp: "Perfect love drives/casts out fear." Again, keeping within the context, the statement does not refer to everyday stresses of life, but rather being "Confident" on that day, of avoiding "Punishment." The fear of punishment comes from a lack of perfected love (1 Jn. 4:17) due to not abiding in Jesus (1 Jn. 4:16). When the believer is truly one with God, His love flows in the sense that the same sap flows through both the vine and the branch, as seen in John's gospel (Jn. 15:4-7). There, Jesus says that the one who abides in Him bears much fruit. That fruit is not so much souls as some teach; instead, it refers to the fruit of the Spirit, the first of which is "Love." Without love, no one will have confidence on the day of judgement

(1 Jn. 4:20). John wraps up this section of his letter with a command that defines the believer's love for God by their love for each other (1 Jn. 4:21).

Four times John uses the word "Confidence" (1 Jn. 2:18, 3:21, 4:17, 5:14). The first and third relates to standing before Jesus, the second refers to the heart, and the last to confidence in prayer, providing the heart is right with God. In the gospel of John, John records the words of Jesus regarding prayer, saying, "We know that God does not listen to sinners, but if anyone is a worshiper of God and does His will, God listens to him" (Jn. 9:31). Again, for this reason (Jn. 9:31), the Gnostics, and anyone who fellowship with them, are without hope.

If the believer has confidence now, due to their heart not condemning them (1 Jn. 3:21) and therefore, confidence that God hears their prayers (1 Jn. 5:14), they will also have confidence when standing before the judgement seat of Jesus Christ (2 Cor. 5:10, Rom. 14:10-12). Only those having confidence in Christ, not in themselves, will be without fear on that day.

Remember, God sent His Son Jesus to redeem humanity so that whoever confesses Him would escape the wrath to come. The wrath refers to both the tribulation (1 Thess. 5:9, Rev. 3:10, 14:10, 15:1, 7, 16:1, 19) and the concluding judgement (Rev. 6:16-17, 19:15). John's reference refers to the judgement seat of Jesus Christ (1 Jn. 4:17), being both the believer's judgement (2 Cor. 5:10) and the judgement of the wicked (Rev. 20:11-15). If anyone lacks confidence in Christ due to their confession or disobedience, the second judgement will be their experience. However, the tribulation will provide one last opportunity to remedy that. When Jesus appears for His bride (the church), removing her from the world before the wrath (tribulation), those failing to abide will "Shrink in shame" (1 Jn. 2:28). Following the rapture, they will have seven years, if they last that long, to repent, and restore their relationship with God, through His Son.

In the tribulation, the confession of Christ and sin is the starting point. Loving one another then flows from true repentance, for John says, "If anyone says, "I love God," yet hates his brother, he is a liar." Remember this theme, which repeatedly reoccurs throughout the letter (1 Jn. 2:9–11; 3:11–24, 4:7–21, 5:2). In the gospel, according to Matthew, Jesus taught on the final judgement of the sheep and the goats (Matt. 25:31-46). The parable refers to those "Left behind" to endure the tribulation. During that time of difficulty, the sheep were those who loved Jesus' brothers (the Jews), while the goats were those who confessed Christ but neglected the Jews in the time of trouble.

How the confessing followers of Christ treated the Jews is likened to their treatment of Jesus: "Whoever loves God must also love his brother" (1 Jn. 4:21). John's gospel states the same, "By this, all people will know that you are My disciples if you have love for one another" (Jn. 13:35). Once more, sacrificial love is the theme and requirement to stand confidently, and without fear before Jesus on the day of judgement, because "Perfect love drives out fear" (1 Jn. 4:17).

CHAPTER 11
Overcoming the World

Everyone who has Been Born of God Overcomes the World

In the previous section, it was stated that the critical point of the passage is "Perfect love drives out fear" (1 Jn. 4:17) and that perfect love is being perfected on this side of Christ's return. Perfect love is being perfected by the one actively responding to God's love while, at the same time, walking in love towards their siblings in Christ (1 Jn. 4:12). John sums up "The Love walk" with the words, "Live through Him" (1 Jn. 4:9). Living through Christ is explained in chapter three, "By this, we know love, that He laid down His life for us, and we ought to lay down our lives for the brothers" (1 Jn. 3:16).

Those living through Jesus Christ are the "Whoever's" who have confessed and committed to Jesus and, consequently, inherit eternal life (1 Jn. 1:12, 2:25, 3:15, 5:11, 13, 20). Twenty-two times John writes the word "Whoever." Five times within the previous section (1 Jn. 4:7, 15, 16, 18, 21). John says, "Whoever confesses that Jesus is the Son of God" (1 Jn. 4:15), "Whoever abides in Him" (1 Jn. 4:16), and "Whoever loves God must also love his brother" (1 Jn. 4:7, 21). Those who do so, they will stand before God with confidence on judgement day (1 Jn. 4:17). John also says whoever does not do those things does not have God, therefore, will not have confidence and do not have eternal life (1 Jn. 5:12b). John enforces his statement by narrowing in on the "Commandments."

Six times John writes the word "Commandments" (1 Jn. 2:3, 4, 3:22, 24, 5:2, 3). John opens this next section with the words, "By this, we know that we love the children of God when we love God and obey His commandments" (1 Jn. 5:2). Remember, nine times John writes the words, "By this, you/we know." Here, John states that we fellowship with God when we obey and keep His commandments. John's gospel records Jesus' sayings, "If you love Me, you will keep My commandments" (Jn. 14:15). Jesus also said, "Why do you call me, 'Lord, Lord,' and not do what I tell you?" (Lu. 6:46). The commandment, again, refers to loving God and one another: "And this is love, that we walk according to His commandments; this is the commandment, just as you have heard from the beginning so that you should walk in it (2 Jn. 6). Those who do what Jesus said, abide/remain in Him (1 Jn. 2:24).

Obeying God's commandments is to do them (cf. Lu. 6:46-49). Keeping His commandments implies keeping watch over, preserving, and guarding them. Jude, likewise, told the church to "Contend for the faith" (Jude 4), meaning to preserve and protect sound biblical doctrine while resisting false teaching. Obeying and keeping the commandment is the critical point of the passage, as seen through the chiastic structure, as follows:

A: Everyone who believes that Jesus is the Christ has been born of God, and everyone who loves the father loves his children as well (1 Jn.5:1)
    B: By this, we know that we love the children of God: when we love God and obey his commands (1 Jn. 5:2)
        C: For this is the love of God, that we keep his commands. And his commands are not burdensome (1 Jn. 5:3)

> C': For whatever is born of God overcomes the world. And this is the victory that has overcome the world - our faith (1 Jn. 5:4)
>
> B': Who is it that overcomes the world? Only the one who believes that Jesus is the Son of God (1 Jn. 5:5)
>
> A': This is the one who came by water and blood—Jesus Christ. He did not come by water only, but by water and blood. And it is the Spirit who testifies because the Spirit is the truth. (1 Jn. 5:6)

As mentioned in the previous section, the structure of the verses is inverted and parallel, with the central idea being in the middle of the arrangement. In this case, C and C' is the central point, stating that the victory of faith is gained and maintained through obedience to God's commands.

Additionally, as has already been said, John uses the phrase "Whoever" twenty-two times in his writing, and nine of those instances make known people who do not follow Christ. For the same reasons that those who do have Christ do, the Gnostic, and those following them, do not. The distinction between the two groups is that those who have God uphold His requirements of faith and obedience. People who do not have Christ do not acknowledge His deity; they have left Him, are apostates, and do not follow His commands, including loving one another.

John's opening statement in verse one: "Whoever believes that Jesus is the Christ has been born of God, and everyone who loves the Father loves whoever has been born of Him" (1 Jn. 5:1, 4). The first part of the verse is a repeat of the previous chapter, where John says, "Whoever confesses that Jesus is the Son of God, God abides in him, and he in God" (1 Jn. 4:15). Again, John had the Gnostics in mind, who do not believe and confess Christ, when writing the statement as mentioned above. In the same way, John confirms the believer in Christ; he also counters and contradicts the Gnostics who are not "Born of God" (1 Jn. 5:1), despite, in their deception, thinking they are (1 Jn. 1:6).

The term "Born of God" refers to the new birth (cf. Jn. 1:12-13, & chapter 3). Because the beloved has been "Born again" (cf. Jn. 3:3, 7, 1 Pet. 1:3, 23), they no longer do the things they used to (1 Jn. 3:9, 5:18); indeed, by keeping the commandments, they have "Overcome the world" (1 Jn. 5:4). Five times John writes the word "Overcome," referring to overcoming the evil one (1 Jn. 2:13, 14), the false prophets (1 Jn. 4:4), and the world (1 Jn. 5:4, 5). The three groups are the same. Satan, the evil one, is the god of this world (2 Cor. 4:4) and the ruler of it (Jn. 12:31, 14:30, 1 Jn. 5:19), while the false prophets are his deceptive ministers (1 Cor. 11:13-15), "They are from the world; therefore, they speak from the world, and the world listens to them" (1 Jn. 4:5). Sadly, many confessing 'Christians' also listen to them, which is why John warns the church, the Gnostics are actively trying to deceive (1 Jn. 2:26, 3:7). The false teachers attempt to deceive by promoting the world and the things of it like Satan did (Matt. 4:8-9), which is again why John says, "Do not love the world or the things in the world" (1 Jn. 2:15).

As mentioned in the section discussing chapter three of John's letter, the Gnostics love the world and the things in the world, evident by not being able to give those things up when another 'brother' is in need (1 Jn. 3:17). In this section (1 Jn. 5:1-5), John developed his criticism of the Gnostics further by saying, "Everyone who loves the Father loves whoever has been born of Him" (1 Jn. 5:1b), again, countering the Gnostics who do not love God, evident by not loving those born of Him. Remember, in the previous section, John said, "If anyone says, "I love God," and hates his brother, he is a liar; for he who does not love his brother whom he has seen cannot love God whom he has not seen" (1 Jn. 4:20). The connection is clear, those who love God, are loved by those who love God. Those who do not love God do not love those who do love God and are loved by God; "By this, we know" (1 Jn. 5:2a).

Recall that John penned "By this, we/you know" nine times. In the previous section, a grid was provided, serving as a checklist of six things for the believer to confirm whether they qualify to know and love God and are thereby known and loved by God. John continues with the same theme in chapter five: God's children are known by their obedience and keeping of the commandments (1 Jn. 5:2-3). The commandment, as stated earlier, is love (1 Jn. 2:7-8, 3:23).

While many state the requirements of God are hard, John anticipates the complaint by saying, "His commandments are not burdensome" (1 Jn. 5:3). Jesus said something similar, "My yoke is easy, and My burden is light" (Matt. 11:30). This saying from Jesus should be understood within the context of Matthew's gospel (Matt. 11:28-30). Jesus is countering the Pharisees who laid heavy burdens on God's people (cf. Matt. 23:4), saying to anyone with "Heavy laden," to take His yoke upon them. The "Yoke" is the confession of Christ, sin, and commitment to Him through active faith, love, and obedience. Contrary to the false claim of charismatics, Jesus is not saying He will give the beloved an easy life, contradicting many other verses of suffering (Jn. 16:33, Rom. 5:3, 8:18, 2 Cor. 1:5, 6, 7, Phil. 3:10, 2 Thess. 1:5, 2 Tim. 1:8, 2:3, 4:5, Heb. 10:32, 1 Pet. 4:13).

If the confessing Christian is of God, the commandment to obey and love God and one another is not difficult because the love of God flows through that person and is made manifest in their response to others, particularly those in need (1 Jn. 3:17). By freely, and sacrificially giving to those in need, the believer proves that they have "Overcome the world" (1 Jn. 5:4a). The things of the world no longer have hold of the one holding fast to God. The famous song, "Turn your eyes upon Jesus," sums John's words up well by saying: "Turn your eyes upon Jesus, look full in His wonderful face; and the things of earth will grow strangely dim in the light of His glory and grace. Through death into life everlasting, He passed, and we follow Him there; Over us, sin no more has dominion for more than conquerors we are!"

Interestingly, the words "Conqueror" and "Overcomer" are used in each of the seven letters to the church in the book of Revelation (Rev. 2-3). Different

Bible translations use one or the other word where Jesus says to each of the seven churches, they must overcome, or conquer, the world, and those from the world, and remain that way if they want to inherit the reward. On each occasion, the reward is eternal life. On the other hand, those being overcome (i.e., KJV) or conquered (i.e., ESV) by the world must repent (turn the situation around) or else experience the loss of their reward.

The chart below shows what each church must overcome or conquer to inherit the promise. On every occasion, Jesus says, "The one who conquers/overcomes, I will grant/give/clothed/make…" The exception is with the church of Smyrna, where Jesus said, "The one that conquers will not be hurt by the second death" (Rev. 3:11b). Again, failing to conquer/overcome, then instead of the eternal reward, judgement will be the everlasting experience. The "Second death" is the lake of fire.

	Loveless	Suffering	False Teaching	Sexual Sin	Idolatry	Worldliness
Ephesus	X					
Smyrna		X				
Pergamum			X	X	X	
Thyatira			X	X	X	
Sardis			X			X
Philadelphia		X				
Laodicea			X			X

In the English Standard Version (ESV), the word "Conquer" is seen eight times, only in the book of Revelation. Each time relates to the churches (Rev. 2:7, 11, 17, 26, 3:5, 12, 21, 21:7). The King James Version also mentions the word "Overcome" eight times within the book of Revelation (Rev. 2:7, 11, 17, 26, 3:5, 12, 21, 21:7). Again, twice more John uses the word in his first letter (1 Jn. 5:4, 5). Luke also uses the word (Lu. 11:22 KJV). The context of Luke's use of the word is within verses fourteen to twenty-three (Lu.

11:17-23). The link between verse twenty-two (Lu. 11:22) and John's letter is seen in chapter three, "The reason the Son of God appeared was to destroy the works of the devil" (1 Jn. 3:8). In the same way, the devil invades the church with his deceptive teaching (Jn. 2:26), Jesus invaded his territory with the truth. The application is "War." While the world is in celestial war, a Christian cannot be impartial (Lu. 11:23). Being impartial would entail opposing Christ. However, faith is never impartial or passive but active in overcoming the world through Jesus Christ (Jn. 16:33, 1 Jn. 4:4).

As previously mentioned in the section of Jude's work, Luke's verse regarding "Overcoming the strongman" (Lu. 11:22) has nothing to do with what charismatics claim, stating that the believer has authority over the devil, and can "Bind him," the "strongman" (cf. Matt. 12:29, Mk. 3:27). The verses hijacked by charismatics refer to Jesus, alone, binding Satan, before returning and judging him (Jn. 12:31). While believers are to wrestle against evil forces (Eph. 6:12), none, apart from Christ, has the authority to bind, and banish the devil who has been given authority over the earth until Jesus returns (Jn. 12:31, 14:30, 2 Cor. 4:4, 1 Jn. 5:19).

The word "Overcome" or "Conquer" also has the English translation, "Prevail" from the Greek word (Nikoa), applying a military conflict. The context is to prevail and have victory through faith in Jesus Christ. Adding to love being evidence of overcoming the world, John says that "Faith" (1 Jn. 5:4b), in Christ Jesus, the Son of God (1 Jn. 5:5), in whom the Spirit testifies of (1 Jn. 5:6), is critical.

Faith in Christ empowers the believer to have victory and overcome the (deception of) world (1 Jn. 4:4). As mentioned beforehand, the first reference to overcoming the world applies to love, and the next refers to overcoming false teaching, further developed in verses six to ten (1 Jn. 5:6-10) where John reiterates that Jesus is the Son of God. Again, John says, "Whoever believes (or has faith) in the Son of God has the testimony in himself" (1 Jn.

5:10, cf. 5:1, 4:15). John, "Writes these things to [those] who believe in the name of the Son of God that [they] may know that [they] have eternal life" (1 Jn. 5:13). Eternal life is only gained through Christ (Jn. 14:6, Acts 4:12).

As mentioned in the previous sections, John twice provides why he is writing the letter to the church. The first reason concerns "Those who are trying to deceive [them]" (1 Jn. 2:26), and the following promises eternal life to those who have overcome Satan, his deceivers, and the world through Jesus Christ (1 Jn. 5:13). Once more, the overcomers have conquered the world through active faith in Christ (1 Jn. 5:4-5) made evident through love (1 Jn. 5:1). However, it was God's love extended towards the beloved, even before any looked to Him (1 Jn. 5:10), enabling them to love, conquer and remain. Paul summed it up this way: "In all these things we are more than conquerors through Him who loved us" (Rom. 8:37). The context of Paul's statement is suffering and tribulation. For those who are loved by God, nothing can separate them from Him (Rom. 8:31-39), other than themselves by failing to abide and obey, and then, walking away (1 Jn. 2:24).

CHAPTER 12
The Testimoney of the Son

The Spirit is the One who Testifies

By now, anyone reading this work should be looking for keywords repeated several times by John. Within this section (1 Jn. 5:6-12), John repeats the word "Testimony" six times (1 Jn. 5:9[x3], 10[x2], 11), also using the word "Testify" (1 Jn. 5:7, cf. 4:14, 1:2). On each occasion the testimony is of Jesus Christ. John mentions Jesus in his first letter twelve times, and the word "Son" is written nineteen times. Noting the number of times, the name "Jesus" is mentioned in a 'Christian' message is a good litmus test, determining whether the message is God-centered. Charles Spurgeon said, "No Christ in your sermon sir? Then go home and never preach again until you have something worth preaching." Someone else said, "Until you have seen Jesus in the passage, you are not yet ready to preach it." However, when Jesus' name is proclaimed, discerning whether His name is used correctly and contextually is also essential.

Further supporting the testimony of Jesus, John mentioned the word "Blood" three times (1 Jn. 5:6[x2], 8, cf. 1:7) and the word "Water" four times (1 Jn. 5:6[x3], 8). The word "Spirit" is also mentioned three times within this section (1 Jn. 5:6[x2], 8), albeit seven times within the letter, referring to the

Holy Spirit (1 Jn. 3:24, 4:2, 6, 13, 5:6[x2], 8). As seen above, verses six and eight are the same, where the Spirit testifies of the Son.

Remembering the previous section, the name of Jesus Christ enabled the overcomers to overcome the world (1 Jn. 5:5), and only those who overcome or conquer have the promise of eternal life. Three times in chapter five, John writes the words "Eternal life" (1 Jn. 5:11, 13, 20); however, he mentions it six times in all (1 Jn. 1:2, 2:25, 3:15, 5:11, 13, 20). On each occasion, John reinforces the point eternal life is not found or gained through any other than Jesus Christ (cf. Jn. 14:6, Acts 4:12, 1 Jn. 5:20). Anyone claiming another way has the spirit of the antichrist (1 Jn. 2:18, 22, 4:3, 2 Jn. 1:7). John goes to great length making this fundamental point as mentioned above, he writes Jesus' name twelve times, and the words "Son" nineteen times. In sum, ten of the twelve times, John essentially says whoever believes in Jesus has eternal life, and twice, whoever does not, does not have eternal life.

Chapter four qualifies who is, and is not of God, saying: "By this, you know the Spirit of God: every spirit that confesses that Jesus Christ has come in the flesh is from God, and every spirit that does not confess Jesus is not from God. This is the spirit of the antichrist, which you heard was coming and now is in the world already" (1 Jn. 4:2-3). Regarding the word "Son," of the nineteen times written, John gives sixteen references indicating who has Jesus and five revealing who does not have Him. Again, remember that the Gnostics, like many today, thought they were in fellowship with God when they were not (1 Jn. 1:6).

As mentioned earlier, a good litmus test is to identify how many times the name "Jesus" is mentioned in any sermon and, indeed, whether, when mentioned, His name is correctly used (cf. 2 Cor. 11:4, Gal. 1:6). John deals with the same issue from the Gnostics where they deny the Son of God. The Gnostics did not say that Jesus did not exist; instead, they rejected His deity and the Trinity. For this reason, John counters them, once again, in verse six, saying, "This is He who came by water and blood—Jesus Christ, not by the water only but by the water and the blood. And the Spirit is the One who testifies because the Spirit is the truth" (1 Jn. 5:6). Note that John says, "Not by the water only." While John agrees with the Gnostics that Jesus came by water, he disagrees with them, adding that He also came with blood.

In John's gospel, three times, he mentioned that Jesus was baptised (Jn 1:26, 31, 33), marking the commencement of His ministry. However, the reference to "Blood" marks the end of His earthly ministry in the flesh. While the Gnostic believed in the man, Jesus, who was baptised, they rejected the work of the cross, therefore, Christ's death, resurrection, and ascension. Essentially, they denied the deity of Jesus, who is Christ. However, God the Father, on four occasions, testified of His Son. When Jesus was baptised, "A voice from heaven said, "This is My beloved Son, with whom I am well pleased" (Matt. 3:7). At the transfiguration of the Mount, just after Jesus foretold of His death and resurrection (Matt. 16:21-23), informing that every follower must also take up their cross (Matt. 16:24-28), "A voice from the cloud said, "This is my beloved Son, with whom I am well pleased; listen to Him" (Matt. 17:5). The words, "Listen to Him" refer to the prophesied death and resurrection. Before the transfiguration, Jesus foretold His disciples of it, and Peter rebuked Him (Matt. 16:22). After the transfiguration, Jesus again said, like with John the Baptist, "The Son of Man will certainly suffer at their (the Jews and the Romans) hands" (Matt. 17:12b).

Another confirmation of Christ was when He was contemplating the cross, God, the Father, was heard again, "Then a voice came from heaven: "I have glorified it, and I will glorify it again." The crowd that stood there and heard it said that it had thundered. Others said, "An angel has spoken to him." Jesus answered, "This voice had come for your sake, not mine, when Jesus died on the cross" (Jn. 12:28-30). A fourth time that God's 'voice' was heard was through the earthquake when Jesus died, causing the centurion and others to say, "Truly this was the son of God" (Matt. 27:54).

Further support for the mention of Jesus coming by blood pointing to the cross is seen in verses six and eight (1 Jn. 5:6, 8), as introduced in chapter one (1 Jn. 1:7). It is by the blood of Jesus Christ, alone, that the sinner is cleansed. Because the Gnostics rejected the redeeming work of the cross, they were disqualified from its cleansing work and eternal life. Note the wording and the condition of chapter one: "But if we walk in the light, as He is in the light, we have fellowship with one another, and the blood of Jesus His Son cleanses us from all sin" (1 Jn. 1:7).

Jesus Christ's appearance and death point to His salvation work. The reason Jesus appeared was to take away sins (1 Jn. 3:5) and to destroy the works of the devil (1 Jn. 3:8). Whoever confesses that Jesus is the Son of God (referring to His virgin birth, death, and resurrection), God abides in him, and him in God (1 Jn. 4:15). The reverse is also true. The Spirit of God testifies to it, as John stated earlier, "By this, we know the Spirit of truth and the spirit of error (1 Jn. 4:6). The "Spirit is the truth" (1 Jn. 5:6b) because He testifies about Jesus (1 Jn. 5:6a), "Bearing witness of Him" (Jn. 15:26). The first and foremost role of the Holy Spirit is to bear witness of the truth about Jesus, countering the spirit of error (1 Jn. 4:6). The truth of Jesus is the original message, heard from the beginning (1 Jn. 1:1, 2:7, 24, 3:11). Remember, if anything changes, everything changes!

The Spirit testifies about Jesus, but not the Spirit only, but "There are three that testify" (1 Jn. 5:7), and "These three agree" (1 Jn. 5:8). The three refer to "The Spirit, and the water and the blood" (1 Jn. 5:8). The "Water and the blood" refer to the works of Jesus. In the gospel of John, Jesus said that His works bear testimony of Him (Jn. 5:36, 10:25), and therefore the work of the cross confirms He is who He said He was due to doing what He said He would (cf. 1 Cor. 15:4).

Joining the triune witness of the Spirit, water, and blood, God, is the Father who also bears witness concerning His Son (1 Jn. 5:9b, 11, cf. Jn. 5:37), countering the "Testimony of men" (1 Jn. 5:9a), when not in agreement. Regardless of what humanity says, "The testimony of God is greater" (1 Jn. 5:9). Even when the testimony of man is good, God's testimony is still greater (cf. Jn. 5:33-36, 1 Jn. 1:1). Further supporting that God's testimony is greater than man's, John repeats chapter four (1 Jn. 4:2-3), saying, "Whoever believes in the Son of God has the testimony in himself. Whoever does not believe God has made him a liar, because he has not believed in the testimony that God has borne concerning His Son" (cf. 1 Jn. 5:10, 12).

The testimony for all who believe in the Son is that of the original message: "What they heard from the beginning" (1 Jn. 1:1, 2:7, 24, 3:11), proclaimed to them by the eyewitnesses of the resurrected Christ (1 Jn. 1:1-3). The message heard from the beginning has also been confirmed by the abiding Spirit (1 Jn. 2:27, 3:24, 4:13, 5:6). John affirms the church, saying, "I write to you, not because you do not know the truth, but because you know it, and because no lie is of the truth" (1 Jn. 2:21). It is repeated in chapter five, "I write these things to you who believe in the name of the Son of God, that you may know that you have eternal life" (1 Jn. 5:13).

As said previously, there is another reason why John writes to the church, as seen in chapter two: "I write these things to you about those who are trying to deceive you." John warns, although you have believed (1 Jn. 2:21, 5:10a), do not become deceived (1 Jn. 2:26)! Should that happen, you will lose your reward (1 Jn. 8). The reward is "Eternal life" (1 Jn. 1:2, 2:25, 3:15, 5:11, 13, 20). Eternal life and Jesus Christ are the same things; no one has one without the other. The Gnostics do not have Christ; therefore, they do not have life (1 Jn. 5:12-13).

The loss of reward is confirmed in chapter five, verse ten: "Whoever does not believe God has made Him a liar because he has not believed in the testimony that God had borne concerning His Son" (1 Jn. 5:10b). Five times John calls the Gnostics liars (1 Jn. 1:10, 2:4, 22, 4:20, 5:10). John says the

Gnostics are liars because they say they have not sinned (1 Jn. 1:10), and do not keep the commandments (1 Jn. 2:4). They deny Christ (1 Jn. 2:22), they do not love their brother (1 Jn. 4:20), and they do not believe God's testimony concerning His Son (1 Jn. 5:10). Remember, the Gnostics once believed, confirming that unbelief is also a process. In context, the Gnostics reject the death and resurrection of Jesus Christ (1 Jn. 5:6, 8).

As stated, the Gnostics did believe in God, thinking they had fellowship with Him (1 Jn. 1:6), but they did not stay with the original message; so, they disqualified themselves through apostasy. At the time of writing, high-ranking members within the Church of England are on the same path and are moving away from the original message (scripture). The second highest ranking member within the Church of England recently justified the shift, stating that "Doctrine develops." In other words, it changes with the times and culture. John warned about this, encouraging his reader to remain in the original teaching (1 Jn. 2:24). Another well known and popular American 'preacher,' Andy Stanley, has also recently shifted following many other departing denominations. Paul warned about these days, saying, "The Spirit expressly says that in the latter times, some will depart from the faith by devoting themselves to deceitful spirits and teachings of demons through the insincerity of liars whose consciences are seared" (1 Tim. 4:1-1).

As previously stated, several times in the letter to the church of Thessalonica, Paul said that the great end time sign was apostasy (1 Thess. 2:3), being fulfilled in our time. The great falling away does not refer to people leaving the church, but rather the church departing from sound biblical doctrine (2 Tim. 4:3-4).

In sum, the promise of eternal life (1 Jn. 5:11) is only afforded to those who have the Son (1 Jn. 5:10, 12). Those who have the Son abide in the original teaching, "What they heard from the beginning" (1 Jn. 2:24). Anyone "Who goes on ahead and does not abide in the teaching of Christ, does not have

God" (2 Jn. 9). "If anyone comes to you and does not bring this teaching, do not receive him" (2 Jn. 10). They are out to deceive you (1 Jn. 2:26). If anyone receives them, they "Take part in [their] evil works" (2 Jn. 11). The primary deceptive teaching that the false prophets bring, causing many to depart, is that Jesus is not the Son of God (the only way to God). Closely connected is that sin has no power over them. In other words, they can do whatever they like, giving license to sin, going against the work of the cross, the testimony of the Spirit and God, the Father. Such a person is damned in their evil works.

CHAPTER 13
That You May Know

All Wrongdoing is Sin, but there is a Sin that Leads to Death

In the previous section, John focused on the testimony of the Spirit, God, the Father, and the beloved. The testimony is of Christ. Jesus Christ's water baptism and shed blood also testify of Him, that is, His deity. The big idea is that Jesus, whom the Gnostics rejected, is the Christ and the only means to inherit eternal life. "Whoever confesses that Jesus is the Son of God, God abides in him and he in God" (1 Jn. 4:15). "Everyone who believes that Jesus is the Christ has been born of God" (1 Jn. 5:1). "Whoever believes in the Son of God has the testimony in himself" (1 J. 5:10). "Whoever has the Son, has life" (1 Jn. 5:12).

John continues his confirmation and affirmation of the beloved by saying, "I write these things to you who believe in the name of the Son of God that you may know that you have eternal life" (1 Jn. 5:13). Remember, twice John says, "I write these things to you" (1 Jn. 2:26, 5:13), again, clearing up any confusion as to whom the letter is written. John's "You" refers to the beloved and children of God who believe, abide, and obey the Son.

As stated, John's letter addresses two groups, the Gnostics and the beloved. The letter in no way refers to unbelievers, as some charismatics suggest, by stating that those in need of repenting (1 Jn. 1:9) are those still yet to confess Christ. Anyone claiming that "1 John 1:9" is for outsiders can be only illiterate; there cannot be any other explanation.

Confessing sin, or repentance, is a way of life for the genuine believer in Christ. Indeed, one of the ways a believer knows that they have eternal life is through the Spirit's continual conviction (1 Jn. 3:21, 24), leading to the confession of sin (1 Jn. 1:9, 2:1). The Holy Spirit initially convicts those who are in the world of their sin (Jn. 16:7-11), resulting in conversion, or rebirth. The Spirit then continues to convict those who are in Christ as sons. The sons of God are led (often into repentance) by the Spirit of God (1 Cor. 2:12-14, Gal. 5:16-18, Eph. 4:30). This is how anyone knows that the Spirit abides within (1 Jn. 3:24). Because the Spirit abides within, the believer is assured that they have Christ (1 Jn. 4:13), and therefore, eternal life. Anyone void of the Spirit, thereby void of conviction and repentance, is without Christ and eternal life.

Repentance is the critical point of this concluding section of John's letter (1 Jn. 5:13-21), seen within the mini chiastic structure, as follows:

A. Statement of Purpose (1 Jn. 5:13)
    B. Belief in Jesus as the Son of God (1 Jn. 5:14-15)
        C. Prayer for the Sinning Brother (1 Jn. 5:16-17)
    B'. Belief in the True God (1 Jn. 5:18-19)
A'. Warning against False Gods (1 Jn. 5:20-21)

Within the concluding passage, there are also four sub-sections (1 Jn. 5:13-15, 16-17, 18-20, and 21). The first deals with knowing through belief and prayer, and the second deals with sin and repentance. The third again deals with the believer's assurance, and the last is a warning about idols. The first and third sections are similar, as are the second and fourth.

Eight times, in five verses, within this section, John writes the word "Know" (1 Jn. 5:13, 15, 18, 19, 20). John writes the word "Know" many more times within the letter, found in thirty-two verses. Twenty-seven of those verses are positive, directed at the one who knows God, and five more times, John refers to those who do not know God.

The distinguishing difference between those who know, and therefore, have God, and those who do not know, and therefore do not have God is summed up in the words, "These things" (1 Jn. 5:13). John says, "I write these things to you," which refers to everything already stated, narrowing in on, "What they heard from the beginning" (1 Jn. 1:1, 2:7, 2:24, 3:11). What they heard from the beginning relates to Christ's crucifixion and resurrection. Those who know the truth and abide in it, they alone have Christ, and therefore, eternal life (1 Jn. 5:13).

Once more, John's reason for writing the letter is to refute the Gnostics, who say they know God when they do not. Jude, likewise, writes his letter, warning of the Gnostics who have crept in unnoticed (Jude 4), claiming to have special revelation through dreams and visions. However, Jude calls them "Dreamers" (Jude 8), meaning they are led by false dreams, revelation, and knowledge, through deceiving spirits. Indeed, they are deceived beyond return (Jude 12-13, 1 Jn. 2:26, 3:7, 2 Jn. 7).

As declared many times before, deception is the leading end times sign, according to the Olivet Discord (Matt. 24, Mk. 13, Lu. 21) and Paul's writings (2 Thess. 2:3, 1 Tim. 4:1-2, 2 Tim. 4:3-4). For this reason, John thought he was living in the final hour (1 Jn. 2:18-19). Within the book of Revelation, the word "Deceived" is seen seven times (Rev. 12:9, 13:14, 18:23, 19:20, 20:3, 8, 10). Those who do the deceiving (within the church) on this side of the tribulation are conditioning and preparing the "Left behind" (from the church) for the ultimate deceiver to come, the antichrist, in the hour of trial (2 Thess. 2:11).

Again, John counters the false teachers, and at the same time, he reassures the beloved, who have become unsteady (cf. 2 Pet. 2:14, Jude 22-23) by false claims and promises (cf. 2 Pet. 2:19). John assures the church that "Those who believe in the name of the Son of God… have eternal life" (1 Jn. 5:13). John's statement is a repeat of his gospel: "But these are written so that you may believe that Jesus is the Christ, the Son of God and that by believing you may have life in His name" (Jn. 20:31). The difference between the two statements is that in the gospel of John, it is evangelistic, aimed at those still in the world, while the letter of John is written to the church. The letter, therefore, serves to "Revive, restore, refresh and renew" what may have become lukewarm or even cold because of false teaching. John revives the beloved by reminding them of what kind of love God has given them (1 Jn. 3:1-2), countering the false promises from the Gnostics. John also reminded the beloved that they have eternal life (1 Jn. 1:2, 2:25, 5:11, 13, 20), whereas the Gnostics do not (1 Jn. 3:15).

Genuine revival is a work of God, calling and causing the church to repent and be "Revived." That is, brought back through confession and repentance (1 Jn. 1:9, 2:1, 5:17). Seventeen times, the word "Revive" is found in the Bible, and six of those times refer to reviving the spirit of the broken, or humble. For example: "When the humble see it they will be glad; you who seek God, let your hearts revive" (Ps. 69:32). Currently, at the time of writing, there is a revival taking place in Kentucky, USA, started by students at Asbury University. Reports have confirmed that hundreds of students are repenting and renewing their faith in Christ; they are being "Revived." Unlike many false revivals, majoring in false signs and wonders, the Asbury revival seems genuine.

A recent example of a false revival is Todd Bentley's Florida revival. Todd Bentley is an arched-heretic, full of false doctrine, accompanied by lying signs and wonders. The evidence for Bentley's false revival, besides his false teaching and lying signs and wonders, is where he twice fell into sexual sin while the so-called revivals were taking place. First, he left his wife and married another (2008/9). Later, he was accused of sexting another male (2020). On both accounts, there was no evidence of Bentley repenting, who, in the latest incident, refused to submit to an investigation and step down from 'ministry'.

True repentance leads to eternal life. In the passage, John writes to the beloved to remind them that they have eternal life, and yet still warns them, it is not over yet (1 Jn. 5:17, 21, cf. 2:26, 3:7). John also encourages them in the here and now, providing they do not sin, by saying they can have confidence in their prayer life (1 Jn. 5:14). When they pray, God hears and answers them (1 Jn. 5:14-15). God answers them when they ask for anything "According to His will" (1 Jn. 5:14).

As stated previously, the only prayer God hears from a sinner is the prayer of repentance (Jn. 9:31). However, once born of God (1 Jn. 3:9, 4:7, 5:1, 4, 9, 10, 18), He hears our prayers when prayed according to His will. As already addressed in chapter three (1 Jn. 3B) of this work, God granting the believer anything they ask for is not biblical, and it is a far cry from what John is saying. Charismatics who name and claim, declare and decree, demand, and command of God, are no better than the Gnostics who have no knowledge. A correlating example of charismatics being without knowledge resulting in their misuse of scripture, is seen through their interpretation of the book of Job. "You will also declare a thing, And it will be established for you" (Job 22:28).

To gain an understanding of the verse, the context needs to be taken into consideration. The one speaking is Eliphaz, who falsely accuses Job of being wicked and pleads with Job to repent. Although Eliphaz's accusations are false, his 'formula' for getting right with God is correct. 1). Submit to God; 2). Make peace with God; 3). Accept God's teaching, 4). Live out God's words; 5). Return to God; 6). Get rid of wickedness, and 7). Quit trusting in wealth!

Interestingly, Eliphaz's last statement runs opposite to how Word of Faith promoters use this verse to suggest, "Declare and decree, that it will come unto me/thee!" In other words, whatever you ask, it shall be established! However, instead of pursuing wealth, or anything else for that matter, Eliphaz says, replace it with God (Job 28:24-25). Jesus echoed the same to the church of Laodicea (Rev. 3:17-22). The condition of the church of Laodicea was that they were wealth-orientated (full of the world) yet completely void of God. On the prophetic calendar, this age (1900s-now) is Laodicean, the last church before Jesus returns.

Job, chapter thirty-one, picks up on Job's response to Eliphaz; Job denies the accusations. Verse twenty-four (Job 31:24) states that Job had not put his trust in wealth; neither had he rejoiced in it (Job 31:25) or pursued any other form of false worship, for that matter (Job 31:26-28). God was first and foremost in his heart. Again, an important observation is to note Job's response, like Eliphaz's accusation, runs in the opposite direction to the false claims and misrepresentation of scripture from the Word of faith proponents. Believers are to seek God, not gold or glory.

After several chapters of false accusations of Job, God finally answers (chapters 38-39), basically saying, "None of you have a clue!" This is true of word-of-faith proponents, too, when twisting scripture to suit themselves like Job's ignorant 'friends.' Word-of-faith proponents make all kinds of arrogant claims, utterly void of understanding due to not loving truth enough to take the time to study the word, and diligently search for and seek God, alone.

Following God's response, Job was brought undone. How could he possibly answer God? (Job 40:4-5). Furthermore, that is true for any in Christ! God continues to challenge Job and says, "Who are you?" "What can you do?" Basically, God is saying, "You are clueless, you are no one, and you are nothing!" (Job 41). In other words, Wake-up! The wake-up call resulted in Job repenting (Job 42:6), realising he uttered what he should not and did not understand (Job 42:3). Job's repentance outcome should be the same for all who claim to be in Christ.

After addressing Job, God turns His attention to Job's friends, stating they, too, knew nothing but had plenty to say, yet should not have done so (Job 42:8). However, God offers a means of forgiveness that they would not be dealt with according to their folly (Job 42:8). God first led Job to repentance and then provided the gift of repentance to his friends, which is also on offer to any who likewise speak foolishly.

Foolishness is precisely what the word of faith movement majors on by declaring and decreeing, even demanding and commanding of God. In other words, they utter what they do not understand. Consequently, their entire 'theology' is built on and centred in 'MEISMs!' Everything revolves around them, what they can be, do, have, multiply, and maintain. However, God says we can do NOTHING, and only He can do ANYTHING. God flips the table; instead of a man making God serve man, God says man must worship Him. Said another way, Man is not the centre and object of worship - God is.

The conclusion of Job could be that when we pursue gold (riches), we forsake God. However, when we seek God, we get God, sometimes even gold (Job 42:11b), but not and never because we declared and decreed it! Connecting the example of Job with the charismatic misuse of scripture and focus on prosperity is seen in John's closing verse, "Keep yourself from idols" (1 Jn. 5:20). Prosperity for many is an idol of the heart (Ezek. 14:1-11). Modern-day idols are fleshly desires that can quickly lead astray (Mk. 4:19; 2 Pet. 1:4b). The very reason why John, Jude, and Peter were writing to the churches.

Another example of the charismatics' abuse of scripture is seen in the verse: "I believed, and so I spoke" (2 Cor. 4:13b) in support of 'naming-and-claiming'. The term, naming-and-claiming, through prayer or otherwise, is also known as 'blabbing-and-grabbing', suggesting that a believer has the authority and the right to call in, even demand certain benefits from God, mostly revolving around one's own 'wealth, health, and happiness'.

As always, context is key, and the surrounding context unsurprisingly offered nothing close to what charismatics claim. The origin of the passage and the verse in question is found in the Psalms (Ps. 116:10), where the interpretation could not be further from the misapplied notion of the (here-and-now) 'health, wealth, and happiness' doctrine. Instead, the application revolves around present-day suffering for faithfully proclaiming the gospel, not prosperity.

As mentioned above, the verse (2 Cor. 4:13b) is directly quoting the psalmist who referred to his personal anguish of the grave (Ps. 116:3) yet had confidence that God would deliver him from death (Ps. 116.:8). In Paul's second letter to the church of Corinth, Paul encourages the saints by saying, "Do not lose heart" (1 Cor. 4:16) in the face of suffering (2 Cor. 4:17). Verse eighteen (2 Cor. 4:18) then encourages the believer in current distress by pointing towards their future state in the Lord. The 'big idea' then revolves around the believer's hope based on the death and resurrection of Jesus (2 Cor. 4:14). Because Jesus conquered the grave, so shall everyone born of Him (2 Cor. 4:14b). However, in the same way, Jesus suffered temporarily (1 Pet. 4:1a), so must His followers (2 Cor. 1:9-10; 4:17; 1 Pet 4:1b-2). The doctrine of suffering is not found within charismatic teaching.

Many more examples could be shared of what the charismatics falsely claim regarding prayer and spoken words. However, for time-sake, it is more important to focus on John's intended message, which is: Those who have confidence in eternal life (1 Jn. 2:28, 3:21, 4:17) also have confidence in their prayer life (1 Jn. 5:14).

As mentioned above, the beloved may be lacking in confidence because of what the Gnostics have been teaching. John aims to re-establish their confidence. John affirms that when the person, born of God, prays, God hears them (1 Jn. 5:14b, 15a), unlike the pagans who heap up empty phrases (babble), God does not hear them (Matt. 6:7). God hears the beloved when they pray "According to His will" (1 Jn. 5:14). Again, charismatics misuse and abuse verses like these (1 Jn. 5:14-15), to suit themselves, deliberately ignoring the context. They state that God's will for them is to be healthy, happy, and wealthy. However, the context says otherwise, precisely revealing God's will, which has nothing to do with what charismatics claim. The will of God is seen in the following verses (1 Jn. 5:16-17), which is to pray for the fellow believer who has fallen into sin, asking God to give him/her life (1 Jn. 5:16).

Four times John writes the word "Ask," and on each occasion, he refers to prayer (1 Jn. 3:22, 5:14, 15, 16) and praying according to God's will. God's will is that all repent and none perish (1 Jn. 5:15-16, 2 Pet. 3:9). When the believer prays for their sinning brother, God hears and grants their request (1 Jn. 5:15), which is according to His will (1 Jn. 5:14). The request granted is giving the sinning brother life, instead of death. "The wage of sin is death" (Rom 6:23a). Instead of getting what the sinning brother deserves, the prayer is that they receive the "Gift of God [which] is eternal life through Jesus Christ" (Rom. 623b). Still, the sinner must confess their sins (1 Jn. 1:9, 2:1-2) to receive forgiveness.

The one praying and the one repenting can both have confidence that God will hear and forgive (1 Jn. 5:15, 1:9). The words, "God will give him life" (1 Jn. 4:16) should be considered alongside John's words in chapter two, "And now little children, abide in Him, so that when He appears we may not shrink from Him in shame at His coming" (1 Jn. 2:28). Those practicing righteousness are born of God (1 Jn. 2:29), while those practicing sin, are not (1 Jn. 3:4). Any 'brother' practicing sin is on the broad road that leads to hell (Matt. 7:13), but still can be saved by snatching them out of the fire (Jude 23), in John's case, through prayer.

As mentioned earlier, the one redeemed from sin is revived or brought back, like with the prodigal son (Lu. 15:11-32). If left alone, the fire, now lapping at their feet, would entirely consume them. To paraphrase the book of Proverbs, Solomon says, "If you play with fire (sin), you will get burned" (Prov. 6:27-28).

Remember again, John is countering the words and work of the Gnostics who have caused some to sin, like with Jude (Jude 22-23). While some are still redeemable, others may not be, for there is a sin that leads to death. Three times John mentions the word "Death" (1 Jn. 5:16, 17, 18). John says, "Do not pray for the one who has committed the sin leading to death." As with reference to God giving life, referring to resurrected life, death also relates to the same, everlasting death, or the second death, being the lake of fire.

Four times John writes the words, "Second death" in the book of Revelation (Rev. 2:11, 20:6, 14, 21:8). The first (Rev. 2:11) addresses the church, telling them if they continue to conquer, then the second death will not harm them. The reverse is also true. Later, John says,

"Blessed and holy is the one who shares in the first resurrection! Over such, the second death has no power, but they will be priests of God and of Christ, and they will reign with Him for a thousand years" (Rev. 20:4). The last two references refer to those being cast into the lake of fire (Rev. 20:24, 21:8). As the faithful follower of Christ will be resurrected for everlasting life (Rev. 20:4), the faithless and the wicked will likewise be resurrected for everlasting punishment (Rev. 20:5). In both accounts, the resurrected receive glorified bodies on their day of resurrection to enjoy/endure whichever eternal outcome they are appointed (Dan. 12:2, Jn. 5:28-29, Acts 24:15).

Note the wording regarding "That [sin]" (1 Jn. 5:16b). Whoever commits a sin unto death is no longer considered to be a 'brother'. However, the 'brother' sinning (not leading to death) should be prayed for, as that brother belongs to God. The other is no longer a brother, instead, he is an outsider and dead to God. Jesus said that He only prayed for His own, not outsiders (Jn. 17:9). To rephrase, the one who has committed the sin leading to death was once a part of the household of God, and now, they no longer are. They are twice dead (Jude 12).

As stated, John's references to life and death do not relate to physical life and death, as the Gnostics and charismatics claim, but instead to eternal life and everlasting death (endless punishment). Charismatics state that if the believer willfully sins, they will not experience the best of what God has for them here and now, but they will still inherit eternal life. John disagrees (1 Jn. 2:24, 3:4-10).

As already seen through the chapters of John's letter, anyone practicing sin is in danger. However, there is a sin that leads to death. Contextually the sin that leads to death is the sin of the Gnostics who deny Christ (1 Jn. 2:22, Jude 4, 2 Pet. 2:1). Anyone who comes to the knowledge of the truth and then falls away commits the sin unto death (Heb. 6:4-8, 10:26-27). Peter says it would have been better for the person to have never known than to know and then fall away (2 Pet. 2:20-21). Once a person has committed the sin of apostasy, there is no longer a sacrifice for their sin, and therefore, all the prayers in the world will not save them. To reject Christ is to reject the saving work of the cross, and to say that Christ is not the only way, is the same. Anyone committing these sins is without forgiveness.

John's instruction not to pray for the one who had committed the sin leading to death is not an isolated case, for God instructed Jeremiah not to pray for Judah, who has turned to other gods (Jer. 7:16–18 11:14, 14:11). Judah, like the Gnostics, never stopped believing in God, but rather, they stopped trusting in Him, and regarding Him as the "One true (and only) God." Anyone committing the sin of accepting many gods (polytheism), such as some ecumenical groups do today, place themselves in the same category as Judah. Even the ecumenical groups who accept the monotheistic God of Judaism, Christianity, and Islam still have the spirit of the antichrist, and therefore, they are without Christ. An example of this is seen with the modern term "Christlam," combining Christianity and Islam.

Interestingly, at the time of writing, the Pope endorsed "The Abrahamic Family House," scheduled to open this year, being constructed on an island in the city of Abu Dhabi in the Middle East. A global peace pact known as the "Document of Human Fraternity for Global Peace," signed by Pope Francis and Sunni Muslim leader Sheikh Ahmen al-Tayeb, inspired the constructed headquarters, also called the headquarters of the "One world religion." The term is a fulfilment of the end times prophecy where the antichrist will create a monotheistic religion connected to monolithic world order and result in the beast's mark (Rev. 13). Anyone who received the mark of the beast is eternally lost (Rev. 14:9-11). John's comment regarding the sin that leads to death is the same.

While there is sin that leads to death, other sins may not (1 Jn. 5:17). John reinforces what he has previously said regarding sin. While all sin, those in Christ confess their sins and thereby are cleansed from wrongdoing (1 Jn. 1:9, 2:1-2). Anyone claiming to have no sin is a liar and makes God out to be a liar and therefore has no forgiveness of sin (1 Jn. 1:8, 10). As mentioned above, John instructs the church to pray for the brother sinning, that God would give him life and not take it away (1 Jn. 5:16). However, and again, for that to occur, the one sinning must repent (1 Jn. 1:9, 2:1-2). The prayer of the church should then be that the one sinning, repents. When the sinner repents, they are "Revived."

Consistent with repentance, the believer "Knows" that they are born of God (1 Jn. 5:18, 19) and, therefore, have "Eternal Life" (1 Jn. 5:13). As a result, God hears their prayers (1 Jn. 5:15), and grants their requests (1 Jn. 5:16). In sum, the believer has an advantage over those in the world, for "God protects them, and the evil one does not touch him" (1 Jn. 5:18). However, for the brother sinning, they remove themselves from the protection of God, for the one who remains in sin does not have fellowship with God (1 Jn. 1:6-7).

John's gospel (Jn. 17:12-15) should be compared with his letter, promising protection for the believer. The promise does not relate to divine protection from worldly harm, as the charismatics falsely claim, but rather their eternal safekeeping. As mentioned above, John has in mind eternal life and death; therefore, the context relates to the believer not losing what they already have (cf. 2 Jn.8). Remember, the church has already overcome the evil one (1 Jn. 2:12-14), who is still out to deceive them (1 Jn. 2:26, 3:7). However, for the one who does not practice sin, they have the promise of protection against the evil one (1 Jn. 5:18), whom the whole world lies in his power (1 Jn. 5:19). Remember, Satan is the ruler of this world until Jesus returns (Jn. 12:31; 14:30; 16:11), debunking charismatics who subscribe to reconstructionism otherwise known as dominionism (the seven-mountain mandate, or kingdom now theology).

As the believer practicing righteousness is protected from Satan, the reverse is also true. Anyone who practices sin is unprotected against Satan and his deception. Anyone falling prey to him, without repentance, will follow him to hell. In context, those being kept safe from Satan are being kept safe from deception. The fundamental protection from God relates to the truth about Jesus Christ, confirmed in verse twenty: "And we know that the Son of God has come and has given us understanding, so that we may know Him who is true; and we are in Him who is true, in His Son Jesus Christ. He is the true God and eternal life" (1 Jn. 5:20). Three times, John writes the word, "True" in verse twenty, countering the Gnostics who deny Christ. Remember again; John continually points his readers back to the message they heard from the beginning regarding the light (truth) and love of Jesus Christ (1 Jn. 1:1, 2:7, 2:24, 3:11).

John concludes the passage and letter with the words "Little children, keep yourselves from idols" (1 Jn. 5:21). As mentioned above, an idol can be anything of the heart. Within the context, the idol relates to anything causing the believer to become apostate. The love of the world and the things of it (1 Jn. 2:15-18) have caused some to depart from the faith (cf. 2 Tim. 4:10). Due to the love of the world, Demas departed from the faith, and committed sin leading to death. When Demas departed, he removed himself from God's protection against deception and therefore became thoroughly deceived, evident by taking up the role of "Priest of idols."

As mentioned earlier, the sin of idolatry leads to death, where some claim that all monotheistic faiths worship the same God. The obvious problem with that ideology is the absence of Jesus Christ in two of the three faiths. John goes to great lengths to say that without Jesus Christ, none have eternal life. As mentioned at the beginning of this section: "Whoever confesses that Jesus is the Son of God, God abides in him and he in God" (1 Jn. 4:15). "Everyone who believes that Jesus is the Christ has been born of God" (1 Jn. 5:1). "Whoever believes in the Son of God has the testimony in himself" (1 J. 5:10). "Whoever has the Son, has life" (1 Jn. 5:12).

In sum, idols refer to anything false, including the false teaching from the Gnostics, who deny Christ, and other modern movements operating under the banner of Christianity. Mormonism and the Jehovah's Witnesses are prime examples. Other "Idols" include self-reliance, seen in those trusting in their works, and self-righteousness. Catholicism is an example of a works-based religion, which is also full of idols, such as Mary, other saints, the rosemary, and the elevation of the Pope. The charismatics are also guilty of idolatry. Kenneth Copeland and associates are an example when they say, "When I read 'I AM' in the Bible, I just smile and say, 'I am too.'" Other examples of idolatry within the charismatic movement include the health, wealth, and happiness gospel, otherwise known as the prosperity gospel. In all cases, John says, "Keep yourself from idols," which would also mean, "Stay away from anyone promoting idolatry through false teaching" (cf. 2 Jn. 10-11).

By staying away from those who promote false teaching, the believer adds another layer of protection against deception (all forms of idolatry). Remember, the critical point of the passage is that "All wrongdoing is sin" (1 Jn. 5:17). Idolatry is a sin leading to apostasy. While there is a sin that leads to death (the denial of Christ), all sin can result in the same when practiced.

John writes the word "Practice" eight times in seven verses (1 Jn. 1:6, 2:29, 3:4[x2], 7, 8, 9, 10). Remember that the critical point of the letter is pinpointed in chapter three, verses four to ten (1 Jn. 3:4-10), determining who belongs to God and who does not. Those who practice righteousness belong to God, while those who make a practice of sin belong to the devil (1 Jn. 3:10).

SECOND JOHN

DOCTRINE MATTERS
Fellowship, Only, with those Walking in Truth and Love

Introduction:

The short second letter of John contains the same message as the first, truth (light), love, and life. There is also a warning against the same deceivers, like with the first letter, who are taking advantage of the kindness of some, expressed through Christian hospitality, to gain access to their homes (churches) and lives. The same is seen in Peter's second letter and the letter from Jude, where false teachers have crept in unnoticed among the believers and are now sitting at the love feast.

Both Peter and Jude call the false teachers blemishes at the love feast, defiling everything and everyone they touch. Peter says they go after unsteadying souls, and Jude says they have caused some to doubt and others to sin. On both accounts, the contaminated are in danger of hellfire, needing to be snatched back.

John writes his second letter to a "Lady," who John says is "Elect" (2 Jn. 1) and "Dear" (2 Jn. 5). She is said to have the gift of hospitality. Showing hospitality is commanded in scripture (cf. Rom. 12:13, 1 Tim. 5:10, Heb. 13:2, 1 Pet. 4:9-10), directly connected with "Walking in love according to the commandments" (2 Jn. 6). Ten times in his first letter John writes the word

"Commandment," and another four times in his second letter (2 Jn. 5, 6[x2]), mostly referring to loving one another (1 Jn. 2:7, 2 Jn. 5).

The commandment of love is "What [the beloved] heard from the beginning" (2 Jn. 5, 6). The warning is not to go ahead of the teachings of Christ (2 Jn. 9). Four times John writes this phrase (What they heard from the beginning) in his first letter (1 Jn. 1:1, 2:7, 2:24, 3:11) and twice more in his second (2 Jn. 5, 6). The purpose of stating the phrase several times is to encourage the believer to remain (abide).

The critical and conditional verse of John's first letter is: "Let what you heard from the beginning abide in you. If what you heard from the beginning abides in you, then you too will abide in the Son and in the Father" (1 Jn. 2:24). The key word is "Abide," seen twice more in John's second letter (2 Jn. 2, 9). Verse nine is like the critical verse mentioned above (2 Jn. 2:24), warning that if anyone does not abide in the original teachings of Christ but instead goes ahead of that teaching, they do not have God (2 Jn. 9). Indeed, they have lost what they once had (2 Jn.8).

John warns that a believer can lose what they once had, referring to Jesus, who abides within, forever (2 Jn. 2). Jesus abides, providing the believer remains in Him (1 Jn. 2:24). On one hand, John says that Jesus abides forever. On the other hand, he warns the believer to "Watch [themselves], so they do not lose what we (the apostles) have worked for" (2 Jn. 8). The warning does not refer to rewards in heaven but salvation. The context of the warning refers to false doctrine spread by the deceivers (2 Jn. 7[x2]), countering the "Truth" (2 Jn. 1[x2], 2, 3, 4). The deceivers have the spirit of the antichrist (2 Jn. 7), spreading false doctrine by manipulating others and abusing the command of "Love" (2 Jn. 1, 3, 5, 6), specifically relating to hospitality to gain access to their lives and homes.

The Gnostics major on the abuse of scripture, twisting it to get what they want. Charismatics do the same thing. From 2005 to 2008, I had an itinerate ministry in London, the UK. While ministering in a particular free evangelical church, I encountered a card-carrying charismatic who was trying to gain access to the London circuit of churches for financial gain. The charismatic was from Africa, promoting the prosperity 'gospel'. On his business card, he had the title, "Apostle" and the Bible verse, which was either: "Behold, I have given you authority to tread on serpents and scorpions, and over all the power of the enemy, and nothing shall hurt you" (Lu. 10:19). He asked me, "How do I breakthrough?" meaning, how can he establish an itinerate ministry in London. I replied, "You can start by removing the word "Apostle" from your business card, followed by the removal of the verse "Luke 10:19," or a similar one from Mark's gospel (Mk. 16:17-18), from memory."

When discussing the matter with the pastor of that church, he justified accommodating the African charismatic by saying, "Do not neglect to show hospitality to strangers, for thereby some have entertained angels unawares" (Heb. 13:2). At the time, the pastor, of this struggling church, was paying for the African's first-class airfare back and forth from Africa. I replied to the pastor's use of scripture (Heb. 13:2), "I was unaware of angels needing to travel by airplane, never mind first class!" Clearly, the African charismatic was a deceiver, who interestingly carried a business card with a Bible verse stating that a believer has authority over demons (snakes) who obstruct the proclamation of Jesus (Lu. 10:17-20). The biblical authority refers to the ability to cast them out (Lu. 10:17, 19, cf. Mk. 16:17), which should have happened to the itinerate individual taking advantage of a gullible yet kindhearted pastor who was seeking to show hospitality.

Preventing the problem in the first place, John says do not let deceivers into your home (2 Jn. 10). For the first few centuries, the church met in houses; therefore, by the believer stopping the deceiver from entering their home, they also blocked them from the church. This was not always happening; as mentioned above, Peter and Jude wrote letters to the churches addressing the problem. Likewise, John's second letter responded to the "Dear lady" (1 Jn. 5), who had the good sense to inquire what she should do.

The story above, is an example of how the itinerate Gnostics and some charismatics manipulate scripture to gain access and make disciples (Act. 20:29-30). Peter, among others, warns that the motive is greed. The Gnostics have their hearts trained on greed (2 Pet. 2:2, 14), helping themselves to the best of everything (Jude 12), and some key leaders and televangelists within the Word of Faith charismatic movement are no different.

Because deception is the greatest of the end time signs, John's ancient warnings are more relevant today than they were two thousand years ago when he thought he was living in the last hour due to the increase of deception (1 Jn. 2:18). Therefore, John's instructions not to give deceivers access to your life and home is even more important today. Today, deceivers gain access through Christian television, the radio, books, and the internet.

CHAPTER 1
Walking in the Truth and Love

Some of Your Children [are] Walking in the Truth

John's second letter is broken up into two main parts, the first (2 Jn. 1-6) addressing truth (the light) and love, with the second part (2 Jn. 7-11) addressing deception. However, the structure of the letter has four parts, as follows:

A. Greeting (verses 1-3)
B. Walking in Truth (verses 4-6)
C. Warning Against Deceivers (verses 7-11)
D. Final Greetings (verse 12)

The letter's purpose urges the recipient (the lady and her children) to continue walking in the truth they have received, which is the commandment they heard from the beginning (2 Jn. 5-6). John's second letter echoes the importance of following the truth by avoiding deceivers. One takes a person away from the other. Specifically, John warns against deceivers who do not confess the coming of Jesus Christ in the flesh (2 Jn. 7). In fact, they have the spirit of the antichrist (2 Jn. 7), implying they also deny Christ's first appearing, and His deity. As with John's first letter, he writes the second to warn about these deceivers (1 Jn. 2: 26, 2 Jn. 7-11).

The recipient of the second letter was an "Elect lady" (2 Jn. 1), later referred to as a "Dear lady" (2 Jn. 5). Her "Children" are most likely referring to the church members, moreover natural sons, and daughters. Interestingly, and consistent with the warning (2 Jn. 7-8, 10-11), only some of her children are walking in the truth (2 Jn. 4) of the commandment and original teaching (2 Jn. 5-6, 9-10). John's comment should remind the reader of the parables, where most have the commonality of the true and the false mixing together until the day of judgement. The illustration serves to warn that not all who confess to know God and follow Christ do (cf. Matt. 7:21-23, Lu. 6:46, 13:22-30, 1 Jn. 1:6). Remember, even within the original twelve followers of Jesus, there was one who belonged to the devil, Judas. The application is that within any church gathering, there will be a mix of true and false converts. Most troubling is that all confessing 'Christians' think they are saved when many are not (Matt. 7:22). While "Some" started on the right foot, they can lose what the apostles worked for, referring to salvation (2 Jn. 8).

Further support for the word "Children" applying to the church is seen in the closing verse: "The children of your elect sister greet you." The term probably refers to the children (members of the church) of another (sister) church greeting them. John writes the word "Children" thirteen times in his first letter, referring to those who belong to God or the devil. Three times more, John writes the word in his second letter (2 Jn. 1, 4, 13) and once in his third (3 Jn. 4), where he says, "I have no greater joy than to hear that my children are walking in the truth."

While John addresses the "Lady" (2 Jn. 1b, 5), who is the owner of the house where the church meets, John is the "Elder" (2 Jn. 1a) and, therefore, overseer of that house church, whom, he "Loves in truth" (2 Jn. 1b). John goes on to say, "Not only (this church) but also all who know the truth" (2 Jn. 1c). John's expression of love applies to all, first referring to the church being addressed (2 Jn. 1:1), the sister church (2 Jn. 13), and every other church of every age, who love and walk in the truth of Christ; that is, the message heard from the beginning (2 Jn. 5, 6).

The promise to those abiding in the truth is eternal life (2 Jn. 2), where truth remains and forever preserves the immortal soul. The reverse is also true; deception blinds, corrupts, and eventually and eternally consumes the eternal soul in hell's fire. Deception is the opposite of the truth. The longer a person remains to be deceived, the further they drift from the truth, entirely departing from what they once knew.

The warning of apostasy is common within the Bible, found several times in the Old and New Testaments. Every prophet warned about deception, as does every New Testament author. The only safeguard anyone has against deception is Jesus. John confirmed it by saying, "He who was born of God protects him, and the evil one does not touch him" (1 Jn. 5:18).

The one submitting to God and resisting the devil (Jam. 4:7) is protected. However, the one practicing sin breaks down and removes that hedge of protection (Job 1:10). The hedge of projection safeguards the sheep (Christians) from the roaring lion (Satan), seeking to devour through deception (1 Pet. 5:8). Those submitting to God have the confidence of God's "Grace, mercy and peace" (2 Jn. 3a), that is, for those who continue to walk in "Truth and love" (1 Jn. 3b, 6b), they alone have the confidence of God's protection and provision of grace, mercy, and peace.

John encourages his readers with these words for two reasons - first to remind them of what they have in and through Christ, and secondly, to counter the false teaching of the Gnostics who do not know the truth (1 Jn. 1:8) and do not walk in love (1 Jn. 4:20); therefore, they do not have God (2 Jn. 9).

As mentioned throughout John's first letter, John's use of the word "Walk" is progressive in Greek, meaning continuous, ongoing action. While some start well, not all end well, which is picked up in the following verse (2 Jn. 4). John greatly rejoices to find "Some walking in the truth," implying not all are, or not all have remained. Some "Children" have departed, no longer abiding in truth (Christ) because of the Gnostics. Again, the specific issue at hand is truth and love; some are no longer walking according to the commandment they heard from the beginning (2 Jn. 5, 6). The primary commandment refers to the Son: "And this is His commandment, that we believe in the name of his Son Jesus Christ and love one another, just as He has commanded us" (1 Jn. 3:23). The next is the commandment of love (1 Jn. 2:7-11).

Instead of abiding, as mentioned sixteen times in the first letter and twice more in the second, some have walked away from the commandments, and therefore, they no longer have God's "Grace, mercy and peace" with them (2 Jn. 3). As for those remaining in the truth, John loves them (2 Jn. 1). Because the truth is "In us" (2 Jn. 2), John states that God's grace, mercy, and peace will be "With us" (2 Jn. 3). One is not without the other.

John's reference to "Walking in the truth" means to live it out, to practice and obey. The Gnostics, at one time, knew the truth yet walked away by practicing sin. They "Went out into the world" (2 Jn. 7). As mentioned above, deliberate, ongoing sin takes a person away from the truth, eventually beyond the point of return. Due to the continuing threat of the Gnostics, aiming to deceive (1 Jn. 2:26, 3:7, 2 Jn. 7), John "Greatly rejoiced to find some [still] walking in the truth." John encourages the church to continue walking in love, the commandment they heard from the beginning (2 Jn. 5-6). John mentioned the commandment of love several times in his first letter (1 Jn. 3:11, 23; 4:7, 11, 12) for obvious reasons. If anyone stops walking in love, they will no longer know God; therefore, they will no longer have God (1 Jn. 4:8, 2 Jn. 9).

John reiterates the commandment of love by saying, "And this is love, that we walk according to His commandments; this is the commandment, just as you have heard from the beginning so that you should walk in it" (2 Jn. 6). Verse six should be compared to similar verses in John's gospel: "If you keep My commandments, you will abide in My love, just as I have kept My Father's commandments and abide in His love" (Jn. 15:10). And: "You are my friends if you do what I command you" (Jn. 15:14). The reverse is also true, where Jesus said, "Why do you call me 'Lord, Lord,' and not do what I tell you?" (Lu. 6:46). In other words, unless the confessing follower of Christ walks in truth and love (2 Jn. 1:2), that one does not belong. Again, the commandment is to love one another (Jn. 15:12, 2 Jn. 5-6).

Christ is "In us" (2 Jn. 2) and "With us" (2 Jn. 3), providing we keep His commandments, that is, we walk "In it (the light/truth)" (2 Jn. 3b, 6b). When the confessing follower of Christ is walking (abiding) in the commandments (2 Jn. 5), Christ walks (abides) with them (1 Jn. 4:16). The reverse is also true. To "Walk in it" refers to walking in the truth. John wrote the word "Truth" five times in his second letter (2 Jn. 1[x2], 2, 3, 4). The importance of walking in the truth is to remain. Verse seven (2 Jn. 7) warns of those who have not remained; instead, they have walked away, they have "Gone out into the world." In other words, they have left the church.

Nevertheless, and in conclusion, John greatly rejoiced to find "Some" [still] walking in the truth (2 Jn. 4), which is repeated in his third letter, where he says, "I have no greater joy than to hear that my children are walking in the truth" (3 Jn. 4). As for the one who has walked away, the opposite is just as true. Instead of joy, grief and sadness is the experience, particularly for the ones unable to be restored (Heb. 6:4-8, 10:26-31, 1 Jn. 5:16). For the ones who have not committed the sin unto death, pray for them (1 Jn. 5:16), and save some by snatching them out of the fire (Jude 23).

CHAPTER 2
Deceivers at the Door

Anyone Who Runs Ahead and Does Not Continue in the Teaching of Christ Does Not Have God

As mentioned in the previous section, John greatly rejoiced to find some still walking in the truth (2 Jn. 4), holding fast to what they had heard from the beginning (2 Jn. 5, 6). The original message and commandments are given in John's first letters: 1). Believe on Christ (1 Jn. 3:23), and 2). Love one another (1 Jn. 2:7-11). Unless a confessing believer has the evidence of Christ within, expressed through the outward manifestation of love, they are deceived and destined to hell. Such was the case for the Gnostics.

John further develops his argument against the Gnostics in his second letter, saying, "If anyone does not confess the coming of Jesus Christ in the flesh, such a one is a deceiver and the antichrist" (2 Jn. 7). The word "Antichrist" is written by John five times (1 Jn. 2:18[x2], 22, 4:3, 2 Jn. 7), and only by John in the entire Bible. John coined the word "Antichrist." Much has already been said about the antichrist in the commentary given to John's first letter. Nevertheless, John repeats the warning in his second; therefore, further consideration must be given to the literal, coming man, who is the antichrist.

In the same way, Jesus Christ is literally coming in the flesh (2 Jn. 7), so is the antichrist. In fact, he is already here. John thought he was at the door in his time, saying he was living in the last hour before the tribulation commences due to the increase of false teachers plaguing the church (1 Jn. 2:18-19).

Although little is mentioned of the coming antichrist today from most pulpits, the Bible has much to say about him. Several names and titles throughout scripture know the antichrist, and these names provide a glimpse into the many facets of his sinister character. For example, he is the beast (Rev. 13:1), the man of sin (2 Thess. 2:3), the lawless one (2 Thess. 2:8), the abomination (Matt. 24:15), the little horn (Dan. 7:8); the prince (of darkness) who is to come (Dan. 9:26); the vile person (Dan. 11:21); and a king [who does] according to his covenant, commencing the tribulation.

While no one knows who the antichrist is, we can confidently assume that he is very much alive and active today (cf. 1 Jn. 2:18-19), preparing for a time, times, and a half a time (Dan. 7:25). Alongside the book of Daniel, the period of a time, times, and half a time, is also mentioned in the book of Revelation, chapter twelve, verse fourteen (Rev. 12:14). According to Revelation twelve, verse six (Rev. 12:6), this time equals 1,260 prophetic days times twice, equalling seven years. The time is confirmed in Revelation chapters eleven and thirteen (Rev. 11:3, 13:5).

In Bible prophecy, one prophetic day equals one literal year (cf. Num. 14:34; Ps. 90:4, Ezek. 4:6, 2 Pet. 3:8), implying the little horn will reign supreme for 1,260 days, or forty-two months times twice, dividing up the first and second part of the tribulation. Again, Revelation, chapter eleven (Rev. 11:2-3), and chapter thirteen (Rev. 13:5) support the same. In sum, the antichrist will rule for seven years (Isa. 26:15, 18, Dan. 7:6b, 25, 9:24-27, 12:7, Rev. 12:14), which is the entire duration of the tribulation.

The coming antichrist will have dominion for seven years, which is also said to be one hour (Rev. 3:10). However, he will not be revealed until after the rebellion comes first (2 Thess. 2:3), which is the great falling away, leading to the tribulation. The great falling away refers to the apostate church, mainstreaming worldly worship, the absence of God (cf. church of Laodicea, Rev. 3:14-22), yet, for a time, promoting (another) Jesus (2 Cor. 11:4), conditioning confessing followers of Christ for the counterfeit christ to come (Matt. 24:5, 23-26, Rev. 3:15-20).

The most significant sign of the antichrist's time is the great apostasy of the church, resulting in the apostates being 'left behind' due to not being ready (Matt. 24:44, Lu. 12:25, 40, 47), therefore missing the rapture. The rapture will remove the obedient, ready believers (2 Thess. 2:7), revealing the antichrist in and through the tribulation. The commencement of the tribulation will be triggered by the signing of the (false) peace treaty (Isa. 28:15, 18, Dan. 9:24-27) simultaneously occurring alongside the rapture. During the tribulation, the antichrist is identified by several prophesied activities.

The fastest way to identify the beast (the antichrist) is by signing a Middle East Peace Treaty between Israel and the Arab nations (Isa. 28:15, 18, Dan. 9:24-27). The man that orchestrates that is the antichrist.

Another way to identify him would be by rebuilding the temple in Jerusalem. The antichrist will authorise the rebuild and then rule from that location, commanding ten nations, mainly in Europe, being the Revived Roman Empire ("Ten horns" - Dan. 7:23-27, Rev. 17:7-14). At the halfway mark of the seven-year test, the antichrist will break the peace treaty (Dan. 9:27), and he will receive a mortal wound to the head. This will kill him, yet he will be resurrected (like Jesus) and then claim to be God (Rev. 11:7, 13:3, 12, 14, 17:8-9, 11). At the same time, the antichrist is resurrected, Satan will embody him, who, at the time, has been cast to the earth (Rev. 12:3-4, 7-9, 13).

The halfway mark is called the "Great Tribulation" (Jer. 30:7, Dan. 12:1, Matt. 24:21). Also, at around the halfway mark of the tribulation (3.5 years in), the antichrist will set himself up to be worshipped as God in the rebuilt temple (2 Thess. 2:3-4). This is the "Abomination of desolation" (Dan. 9:27, 11:31, 12:11, Matt. 24:15). Another way to identify the antichrist is through the number of his name—666 (Rev. 13:18). The letters of his name, and character, are a numeric code. The number is that of the "Beast."

Again, from the list above, the coming antichrist is a literal man, not a system. The antichrist is a counterfeit Christ; in the same way, Jesus Christ was a literal man. The antichrist will be, too, again revealed by successfully signing a false covenant of peace within the Middle East, triggering the tribulation. The antichrist will break this (false) peace treaty forty-two months later, essentially halfway through the seven years (Dan. 9:27b).

To summarise and add to the antichrist's activities as listed above, during the tribulation, he will rule the New World Order (Dan. 7:23, 8:19-23; Rev. 13:7; 17:12-13). He will come in his own name (Jn. 5:43b); he will be eloquent and persuasive of speech (Dan. 7:20); he will be a leader of great charisma (Dan. 8:23), and he will operate in supernatural signs and wonders (2 Thess. 2:9; Rev. 13:13; 16:16; 19:20). The antichrist will have no regard for the God of his fathers, being any god at all; neither will he have a desire for women (Dan. 11:37). Having no desire for women does not necessarily characterise him as a homosexual, although it is possible, or at least bi-sexual, instead it suggests he will be anti-women regarding the Messianic hope (Gen. 3:15).

Furthermore, the antichrist will rise from the Mediterranean world. He will be a Jew, not a Muslim, as some suggest - for a reason, Jews will only accept a Jewish Messiah. Therefore, the antichrist is of Jewish heritage, living and or even being born in the revived Roman Empire (Dan. 7:8, 24). In fact, the antichrist is prophesied to be from the tribe of Dan, who judges Israel during the tribulation. The ancient prophecy states that "Dan shall judge his people one of the tribes of Israel. Dan shall be a serpent in the way, a viper by the path, that bites the horse's heels so that his rider falls backward. I wait for your salvation, O Lord" (Gen 49:16-18). The name Dan means judgement (cf. Gen. 30:6). Jacob's prophecy involves a play on words, "Dan shall judge . . ." The Hebrew expression is dan yadin. Yadin is the future tense of the verb conjugated in the third person, meaning "(he) will enact justice," "(he) will make law" or "(he) will judge."

The "Serpent" (Satan), who was cast to the earth to deceive the whole world, will embody the antichrist (Rev. 12:9), who is a descendant from the tribe of Dan. Jacob's prophecy suggests that Satan will operate through a man from the tribe of Dan during the tribulation. The primary issue with the tribe of Dan was idolatry. They "Set up the carved image for themselves" (Judg. 18:30). The antichrist will also have an image (idol) of himself during the tribulation (Rev.13:14-17). For this reason, John warned the church, "Keep yourselves from idols" (1 Jn. 5:21).

The complete absence of Dan from the comprehensive tribe genealogy of First Chronicles 2–10 is noteworthy. While addressing the frequently posed topic of why Dan is left out of the 144,000 Jews who will be sealed during the tribulation period (Rev. 7:4-8), it is important to bear in mind the consequence of idolatry that has afflicted the tribe of Dan throughout its history.

As stated earlier, no one will know who the antichrist is until the tribulation commences, and then, only the wise will be able to identify him (Dan. 12:10, Rev. 13:18) and warn others about him (11:23, 12:3). However, what can be known now, is the nearness of his appearing, by the increase of deception.

Increased deception within the church is what John is concerned about (1 Jn. 2:18-19, 2:26, 3:7, 4:1-3, 2 Jn. 7-11), and is the reason why he wrote his first and second letters (1 Jn. 2:26, 2 Jn. 7). The reason for writing the second letter is seen through the chiastic structure, as follows:

A - Introduction (v. 7a)
    B - Description of false teachers (v. 7b)
        C - Exhortation to hold fast to the truth (v. 8a)

D - Promise of reward (v. 8b)
  E - Contrast between those who remain in Christ's teaching and those who do not (v. 9)
 D' - Warning against receiving false teachers (v. 10)
 C' - Prohibition against participating in the works of false teachers (v. 11a)
 B' - Warning against supporting false teachers (v. 11b)
A' - Conclusion (vv. 12-13)

The central point of the chiasm is the warning against false teachers, which is surrounded by related ideas on both sides. The structure emphasises the importance of avoiding false teachers and holding fast to the truth of Christ's teaching. Overall, this chiastic structure emphasises the need to remain faithful to the true teachings of Christ and to be wary of those who would lead believers astray. As mentioned earlier, "Some" have already departed" (2 Jn. 4, 9, 11).

While some scholars state John's reference to "Some" remaining to walk in the truth does not suggest that some are not, the context clearly says otherwise. If all were abiding, John would not have said, "Some," instead he would have said, "I greatly rejoice to find your children walking in the truth" (2 Jn. 4). Verses nine and eleven (2 Jn. 9, 11) further support that some have departed from what they heard from the beginning (cf. 2 Jn. 5, 6). While they have departed from the truth and Christ, they have remained within the church, corrupting others.

John's statement regarding the deceivers departing the church and returning to the world (1 Jn. 2:19, 4:1, 2 Jn. 7) does not mean they no longer mix with believers. Instead, John's letters, like Peter and Jude, warn the church that the deceivers are among them (cf. 2 Pet. 2:1, 13, Jude 4, 12), with others still trying to gain access to their homes and churches (2 Jn. 10), seeking to deceive (1 Jn. 2:26, 3:7, 2 Jn. 7).

As mentioned earlier, the primary deception is to deny Christ. Verse seven (2 Jn. 7, cf. 1 Jn. 2:28, 3:2) points to the return of Jesus Christ, which is linked to His first appearance (1 Jn. 3:5, 8). One cannot be separated from the other. As stated in the commentary for the book of Jude, the scoffers rejected the return of Christ, also dismissing the coming judgement (Jude 18, cf. 2 Pet. 3:3). Jesus first appeared to deal with the sin problem, and His next appearance will deal with the problem of sinners.

The Greek word John uses for the coming of Jesus is "Parousia." A common word used for the coming of Christ (Matt 24:3; 1 Cor. 15:23; 1 Thess. 2:19; 2 Thess. 2:8; 2 Pet 3:4; 1 Jn. 2:28); the Son of Man (Matt. 24:27, 37, 39); the Lord (1 Thess. 3:13, 4:15, 5:23, 2 Thess. 2:1, Jam. 5:7-8, 2 Pet. 1:16), the day of God (2 Pet. 3:12). In sum, the term Parousia refers to the Second Coming of Christ. The return of Jesus Christ occurs at the end of the seven-year tribulation period, described by Jesus in the Olivet Discord (Matt. 24:15-22, 32-34, Mk. 13:14-23, 29-30, cf. Lu. 19:41-44, 21:20-23, 32-33, 23:28-30).

The Gnostics, who were former members of the church community, denied both the first and second appearing of Christ and are therefore "Antichrist" (2 Jn. 7). As stated in chapter four of John's first letter, the fastest, most straightforward, and cleanest way to identify a false teacher is by their rejection of Jesus Christ (1 Jn. 4:1-3). Anyone coming with a 'gospel' void of Christ is a "Deceiver" (2 Jn. 7), preparing for the ultimate deceiver to come, the antichrist. Seven times John writes the word "Deceive" in the book of Revelation, warning of the activities of Satan, his son the antichrist, and his end time harlot church (Rev. 12:9, 13:14, 18:23, 19:20 20:3, 8, 10).

Like verse four (2 Jn. 4), verse eight (2 Jn. 8) also supports that some have been deceived by the Gnostics and have departed from the truth, having lost what was previously worked for. Therefore, John says, "Watch yourselves!" (2 Jn. 8). The warning can be confusing due to the variation found in varying Bible translations and versions (versions are not the same as translations).

The variation in part A of the verse (2 Jn. 8a) is with the word "We," sometimes written as "You." The ESV says: "Watch yourselves, so that you may not lose what <u>we</u> have worked for," also supported by the NIV, KJV, NKJV, NTL, ASV, NRSV, and NASV. However, the NIRV says: "Watch out that you don't lose what *you* have worked for." The Amplified Version (not a translation) says, "Watch yourselves so that you do not lose what <u>we have accomplished together</u>."

If the NIRV is correct, the reader is in danger of losing what they have worked for; however, if most translations are accurate, then the apostles are in danger of suffering loss. If the reader is in danger, the loss will refer to their faith in Christ and salvation (cf. Jn. 6:27, 29). If most of the versions are correct, then the apostles are in danger of losing what they have worked for, meaning the souls of those they have discipled.

Most Bible translations imply that John, and every elder of the church, throughout the ages are at risk of suffering loss when what they have worked for is snatched away by the deceivers. If the elders suffer loss, the loss of salvation for the reader is also implied. In sum, John's reference to "Full reward" (2 Jn. 8b) refers to the elder's reward for delivering souls safely into the hands of Jesus and eternal life for the believer. It is the elders of the church who have "Worked" to make Christ known (cf. 1 Jn. 1:1-3, 2:21), to disciple and protect the beloved from deceivers (1 Jn. 2:18-19, 2:26, 3:7, 4:1-4, 2 Jn. 7-11). The first thing to guard against is the Gnostics, and their main aim, which is to corrupt the teaching of Christ through the corruption of scripture (2 Jn. 9-10), moving away from what was heard from the beginning (2 Jn. 5, 6).

Strengthening the above argument, there is another variation in part B of the verse (2 Jn. 8b) within varying translations. Several translations present the verse this way: "Be diligent so that <u>you</u> receive your full reward" (2 Jn. 8b, NLT, cf. NIV, ASV, NASV, GNT, MSV, NRSV). However, the ESV says: "Watch yourselves so that you may not lose what <u>we</u> have worked for but may win a full reward." The KJV is similar, saying, "Look to yourselves, that <u>we</u> lose not those things which <u>we</u> have wrought, but that we receive a full reward." The NKJV says: "Look to yourselves, that <u>we</u> do not lose those things <u>we</u> worked for, but that <u>we</u> may receive a full reward."

After considering all the principal translations, John clearly warns of loss for himself and every other elder of the church and his reader if they depart from the truth. Salvation is either received in full or not at all. John's warning (2 Jn. 8) first refers to the loss for the elder when their disciple departs. However, both suffer loss. The elder's loss will be when he stands before Jesus on the day of judgement, with fewer souls than entrusted with.

Guarding against any potential loss, the elder should aim to follow the example of Jesus, the Good Shepherd, who does not lose what He has been given: "I give them eternal life, and they will never perish, and no one will snatch them out of My hand. My Father, who has given them to Me, is greater than all, and no one is able to snatch them out of the Father's hand. I and the Father are One" (Jn. 10:28-30).

Regarding Judas, Jesus did not "lose" him in the sense of losing control over him or being unable to keep him safe. Instead, Judas chose to betray Jesus and ultimately took his own life, as we see in Matthew's gospel, "When Judas, who had betrayed Him, saw that Jesus was condemned, he was seized with remorse and returned the thirty pieces of silver to the chief priests and the elders. 'I have sinned,' he said, 'for I have betrayed innocent blood.' – 'What is that to us?' they replied. 'That's your responsibility.' So Judas threw the money into the temple and left. Then he went away and hanged himself" (Matt. 27:3-5).

While Jesus had the power to prevent Judas from betraying Him, He allowed Judas to exercise his free will, just as He allows us to make our own choices, even if those choices are not in line with His will. However, Jesus did not "lose" Judas in the sense that Judas was snatched out of His hand against His will, which is also the case for John's readers and anyone else.

The responsibility is, therefore, twofold; while Jesus was able to protect what He was given from the enemy and still does through church pastors, if they are doing their job, it is up to the confessing follower of Christ to remain. However, for the pastor failing to do their job, and where loss occurs, namely souls, then they will answer for it. This is why James says, "Not many of you should become teachers, my brothers, for you know that we who teach will be judged with greater strictness" (Jam. 3:1). For those failing to teach sound biblical doctrine, there is a double judgement, those failing pastors will give an account for themselves and for others.

Regardless of the reason for the loss, the elder's reward in heaven on the day of judgement may not be full. If the elder lost none, then he would be "Fully rewarded" (2 Jn. 8). If the elders lost some, then not only is he not fully rewarded, but the one missing is without salvation. While reasons for the loss may vary, John narrows in on the deceivers who add and take away from scripture (2 Jn. 9-10). Anyone who changes or fails to "Abide in the teachings of Christ, does not have God" (2 Jn. 9). If they do not have God, they will not be standing before Jesus at the Bema Seat judgement (1 Cor. 3:10-15, 2 Cor. 5:10, Rom. 14:10-12).

While standing at the Bema Seat judgement, some will still suffer loss; however, they will still be saved (1 Cor. 3:13-15). Naturally, if someone suffers a loss, their reward will not be full; this is different from what John has in mind when warning his readers. Again, anyone who does not have God will not be standing before the Bema Seat, but rather the Great White Throne of Judgement (Rev. 20:11-15). The Gnostics, and anyone following them, are reserved for the latter (Jude 10-13).

"Anyone who runs ahead and does not continue in the teaching of Christ does not have God." John could not have made it more straightforward because "Some" of his readers (2 Jn. 4) had run ahead, following in the footsteps of the Gnostics. By running ahead of the original teaching, the offender departs from Christ, and if not rescued, they will arrive at the point of no return (1 Jn. 5:16-17, Jude 22-23); hence, they no longer have God (Jn. 9). On the other hand, "Those who remain in the teaching, have both the Father and the Son" (2 Jn. 9).

The purpose of the warning is to protect the reader against deception, guarding against any temptation to change the Word of God. As mentioned, the great end times sign is deception. Paul prophesied that there would be a great falling away before the tribulation commences, where entire church denominations and movements depart from sound biblical doctrine (2 Thess. 2:3, 1 Tim. 4:1-2, 2 Tim. 4:3-4). Paul's prophesy is being fulfilled in our time, where churches are accommodating and even celebrating same-sex marriage, the ordination of LGBTQ+ clergy, abortion, and euthanasia. Other concerns are with ecumenicalism, including the fellowship of interfaith, namely those rejecting the deity of Christ. John expressly says not to mix with them (2 Jn. 10-11). Anyone committing any of the above has departed from the teachings of Christ and therefore does not have God (2 Jn. 9).

The method of protection provided by John is to shut the Gnostics out, show them no hospitality, give them no greeting in the street, and no access to homes and churches (2 Jn. 10). Specifically, John is targeting those who do not bring the teachings of Christ (2 Jn. 10); however, the passage also includes anyone who has changed the original teachings. John goes on to say, "Whoever greets [that one] (the false teacher) takes part in his wicked works" (2 Jn. 11). The danger of greeting false teachers is that any sign of acknowledgment can be seen as an endorsement. Anyone giving an endorsement of the false teacher promotes them, thereby shares in their wicked works (2 Jn 11), which is why John said in his first letter, if you want to have fellowship with us, you cannot have fellowship with them (the Gnostics). Anyone with a foot in both camps will be considered as lost as those who have departed.

In John's words, the evidence is that they "Take part in his wicked works" (2 Jn. 11).

John concludes his second letter, saying, "I have much to write to you; I would rather not use paper and ink. Instead, I hope to come to you and talk face to face, so that our joy may be complete" (2 Jn. 12). John's joy being complete refers to finding "Some children [still] walking in the truth" (2 Jn. 4), John greatly rejoiced over that testimony (3 Jn. 3-4). John wrote his first letter to complete his joy (1 Jn. 1:4), safeguarding the beloved from the deceivers. John loves the church walking in the truth, and love (2 Jn. 3), including the ones being addressed, the sister church (2 Jn. 13), and any other within the church age. As for the rest, he warns, have nothing to do with them, lest you be like them and share in their "Reward." Remember Judas, "Who was allotted his share in this ministry," he was "Rewarded" for his wicked works (cf. Acts 1:17-20).

In conclusion, the critical point of the passages (2 Jn. 7-13) is that within any groups, there will be a contrast between those who remain in Christ's teaching and those who do not (2 Jn. 9). To safeguard the household of God, John warns, "Anyone who runs ahead and does not continue in the teaching of Christ does not have God" (2 Jn. 9). Therefore, "If anyone comes to you and does not bring this teaching, do not receive him into your house or give him any greeting" (2 Jn. 10). These are John's instructions to the "Elect" and "Dear lady and her children" (2 Jn. 1, 5), "Some" of whom are still walking in the truth (2 Jn. 4), implying that some no longer are.

THIRD JOHN

FRIENDS AND FOES
Diotrephes and Demetrius

Introduction:

John's third letter is like his second, written to the elder of the church, Gaius, who John loves in the truth (3 Jn. 1). Gaius is known for his hospitality towards travelling missionaries by living out John's teaching of truth and love. The introductory greeting echoes the second letter (2 Jn 1-2). Verses three and four (3 Jn. 3-4) repeat John's joy when finding some [still] walking in the truth (2 Jn. 4). John greatly rejoices over those who have remained, for "Some" [others] have clearly departed, falling prey to the deceptive Gnostics. Deception is the critical point of each of John's letters. In his third letter, John distinguishes between Diotrephes and Demetrius, which is pinpointed through the chiastic structure.

The chiastic structure of Third John can be outlined as follows:

A. Greeting and commendation of Gaius (verses 1-8)
    B. Praise for Gaius' hospitality (verses 5-6)
        C. Gaius' faithful conduct and support of the gospel (verse 3)
            D. Warning against Diotrephes (verses 9-10)
                E. Contrast between Diotrephes and Demetrius (verse 11)
            D'. Praise for Demetrius (verse 12)
        C'. Gaius' reputation for truth and love (verses 1-4)

 B'. Request for continued support (verses 7-8)
A'. Farewell and final greetings (verses 13-15)

In this chiastic structure, the focus is on Diotrephes and Demetrius; Demetrius is praised for his hospitality, faithful conduct, and support of the gospel. On the other hand, Diotrephes is rebuked for his rejection of John's apostolic authority, his intent of harm, and his self-serving lack of hospitality. While the overall contrast is made between Gaius and Diotrephes, where the latter is warned against, John narrows in on the distinction between Diotrephes and Demetrius. The structure emphasises the importance of supporting those faithful to the gospel while avoiding those not walking in the truth and love. All three of John's letters major on truth and love. John warns, without truth and love, no one has Christ, therefore, eternal life.

Noteworthy is that Diotrephes is the church leader, like Gaius and Demetrius. Despite Diotrephes' position within the church, he is heading in the opposite eternal direction to Demetrius because he does not have fellowship with the apostles; therefore, he does not have fellowship with the Father and with His Son, Jesus Christ (1 Jn. 1:3). The second reason that he does not have eternal life is that he does not walk in love. John says the one who does not love his brother does not have God; the lack of love proves they are without God (1 Jn. 3:10, 4:20-21).

As mentioned above, like with John's first and second letters, his third majors on truth and love. One is without the other for the genuine follower of Christ. Again, the lack of love, outside the denial of Jesus Christ, is the evidence that a confessing believer does not have God: "This is how you/we know" (1 Jn. 2:3, 4, 3:16, 19, 24, 4:2, 6, 13, 4:2). Nine times John provides the means to identify who of the confessing believers belong to God, and who does not. The nine verses narrow in on two things, 1). Listening to, keeping, and abiding in God's word, and 2). Loving one another. The nine verses are reinforced through six more, "What they heard/had from the beginning" (1 Jn.1:1, 2:7, 24, 3:11, 2 Jn. 5, 6).

From the beginning, the beloved had the message of Jesus Christ proclaimed through the apostles (1 Jn. 1-3), expressly commanding the hearer/reader to believe in Him and to love one another (1 Jn. 3:33). John's conditional statement in chapter two of the first letter clearly states that unless the confessing believer in Christ remains in the original teaching, evident by their confession and love walk, then they do not have eternal life, regardless of their position within the church (1 Jn. 2:24, 25). Today, many in high-ranking church positions, having titles, accolades, fame, and fortune, going by the requirements John provides, do not have God, and neither do many more following them. Here lies the danger and the reason for John's letters.

John writes each of his three letters, warning about self-serving false teachers who aim to deceive (1 Jn. 2:26, 3:7, 2 Jn. 7-11, 3 Jn. 9-10). In his second letter, John warns his readers that if they follow, or give hospitality to the false teachers, then they will share in their wicked works (2 Jn. 13). For this reason, John essentially writes in his first letter, "If you want to have fellowship with us, then you cannot have fellowship with them" (1 Jn. 1:3, paraphrased). It is either one or the other. No one can follow or fellowship with the false teachers who deny Jesus Christ, twist scripture, and then still remain in fellowship with the apostles and God. To remain in fellowship with the apostles, post the first century one must remain/abide in God's written word. That is, "What they have heard from the beginning." In other words, the original message that is contained in the sixty-six books of the Bible.

CHAPTER 1
Walk In The Truth

The Truth Attracts Trouble

John's third letter is addressed to the church elder, Gaius, who is well-known in the community of believers. Gaius was a fellow workman alongside Paul, primarily known for his faithfulness and hospitality (Acts 19:29, 20:4, Rom. 16:23). In fact, Paul baptised him (1 Cor. 1:14). As seen through the listed passages, Gaius was no stranger to hostilities, nor false teachers.

In the book of Acts, chapter nineteen, a troublemaker called Demetrius (Acts. 19:23) became rich by making idols of Artemis (Acts. 19:24, 25). When Paul came preaching the gospel of Jesus Christ, Demetrius rallied forces against him. Paul had a reputation for turning many away from idols, converting them to Christianity (Act 19:26). Because of this, Demetrius inspired an angry mob (cf. Acts 19:40) to kill Paul, and his companions, which included Gaius. Gaius was caught by the crowd and dragged to the temple. Paul, and his fellow companions, including Gaius, escaped the mob at Ephesus, only to run into trouble again in Greece (Act. 20:2). There, the Jews wanted to kill Paul (Acts 20:3); though, Paul again slipped away, departing for Syria.

Paul's next mention of Gaius is in the letter to the Romans. Like the book of Acts accounts, the passage's context is conflict. Within the context of internal church conflict, **Paul "Appeals to the brother [telling them] to watch out for those who** cause divisions and create obstacles contrary to the doctrine [they] have been taught." (Rom. 16:17, in context of verses 17-23).. Like John (2 Jn. 1-11), Paul says, "Avoid them" (Rom. 16:17). Paul goes on to say, "Such people do not serve our Lord Jesus Christ, but their own appetites, and by smooth talk and flattery, they deceive the hearts of the naïve" (Rom. 16:18). Peter says something similar, warning that the Gnostics "Have eyes full of adultery, insatiable for sin. They entice unsteady souls. They have their hearts trained on greed. Accursed children!" (2 Pet. 2:14).

Paul's critical point of his appeal in the letter to the Romans is seen in verse nineteen (b), saying, "I want you to be wise as to what is good and innocent as to what is evil" (Rom. 16:19b). Paul closes his letter by encouraging the church with the words, "The God of peace will soon crush Satan under your feet" (Rom. 16:19a), implying, until then, Satan will continue to trouble you (cf. Jn. 16:33), mainly through those causing division, namely by twisting scripture (Rom. 16:17). Paul then lists those who are with him, Timothy, Lucius, Jason, Sosipater, Gaius, Erastus and Quartus (Rom. 16:21-23).

While some say that the person Gaius, mentioned three times throughout scripture, may not be the same person, there is no reason to doubt that he is. He is mentioned once to be Gaius, the Thessalonian (Acts 20:4). If there were others by the same name, it would be expected that the others would have been addressed in connection to their location.

An example in the Bible is where two people with the same name come from different locations, as in the name "James." In the New Testament, there are two apostles named James. The first is James, the son of Zebedee, one of the twelve apostles and brother of John, the apostle (Matt. 4:21). He was martyred by King Herod Agrippa I in Jerusalem in AD 44 (Acts 12:1-2).

The second James is the son of Alphaeus, who was also one of the twelve apostles (Mk. 3:18). He is sometimes referred to as "James the Less" or

"James the Just" to distinguish him from James, the son of Zebedee. He became a leader in the church in Jerusalem. He played a prominent role in the Council of Jerusalem, which dealt with the issue of whether Gentile converts to Christianity needed to be circumcised (Acts 15:13-21).

It is believed that James, the son of Zebedee, was from Bethsaida in Galilee, while James, the son of Alphaeus, was from either Nazareth or Capernaum. Despite sharing the same name, these two apostles came from different locations and played different roles in the early Christian church.

Another example in the New Testament where two people with the same name come from different locations is the name "Simon." The first Simon in the New Testament is Simon Peter, one of the twelve apostles and a prominent leader in the early church. He was born in Bethsaida, a fishing village on the north-eastern shore of the Sea of Galilee (Jn. 1:44; Matt. 17:24). He was called by Jesus to be a disciple and was later named "Peter," which means "Rock" (Matt. 16:18).

The second Simon in the New Testament is Simon the Zealot, another of the twelve apostles. He is also called "Simon the Cananaean" or "Simon the Zealot" to distinguish him from Simon Peter (Lk. 6:15; Acts 1:13). The exact location of Simon the Zealot's birthplace is unknown, but some scholars believe that he may have been from Cana, a village in Galilee (Jn. 2:1-11).

Despite sharing the same name, Simon Peter and Simon the Zealot came from different locations and had different backgrounds. They were both chosen by Jesus to be His disciples and played important roles in the early Christian church, but they are often distinguished from each other to avoid confusion.

The conclusion is that all three references of Gaius refer to that same person. The conclusion is supported by that person, Gaius being an important figure in the early church; he was a host to Paul, and the entire church (Rom.

16:23), as seen again in John's letter (3 Jn. 1). Gaius was a close friend of both Paul and John (3 Jn. 15), he had intimate fellowship with them and Jesus Christ due to loving the truth, and walking in love, evidenced by his hospitality.

Because Gaius loved the truth, John loved him (3 Jn. 1). John loved anyone who was, and is, walking in the truth (2 Jn. 1:1), which included Demetrius. Gaius and Demetrius loved the truth and held important roles within the church. Diotrephes also had an important role within the church; however, he was nothing like Gaius and Demetrius. Diotrephes did not love the truth, evident in rejecting John's authority, and he did not walk in love toward others, seen through withholding hospitality (cf. 1 Jn. 3:11-24, esp. verse 17).

Within the context of the abovementioned, John writes a prayer of blessing over Gaius, which is an extension of traditional greeting. Verse two (3 Jn. 2) is well-known within the charismatic circles, "Beloved, I pray that all may go well with you and that you may be in good health, as it goes well with your soul" (3 Jn. 2). The Word of Faith camp hijack the verse in support of their erroneous wealth, health, and happiness doctrine. As mentioned earlier, the Christian expectation and experience in this life is persecution and suffering, not physical prosperity (Acts 14:22, Rom 8:18, Phil 3:10-11, 2 Tim 3:12, 1 Pet 4:13, 5:1).

Clearing up the charismatic confusion, as mentioned, Gaius, whom John loves, received a greeting accompanied with good wishes in the same way we might today (i.e., I hope, and pray that you are doing well, my friend and are in good health). That is a standard way to greet someone, and in no way implies that God promises health, wealth, and happiness. In other words, "Your Best Life Now." The false teaching that promises "Your Best Life Now" serves as an example of how far some have wandered from the truth, the original teaching, by twisting scripture for greedy gain.

As written above, included in the greeting for his friend, Gaius, John offers a prayer for his friend, which has nothing to do with promising prosperity from God. Again, John does this in response to his friend's love and testimony of the truth (3 Jn. 3-4). That is the truth of the gospel, relating to Jesus Christ, who died for sinners so that their souls might be saved from hell. Jesus did not endure the horrific suffering of the cross so that His followers' pockets might be filled.

Furthermore, the context of John's prayer (3 Jn. 2), accompanying his greeting toward his brother, Gaius, considers the brothers (missionaries) who testify of Gaius' faithfulness, who have gone out for the sake of the name (Jesus), by faith, with nothing, spreading the truth of the gospel (3 Jn. 6-8). John asks Gaius to further support them (3 Jn. 6) like the church should support missionaries sent by the church today.

Noteworthy is that the faithful brothers have gone out preaching the gospel, with nothing (3 Jn. 7), following the instructions Jesus gave to His disciples (Matt. 10:8-10, Mk. 6:8, Lu. 9:3). Indeed, verse seven (3 Jn. 7) crushes the prosperity preachers' claim that verse two (3 Jn. 2) proves that God wants His followers to be rich. If that were the case, what should be concluded of the poor missionaries who went out with nothing? Paul answers this same nonsense of believers thinking God wants them to be rich in his letter to the church of Corinth, which is another verse that charismatics misuse to support the false prosperity 'gospel'.

The verse in question is: "Already you have all you want! Already you have become rich! <u>Without us</u>, you have become kings! And would that you did reign, so that we might share the rule with you!" (1 Cor. 4:8). Once again, and completely ignored by the Word of Faith camp, is that the context, instead of health, wealth, and happiness, suffering, and humility is the theme.

As already stated, Paul was no stranger to suffering and humility (1 Cor. 4;9, 11-13), following the example of Jesus. In his despair, he urges the church of Corinth, and the church of all ages, to endure the same (1 Cor. 4:16). In doing so, there is a crown laid up (2 Tim. 4:8). The crown is laid up for those (alone) who commit to the call and remain faithful to the cause, while suffering (bearing your cross), until the end, and even unto death if necessary (2 Tim. 4:5-6).

Again, as mentioned above, confessing Christians from the prosperity camp do not 'receive' suffering as a part of their 'gospel'. Instead, they confess the blessings and benefits of the coming kingdom now. Otherwise known as Kingdom Now 'theology.'

Similarly, the Corinthian Christians were chasing and claiming their best life now, believing they could reign as kings in this life. Paul responds by saying, "I wish it was true! I wish you were right, and I, too, could share in this make-believe fairy tale!" (v. 8b). Yet he goes on to say - But you are wrong! You are so, very, very wrong, and here is the reason why: Persecution, not prosperity, is the mark of the true believer in Christ (1 Cor. 4:9, 11-13, 16). And it is through enduring persecution the sweet spreading fragrance of the gospel makes God known (2 Cor. 2:14-17, cf. Rev. 2:8-11).

Sadly, the prosperity 'gospel' is nothing new. As Paul and John did, Christians should confront and correct it and should expect to be criticised for doing so. Paul knew some would resist his teaching, such as certain arrogant leaders among them (1 Cor. 4:18). The arrogant leaders were the so-called 'super-apostles' (2 Cor. 11:5, 12:11) who had infiltrated and deceived many within the church with their eloquent speeches and clever arguments (2 Cor. 10:4-6). They preached "Another gospel" (2 Cor. 11:4), albeit powerless (1 Cor. 4:19), due to being void of the biblical Jesus.

Like many within the charismatic camp, the boastful "Super-apostles" went opposite to Paul and Jesus' example of humility through suffering. Those who go beyond what is written (1 Cor. 4:6), who fail to take care of how they build (1 Cor. 3:10), and by running ahead of Christ's teachings (2 Jn. 9), they do not have God (1 Jn. 2:19, 2 Jn. 9).

Regarding John's letter, mentioning the missionaries who had nothing, the Word of Faith camp would argue that God is their provider; therefore, the missionary did not have enough faith to live the life God intended. An abundant life, full of everything their hearts desires! Those at the top of the chiasmatic Ponzi-scheme who do obtain such a lifestyle have done so by fleecing the flock, extracting funds to finance their desires, such as multi-million-dollar airplanes (e.g., 54m) and mansions, alongside every other luxurious item that this world offers.

Aptly aligned with many charismatics is Diotrephes, mentioned in verses nines and ten (3 Jn 9-10). There, John names and shames him as one who likes to put himself first, like Jude's Gnostics (Jude 12). Specifically, as mentioned above, Diotrephes failed to acknowledge John's apostolic authority, therefore God's word (scripture), and instead talked "Wicked nonsense" (3 Jn. 10). John's accusation of Diotrephes "Talking" (idol babble) "Wicked nonsense" refers to his intention to do John harm. Interestingly, Diotrephes's name means "Nourished by Jupiter," and the name fits the man. In Roman mythology, Jupiter was the chief of the gods, and among the planets, Jupiter is the largest! By comparison, the name Paul is also Roman, meaning "Small."

John's reason for mentioning Diotrephes is to warn, saying: "Do not listen to him, neither fellowship with him, who imitates evil" (3 Jn. 11, cf. 2 Jn. 11). Instead, be like Demetrius, who, like Gaius, testifies and walks in the truth, and love (3 Jn. 12). Following the rebuke, John closes with the word "Peace be with you" (3 Jn. 15). John prays a prayer of peace over the one loving, testifying, and walking in the truth, who also offers open-handed hospitality towards others, even strangers in the faith. In sum, John contrasts the difference between Gaius, Diotrephes, and Demetrius.

John's closing prayer is like his opening greeting and blessing that Gaius is in good health and that his soul "Prospers" (3 Jn. 2). As mentioned above, the words "Just as your soul prospers" clearly imply that John wishes his friend well. The Greek word for prosper (Gk. Eudoo/eudow) supports the meaning as mentioned above: "To accomplish, to do, to make, to finish, or to further (as on a journey)." The same is seen in verse six (3 Jn. 6). The primary sense and use of the word and intention within the letter implies that John is wishing his friend that his spiritual journey goes and continues to go well, even under (anticipated) trial, until the end.

On this side of Christ's return, Christians live in this world whose god is Satan (2 Cor. 4:4); hence, Christ's followers must expect persecution, for that was the experience of Christ and His disciples. It was also the promise of Christ to those following. For example, Jesus said, "Then they will deliver you up to tribulation and put you to death, and you will be hated by all nations for My name's sake (Matt. 24:9), and "If the world hates you, know that it has hated Me before it hated you. If you were of the world, the world would love you as its own; but because you are not of the world, but I chose you out of the world; therefore, the world hates you" (Jn. 15:18-19). Persecution is a part of the package; nevertheless, no follower of Christ would pray for it or wish it on others, but rather, all in Christ should be prepared for it.

The danger with the prosperity gospel (which could be defined as another gospel, 2 Cor. 11:4) is that when persecution comes (and it most likely will come), prosperity followers fall away, saying, "It did not work! I did not get what I signed up for!" Many of them are false converts, to begin with, due to "Signing up for another gospel." Nevertheless, they fall away altogether, abandoning whatever little faith they might have had because they embraced the prosperity gospel and its false teaching that places the focus on them and theirs instead of Jesus and others. Simply put, the prosperity gospel motivates those subscribing to it to chase comfort in this world, which often comes at the expense of negating Jesus and ignoring the signs of the time, leading to His return.

In sum, God does not care as much about physical wealth and health for His followers as He does about their spiritual well-being, leading to eternal life. In this life, genuine followers of Christ are guaranteed trials and tribulations through which they are being saved (Acts 14:22). Those (only those) who endure such hardship until the end will be saved (Matt. 10:22, 24:13).

CHAPTER 2
Do Not Imitate Evil

Do Not Be Like Diotrephes

In the previous section, much time was spent in and around verse two (3 Jn. 2), debunking the false charismatics teaching of guaranteed divine health and wealth. To recap, John wishes his friend Gaius, "Well." The Greek word can also be translated as "Favour" as on a journey, therefore, wishing "Safe travel," which would be the equivalent modern-day saying.

John uses the word "Well" three times in two verses (3 Jn. 2[x2], 6), each time applying to Gaius. John first prays a blessing over him and then further encourages his friend to continue in good works, that he would "Do well to send [the missionaries who have nothing] on their journey in a worthy manner" (3 Jn. 6). In sum, hospitality and generosity is the mark of a genuine follower of Christ. It attracts the continued favour of God. A lack of hospitality will attract God's disapproval and even condemnation (1 Jn. 3:17).

Where there is no sign of generosity and hospitality in a confessing believer, John would question that person's salvation (1 Jn. 3:10-20). John says, "By this (acts of generosity) we shall know that we are of the truth" (1 Jn. 3:19). When a genuine believer holds back from their brother in need, their heart will condemn them (1 Jn. 3:20). If there is no love (generosity) and no conviction, it is because the Spirit of God does not abide within. Therefore, the loveless person, void of conviction, does not abide in God.

As mentioned in the previous section and above, the word "Journey" is applied to John's blessing over Gaius. John wishes that all would go well with his soul/life (2 Jn. 2). John uses the word "Journey" in verse six (3 Jn. 6) regarding the travelling missionaries. As stated, the Greek implies that John requests his friend to help the needy missionaries by sending them off, or forward, with some money. Paul makes a similar request in his letter to the Romans: "I hope to see you in passing as I go to Spain, and to be helped on my journey there by you, once I have enjoyed your company for a while" (Rom. 15:24). Paul's request for help is the same as John's request for Gaius to "Send [the missionaries] on their way."

Following his greeting and prayer of blessing over Gaius, John's words express great joy to find him and others walking in the truth (3 Jn. 3-4). The truth of the gospel and love towards others are inseparable. No one can claim to be in fellowship with God when one of the two requirements is missing. The evidence is seen with Diotrephes (3 Jn. 9-10), who imitates evil (3 Jn. 11).

In contrast to Diotrephes, John continues to praise his brother Gaius in verse five (3 Jn. 5), motivated by the good testimony from the missionaries (3 Jn. 6). The missionaries have reported back to John, informing him of Gaius' hospitality and quite possibly, the lack of hospitality from Diotrephes. The report results in John's praise for Gaius (3 Jn. 3) and his rebuke for Diotrephes, who imitates evil (3 Jn. 11). John's accusation of imitating evil is directly linked in his first letter, where he likens the Gnostics to Cain, "Who was of the evil one" (1 Jn. 3:12). John says, "The message that you heard from the beginning [is] that we should love one another" (1 Jn. 3:11), therefore, do not be like Cain.

Interestingly, John's third letter mentions the sent missionaries of God, who have "Gone out for the sake of the Name (Jesus), accepting nothing from

Gentiles" (3 Jn. 7), who are in direct contrast to the 'missionaries' in his second letter (2 John). Those 'missionaries' are otherwise called "Deceivers" and "The antichrist" (2 Jn. 7). The deceivers are denying Christ (2 Jn. 7), specifically His first and second appearances (the two are inseparable). They have gone ahead of the teachings of Christ (2 Jn. 9). John says, "Everyone who goes on ahead and does not abide in the teaching of Christ, does not have God" (2 Jn. 9). As mentioned earlier, the one who does not love their brother, does not have God (1 Jn. 3:10, 4:20), and the one who does not abide in the original written word, likewise, does not have God (2 Jn. 9).

A distinction between the missionaries, who were 'sent' out for the sake of the Name (3 Jn. 7), and the deceivers (2 Jn. 7-11) is that they 'went' out for their own sake. The sent missionaries report back to John; therefore, he is their direct oversight and sender. Gaius also sends them. Whereas the deceivers belong to Satan, being antichrist, therefore he sends them (2 Cor. 11:14-15).

Another distinction between the two groups is that the Christian missionaries went out with nothing and accepted nothing from the Gentiles (3 Jn. 7), whereas the false teachers are known for their greedy motives. Peter warns, "And in their greed, they will exploit you with false words. Their condemnation from long ago is not idle, and their destruction is not asleep" (2 Pet. 2:3). Jude likewise says, "Woe to them! For they walked in the way of Cain and abandoned themselves for the sake of gain to Balaam's error and perished in Korah's rebellion" (Jude 11). Paul provides similar warnings (1 Tim. 6:5, Tit. 1:11). The above distinctions should cause the prosperity-driven charismatics some concern.

Yet another distinction seen between the two groups is where one should be received into the home and church (3 Jn. 7), and the other shut out (2 Jn. 10). Gaius' hospitality towards the missionaries meant receiving them into his home, feeding them and providing a place to sleep. Gaius' hospitality also endorsed them. However, in his second letter, John warns the church not to receive false teachers into their homes and, therefore, churches due to the implied approval.

As a result of Gaius' hospitality, the missionaries testified before the church (3 Jn. 6); likewise, when hospitality is given to false teachers, that also results in a testimony. This is why John said if anyone greets the false teachers in the street or gives them access to their homes and churches, they share in their wicked works (2 Jn. 10-11). Essentially, greeting and receiving false teachers help to spread their false version of the gospel; therefore, the one showing hospitality towards them shares in the same 'reward' on the day of judgement. Once more, John's letters are eschatological.

Albeit, unlike the previous letters (1 and 2 John), the third letter of John does not have a strong eschatological theme; however, there is still a reference that could be considered that way. In verse eleven, John writes, "Anyone who does what is good is from God, and anyone who does what is evil has not seen God" (3 Jn. 11). This could be interpreted as a reference to the final judgement, where believers will be separated from unbelievers based on their actions.

One more distinction between the two groups is seen with reference to the "Church" (3 Jn. 6, 9, 10). John only uses the word church in his third letter and the book of Revelation (x19). In the book of Revelation, the church is never mentioned during the tribulation. She is not directly mentioned by name past chapter three, nor again until chapter twenty-two. However, chapter four (Rev. 4:1, cf. 11:12) reveals her departure (rapture), and chapter nineteen, her return (Rev. 19:14). The reason the church is not mentioned during the seven-year tribulation on the earth is that she has been taken out of the way (Rev. 3:10). When the church is removed, many who now stand behind pulpits and warm church pews will be left behind. Instead of being caught up in the air (1 Cor. 15:51-55, 1 Thess. 4:7), they will be "Thrown into the great tribulation" (Rev. 2:22), because they were not ready for Jesus' return (Rev. 3:3). The likes of Diotrephes will go into the tribulation. While Diotrephes is a leader within the church, he is not of it. He was of another community, who have "Gone out into the world" (1 Jn. 2:19, 4:1, 2 Jn. 7) spiritually while physically remaining within the church community. The Gnostics Peter and Jude addressed did the same, participating in the love feast (2 Pet. 2:11, Jude 12).

Interestingly, John writes the words "Gone out" three times within his letters - once for each, twice referring to those who have gone out (from the church) into the world (1 Jn. 4:1, 2 Jn. 7), and once more referring to the missionaries who have "Gone out for the sake of the Name" (3 Jn. 7). Besides John's reference of the missionaries going out "For the sake of the "Name" (Jesus), the phrase is seen five more times within the New Testament (Acts 5:41, 9:16, 15:26, 21:13, Rom. 1:5), and on each occasion, the context is suffering. Those "Going out for Christ's sake" did/do so at high personal cost, unlike the false teachers who deny the Name and were/are motivated by greedy gain, promising false freedom (2 Pet. 2:19), preaching greasy grace (Jude 4), while denying the literal return of Jesus Christ (2 Jn. 7).

Two of the primary things the sent missionaries proclaimed were Christ's first and second appearing (1 Jn. 2:28, 3:2, 2 Jn. 7). The first points to Christ's salvation work through the cross, and the next point toward His judgement, when He returns. The end time judgement of a person depends on which group they belong to, the church of Christ or the end time harlot church (Rev. 17). Those abiding in Christ are judged righteous, as opposed to the apostates, and those Jesus never knew; they will be judged, wicked. At the final judgement, one will be separated from the other, although, until then, they remained mixed (Matt. 13:24-30, 25:31-33). Although the groups remained mixed, John instructs the church to distinguish one from the other (This is how we/you know x9), warning the beloved about deception (1 Jn. 2:26) and against helping false teachers (2 Jn. 10-11).

In support of the warning against helping false teachers, John provides an example where the missionaries accepted nothing from the Gentiles (3 Jn. 7). John's reference to the Gentiles means pagans. The missionaries did not rely on pagan support but entirely on the church, as they had "Gone out [with nothing], for the sake of the Name" (3 Jn. 6). By rejecting pagan support, the missionaries denied them any form of endorsement. John's endorsement of the missionaries (3 Jn. 8) is the opposite of his warning in his second letter not to endorse false teachers (2 Jn. 7-11). As mentioned earlier, the warning from the second letter is picked up again in his third when addressing Diotrephes (3 Jn. 9-10).

After praising Gaius and endorsing the missionaries, John turns his attention to Diotrephes, accusing him of five things: 1). Putting himself first, 2). Rejecting apostolic authority, 3). Talking wicked (harmful) nonsense against the apostles, 4). Refusing the missionaries by withholding hospitality, and 5). Diotrephes was putting those who wanted to help the missionaries out of [his] church.

The missionaries being refused hospitality are the same who were sent and endorsed by the apostles. If they had been sent and endorsed by the apostles, they also had God's approval, putting Diotrephes in direct opposition to God. Remember, the missionaries had gone out with nothing, preaching Christ, and Christ alone (Jn. 14:16, Acts 4:12). The false teachers had also gone out, promoting a false gospel for greedy gain. If Diotrephes rejected one, it would stand to reason; he supported the other. His support, and therefore, endorsement of the false teachers, automatically put him in danger of the final judgement (2 Jn. 11).

John's charges against Diotrephes were first put to the church, and him, in writing (3 Jn. 9), with the intention of following up face to face. John informs Gaius that he has already addressed Diotrephes and will again. John's rebuke provides Diotrephes with an opportunity to repent; however, the letter indicates that he was not open to correction; instead, he was a power-hungry, self-serving imposter.

John's statement of where Diotrephes likes to put himself first uses the Greek word "Philoproteuo," meaning that he wants to be the leader, desiring to lord over others, like the Nicolaitans, who did what Jesus hates (cf. Rev. 2:6, 15). Peter addressed the same issue, saying, "So I exhort the elders among you, as a fellow elder and a witness of the sufferings of Christ, as well as a partaker in the glory that is going to be revealed: shepherd the flock of God that is among you, exercising oversight, not under compulsion, but willingly, as God would have you; not for shameful gain, but eagerly; not domineering over those in your charge, but being examples to the flock. And when the chief Shepherd appears, you will receive the unfading crown of glory. Likewise, you who are younger be subject to the elders. Clothe yourselves, all of you, with humility toward one another, for God opposes the proud but gives grace to the humble" (1 Pet. 5:1-5). Following John's rebuke, the absence of any record of Diotrephes suggests that he did not repent and therefore continued to imitate evil (3 Jn. 11).

Diotrephes selfishly desired to be first (3 Jn. 9) and successfully obtained authority within the church (3 Jn. 10). He rejected John's authority, refused to welcome visiting brothers, and excommunicated anyone who did not follow and obey him. Diotrephes displayed controlling and cult-like behaviour. Similar allegations of controlling behaviour have been levelled against several charismatic churches, including, but not limited to: Hillsong, C3 Church Global, Revival Centre, and Bethel Church, which the media have investigated. Celebrity status preachers, such as Mark Discal of Mars Hill, Bill Hybels of Willow Creek Community Church, Brian Houston, and Carl Lentz of Hillsong, and Ravi Zacharias, the Christian apologist, to name a few, are examples of leaders who once had favour yet suffered a spectacular fall, but not from grace (Gal. 4:5). God's grace is still evident even in, and through their fall, providing an opportunity to repent. Sadly, Ravi Zacharias went to his grave, harbouring his unconfessed sins, which were exposed later. Diotrephes most likely shared the same fate, despite having a chance to turn around. As mentioned above, the evidence suggests that he did not. Like many others, Diotrephes loved the world, and the things of it, which disqualified him from having God (1 Jn. 2:15-17).

In verses ten and twelve (3 Jn.10, 12), John makes another distinction between those belonging to God and those who do not. On the one hand, Diotrephes "Refused" to welcome anyone outside of his authority and, therefore, his control (3 Jn. 10). On the other hand, Demetrius "Received" a good testimony, like Gaius, for his open-handed hospitality (3 Jn. 12). Verse eleven (3 Jn. 11) readdresses Gaius, as beloved, used three times previously (cf. 3 Jn. 1, 2, 5), warning him, who is doing well, not to follow in the footsteps of Diotrephes, who imitates evil. Once more, John highlights the potential to fall (cf. 1 Jn. 2:15-17, 2:24, 26, 3:7) and the danger of losing what has been worked for (2 Jn. 8).

In support of the warning, John almost repeats what he said in his first letter: "Little children, let no one deceive you. Whoever practices righteousness is righteous, as he is righteous. Whoever makes a practice of sinning is of the devil, for the devil has been sinning from the beginning." (1 Jn. 3:7-8). However, in his third letter, he says, "Whoever does good is from God; whoever does evil has not seen God" (3 Jn. 11b). The difference is with the words "Righteous" and "Good," albeit both are the mark of the one belonging to God, and absence of these qualities also marks those who do not have God. The difference between the two words, contextually, is that doing "Right" is talking about resisting and refraining from sin, in contrast against those who wilfully sin.

Doing "Good" refers to generosity and hospitality, in contrast to those lacking these gifts and qualities (i.e., Generosity: Rom. 12:8, 2 Cor. 9:13. Hospitality: Rom. 12:13, 1 Tim. 5:10, Heb. 13:2, 1 Pet. 4:9). Generosity and hospitality are spiritual gifts (Rom. 12:4-8, 1 Cor. 12:4-11, 28); yet greater than the gifts, is love (1 Cor. 13:13, 14:1). Diotrephes, and those like him, "Who like to put themselves first" lack love for others, while having plenty of it stored up for themselves. Being a lover of self is an end time sign; those guilty of loving themselves are to be avoided (2 Tim. 3:1-6).

Again, because Diotrephes lacked love for others and instead did what was evil, he did not have God (3 Jn. 11). The contrast and critical point of the letter is that Diotrephes did not have God, while Gaius and Demetrius did. The three church leaders are an example of what to do and what not to do. In sum, do not be like Diotrephes, do not imitate evil, and do not take anything from pagans (Gentiles), who might then put a claim on the gospel or restrict it in some way.

The Gnostics were categorised as Gentiles due to going ahead of scripture and therefore being without God (2 Jn. 9). John says, have nothing to do with them, including receiving nothing from them. Today, many churches, ministries, Bible Colleges, and Christian Universities have restricted themselves by obtaining grants and other financial support from the government (Gentiles). For this reason, John says not to do it. Instead, the work of God should be funded by the people of God.

John ends his third letter the same way he finished his second, saying, "I had much more to write to you, but I would rather not write with pen and ink. I hope to see you soon, and we will talk face-to-face" (3 Jn. 13, cf. 2 Jn. 12). John also adds a blessing of peace, informing the church that others are greeting them also (3 Jn. 15, cf. 2 Jn. 13). Specifically, John says, "The friends greet you" (3 Jn. 15), which could be drawn from his gospel, where Jesus said, "Greater love has no one than this, that someone lay down his life for his friends. You are My friends if you do what I command you. No longer do I call you servants, for the servant, does not know what his master is doing;

but I have called you friends, for all that I have heard from my Father I have made known to you" (Jn. 15:13-15).

The condition of being called a friend of Jesus is to do what He has commanded: to believe in Him and love one another (1 Jn. 3:23). The context is sacrificial love, even laying down one's life. The closing contrast, therefore, is between Diotrephes, who put himself first (3 Jn. 9), and the missionaries who went out for the sake of the Name (Jesus), accepting nothing from the Gentiles. (3 Jn. 7). The missionaries quite possibly also went out with nothing, as instructed by Jesus (Matt. 10:8b-10, Lu. 22:35).

CONCLUSION
Jude And John

The letters of Jude and John (1, 2, 3), along with the letter of Second Peter, provide a firm warning against false teachers and the imminent return of Jesus Christ. These letters stress the need for believers to be vigilant and to hold fast to the truth of the gospel, "What [the church] heard/had from the beginning." The church must remain watchful, contending for the faith as there are deceivers at the door and even within, seeking to lead some of its members astray.

Jude, John, and Peter warn their readers of the danger posed by false teachers who seek to falsify the truth and deceive believers. In Jude (verse 4), it is written, "For certain individuals whose condemnation was written about long ago have secretly slipped in among you. They are ungodly people who pervert the grace of our God into a license for immorality and deny Jesus Christ, our only Sovereign, and Lord." Similarly, it is stated, "Many deceivers, who do not acknowledge Jesus Christ as coming in the flesh, have gone out into the world. Any such person is the deceiver and the antichrist. John warns, "Watch out that you do not lose what we have worked for, but that you may be rewarded fully" (2 Jn. 1:7-8).

As mentioned above, the letters of Jude and John are eschatological, emphasising the nearness of Jesus Christ's return and the importance of being prepared for that day. Peter adds, "The Lord is not slow in keeping his promise, as some understand slowness. Instead, he is patient with you, not wanting anyone to perish, but everyone to come to repentance." However, in the same chapter, Peter, under the inspiration of the Holy Spirit, also warns that the day of the Lord will come like a thief in the night (2 Pet. 3:9). In other words, when Jesus returns, it will be suddenly, and at an hour no one expects.

In conclusion, the letters of Jude and John convey a powerful message that emphasises the importance of staying true to the gospel and standing firm against false teachings. They also serve as a reminder that the return of Jesus Christ is imminent, stressing the need for the church to remain vigilant and committed to living holy lives. These letters encourage the church, living in the end times, to be prepared, ready, and eagerly awaiting the coming of our Lord.

May all in Christ be strengthened by these words, continuing to walk in faith, truth, and love until the end.

www.ingramcontent.com/pod-product-compliance
Lightning Source LLC
Chambersburg PA
CBHW070553100426
42744CB00006B/266